To Isaac and Esmée

Text © Bernard Williams 2021
ISBN: 9798744540418

Although every precaution has been taken to verify the accuracy of the information that is contained herein, the author and publisher assume no responsibility for any errors or omissions.

First printing:
May 2021

ACKNOWLEDGEMENTS

With thanks to the following for permission to reproduce photographs and other copyright material in this book:

American National Red Cross photograph collection/Lewis Wicks Hine: 186; **Cantal Liens - association de liaison pour la généalogie et l'histoire populaire du Cantal:** 3 (right), 10 (bottom left), 31, 58 (top right), 65 (bottom left), 74, 78; **Corning Museum of Glass:** 35 (top left); **Bertrand Laporte:** 5 (bottom), 23 (bottom left), 35 (right), 44 (bottom right), 140 (top left), 149 (top right), 162 (left); **Jérôme Maugat:** vi (middle top), 89 (bottom left), 147 (left), 158 (bottom left); **Peter Silk:** vi, vii (top right), 9, 16, 17, 24, 27, 34 (left), 35 (bottom left), 44, 47, 53, 56 (bottom right), 60, 62, 64, 65, 68, 77; **TopFoto/Roger-Viollet:** iv, 71 (bottom), 77 (bottom right).

Every effort has been made to contact copyright holders. The publisher apologises to anyone whose rights have been inadvertently overlooked and will be happy to rectify any errors or omissions.

CONTENTS

Journées - Nationwide Fundraising Days

When the French Government decided to declare a general mobilisation on the 1 August 1914, no one who witnessed the scenes of great exuberant patriotism, could have anticipated the speed with which the mood of the nation would deteriorate. Approximately 8,500,000 troops were mobilized in France during the conflict, out of which 1,397,800 died and over 4,000,000 were injured[1]. In addition to these horrific statistics, after returning home, a further 70,000 died of war-related illnesses. The First World War decimated families throughout France and created many new vulnerable classes of people - former soldiers who found themselves permanently incapacitated by injury, prisoners of war, those stricken with tuberculosis, refugees, orphans and widows.

The war was unprecedented in its conditions and ferocity. The effect on the psyches of the soldiers, mired in the cold and filthy trenches and facing the deadly efficacy of defensive weapons, was hardly difficult to measure.[2] The deadly war of attrition undermined troop morale and engendered a high level of psychological stress. The French front line troops were often filthy, unshaven and exhausted. They soon acquired the detested nickname of *poilu*, which literally meant a "hairy beast".[3] Many soldiers soon developed what can only be described as a pervasive 'us and them' mentality. It is fair to say this belief involved a certain amount of envy as well as a sense of moral superiority. As the war proceeded into a bloody stalemate, a clear sense of betrayal developed amongst the troops, that their officers, the press, politicians, and many civilians cared very little for them.[4]

This view was often reinforced on the rare occasions when troops were granted three to ten days leave from the frontline trenches. The *permissionnaires* were given leave two to three times per year and when journeying home, they would often complain that they were being treated like 'cattle', having to stand for hours during their journeys in poorly heated and very slow moving trains.[5] Many soldiers on leave also bitterly resented what they perceived to be a massive gap between the living conditions of civilians and those of combatants.[6]

The French authorities quickly realised the importance of raising morale, not just amongst the frontline troops but also the civilian population. In an attempt to improve the lives of the soldiers and to actively involve the French general public, it was decided to set about organizing fundraising events. Previously, charitable fundraising in France for any given cause was accomplished mostly through soliciting a handful of wealthy donors. It was now considered essential, faced with a 20th century conflict devastating the lives of millions, to pioneer a variety of fundraising campaigns which not only targeted the masses but also actively involved people across all social strata, involving the smallest villages to the largest cities.

Right:
Permissionnaires who felt lucky to be on leave from the appalling conditions they were facing at the front were amazed to discover that less than 150 miles away Parisian social life was continuing relatively untouched.

These "Œuvres de guerre" were intended to come to the aid of all victims of war - refugees, wounded, mutilated, widows and orphans. There is little doubt that some of these large scale charity campaigns were immensely successful. That said, despite raising huge amounts of money for their cause, some discovered that they were not above criticism. Certain organizations were accused of mismanagement (see pages 86-87). Charges for administration costs were a particular area of concern and questions were also raised regarding the commissioning of famous artists. Undoubtedly their involvement succeeded in raising the profile of the event but their 'expense claims' often led to a significant increase in overhead costs thereby depleting the net revenues. Sadly it also transpired that some fundraising organisations were no more than nefarious scams with fraudsters taking advantage of the generosity and patriotic sentiment of the general public.

To ensure that fraud was minimised and that the organizations involved were regulated and far more rigorously managed, the French government passed a law on 30 May 1916 which not only limited the number of recognized charities to 3,242 but also gave the Minister of the Interior the power to examine all fundraising applications and oversee the receipts and expenses of all fundraising bodies.

The most popular of the fundraising campaigns became known as the *Journées* - particular days set aside to raise money throughout France for certain authorised, specific and well-publicised causes. The actual organizational logistics that lay behind the successful implementation of all the *Journées* required an incredible degree of co-ordination. Vast numbers of items including medals, insignias, brooches and lapel pins were mass produced so that they would be affordable to the general public. Promotional posters for these events were distributed to all Departments and thousands of volunteers were recruited across the country to solicit donations from passers-by in the streets. In return the donors would often receive a cardboard insignia, medal or lapel pin related to the particular cause. Despite being produced in vast quantities many of these items have long since been destroyed or lost but today there appears to be renewed interest in the items probably stemming from the recent World War One centenary events and exhibitions. Up until this time, very little scrutiny was afforded by historians to this particular field but

Right:
Despite the regulations that were set out under the law of 30 May 1916, there remained a certain amount of confusion regarding the legitimacy of certain organizations involved in the fundraising. When the issue was raised by député Abel Gardey on 29 May 1917, a written response to his question was given in the Senate in Note 15882.

Far right:
Posters setting out these powers and outlining the key provisions of the new law were sent to all the Préfectures and were prominently displayed.

thanks to the work of one individual and a growing number of impassioned collectors, interest in the *Journées* has steadily gathered momentum.

Undoubtedly the most detailed reference book on the subject of the national and regional *Journées* is *Les insignes de journées de la guerre 1914-1918,* written by the historian Roger de Bayle des Hermens and published in 1985.[7] This study alone has contributed significantly to stimulating the passion that so many individuals have for this particular topic.

Sadly for researchers, many of the archive records of the organisations which were directly involved in the fundraising campaigns such as La Croix Rouge française, as well as those of the three great Parisian publishing companies (Devambez, Lapina and Chambrelent), were lost/destroyed by the end of World War Two. Fortunately, for the purposes of my research, historical archives in France such as those held by the Bibliothèque nationale de France and several French Departments have been instrumental in allowing me to glean information from many primary sources, giving me a privileged insight into several of the most prominent French nationwide fundraising campaigns of World War One. Today, websites built by the likes of Christian Doué and Bernard André[8] also serve as invaluable sources for any individual researching this area of interest.

Even today, large numbers of the insignias and other items sold to raise money for the *Journées* have never been fully inventoried. Apart from the problems mentioned above, an additional obstacle stems from the fact that some of the insignias bear no dates or even a brief legend that might give the researcher some clue as to which campaigns the insignias were produced for.

Right:
Frequently the exact same design would be used for a variety of different causes.

Above:
Some insignias carry no legend on the obverse or reverse which makes identification very difficult.

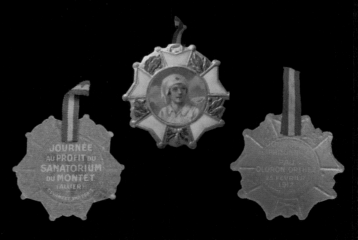

Below:
Certain insignias are so obscure (such as the *Journée du 3e Zouaves*) that there are no records whatsoever to better inform us about them.

Above:
According to de Bayle des Hermens, this insignia was actually designed as a blank template and the appropriate date and legend - in this case for the *Journée des Rapatriés* - would be added.

Quite simply this work is intended to be a helpful and handy-sized up to date reference and guide book for the person who is interested in the various national as opposed to the regional fundraising *Journées*. It is impossible to detail within a single volume the vastness of this topic. Readers well versed in the work of de Bayle des Hermens will immediately note that some of the *Journées* have been left out. Research has shown that the majority of those that have been omitted were almost certainly organised on a regional rather than national basis by associations such as La Croix Rouge française. Quite often charitable organizations were decentralized and relied heavily on local Comités de Bienfaisance and Secours National for most of their operations across France and Belgium. Few references about them could be found in the daily newspapers of that era and nor do any of the Department Archives contain much information on them.

For the purposes of this study I have chosen to focus on the acknowledged national *Journées* but I have included 'Section Two' which examines some of the lesser known *Journées* which could be described loosely as 'national'. I also took the decision to make one exception and include a 'regional' fundraising event - in my opinion it would have been remiss of me to ignore the three *Journées de Paris*. Although technically these were regional events, they were superbly organised and highly successful in raising funds for the frontline troops.

It is customary to acknowledge the assistance one has received in the preparation of a book of this nature. I am especially indebted to Mr Peter Silk, Mr Jérôme Maugat and Mr Bertrand Laporte all of whom have kindly given me much invaluable assistance with my research. As always, I owe a great deal to my wife Rachael for her forbearance and unbelievable patience.

The book sustains a chronological framework and seeks to establish and reflect upon the context of events, hopefully throwing some light on this fascinating historical and cultural period. I hope, too, that the information provided may be of some service in bringing to light, and restoring to its rightful place, an often neglected and forgotten subject in the French history period 1914-1919. In the interests of clarity, I have imposed some arbitrary stylistic forms and for the general interest of those readers who might not be familiar with the French language but wish to have a clearer understanding of all the notes referred to in the book, I have also included translated 'English sections' in Appendix 2.

Bernard Williams

La Journée du Petit Drapeau Belge
20 and 25 December 1914

La Journée du Petit Drapeau Belge
20 and 25 December 1914

The enormous upheaval that followed the German invasion of Belgium and Northern France resulted in nearly two million French and 325,000 Belgians being forced to leave their homes. As well as being homeless, they also suffered from lack of food and supplies. Many of the Belgian refugees as well as civilians in northern France were often mistreated by the occupying forces. Sadly many of them, as well as the vast numbers of individuals who were repatriated from the invaded regions, were seen by some as 'opportunists', who opted for the easy way out rather than attempt to face the enemy onslaught. The demeaning and derisive term Boches du Nord (literally 'Germans of the North') came to be used, especially in Northern France, to describe those who were suspected for various reasons of being cowardly or seen as taking some sort of perverse advantage to receive government benefits.

Deserving 'victims of war' received financial help as well as additional assistance from the French government and several charitable enterprises. In fact, the first national fundraising day organized in France was held to raise money to help the Belgian refugees. Small Belgian flag pins were sold on *La Journée du Petit Drapeau Belge* held throughout France on Sunday 20 December 1914.

An extract from the *Le Figaro* 20 December 1914 reveals that over four million flag pins had been ordered for *La Journée du Petit Drapeau Belge* just for Paris with an additional 700,000 required for the outskirts of the city.

Above:
Villages were abandoned by their inhabitants as over one million Belgian refugees fled from the invading German forces.

Below:
Young *Journée du Petit Drapeau Belge* collectors, along with many adults, helped to make the two fundraising days an enormous success.

LE PETIT DRAPEAU BELGE

Rappelons que la journée d'aujour-d'hui, par toute la France, appartient aux Belges. Le chiffre des petits drapeaux demandés par la province ne s'élève pas à moins de dix millions!

A Paris, les sociétés de la Croix-Rouge ont mis spontanément à la disposition du comité, pour la vente, son admirable personnel ; 4 millions de drapeaux ont été réservés pour Paris et 700,000 pour la banlieue.

Dimensions: 300 (H) x 500 (W) mm

Above:

An example of one of the thousands of posters which alerted the general public to the fundraising event.

Below:

An extract from *Le Petit Journal* which is dated 20 December 1914. The emotive article, setting out the plight of the Belgian people, was written by Maurice Maeterlinck (1862-1949) the brilliant Belgian poet, playwright and essayist who won the Nobel Prize for Literature in 1911.

Below:

A letter sent by the Comité Central Franco-Belge to the Prefecture of Cantal (a department situated in the Auvergne-Rhône-Alpes region of France). It acknowledges receipt of a letter in which le Préfet informed the Comité how much had been raised for the *Le Petit Drapeau Belge* in Cantal.

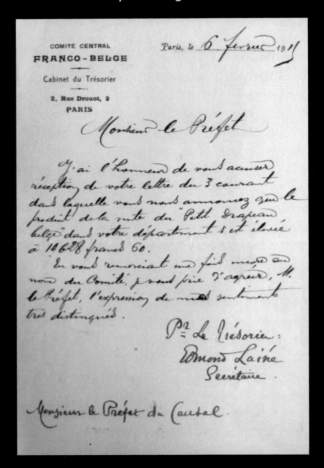

LA JOURNÉE
DU
DRAPEAU BELGE

Il faut que ce jour où notre drapeau va palpiter comme un symbole d'amour et de reconnaissance dans toutes les mains françaises, soit un jour d'espérance et de gloire pour toute la Belgique.

Oublions un instant notre affreuse détresse, nos campagnes, les plus belles, les plus fertiles de l'Europe, à ce point ravagées, que tout ce qu'on en dit ne peut donner l'idée d'une désolation qui semble irrémédiable. Oublions, s'il se peut, les femmes, les enfants, les vieillards, les innocents, les pacifiques massacrés par milliers, dont le compte étonnera le monde, lorsque sera brisée la sinistre barrière derrière laquelle se passent tant de secrètes horreurs. Oublions ceux qui meurent de faim dans notre pays sans moissons, sans maisons, méthodiquement rançonné, pillé et pressuré jusqu'à la dernière goutte de sa vie. Oublions le reste de notre peuple dispersé par les routes de l'exil, vivant de la charité publique qui, si fraternelle, si affectueuse qu'elle se montre, est cependant si lourde à des mains entre toutes laborieuses, qui ne connurent jamais le poids déprimant de l'aumône. Oublions enfin nos dernières villes menacées, les plus belles, les plus fières, les plus chères, celles qui forment le visage même de la patrie et qu'un miracle seul pourrait encore sauver. Oublions, en un mot, la plus grande calamité et la plus criante injustice de l'histoire, pour ne songer qu'à notre délivrance qui s'approche. Il n'est pas trop tôt pour la saluer. Elle est déjà dans toutes les pensées comme dans tous les cœurs. Elle est déjà dans l'air que nous respirons, dans tous les yeux qui nous sourient, dans toutes les voix qui nous acclament, dans toutes les mains qui se tendent vers nous en agitant des palmes; car c'est vraiment l'admiration du monde entier qui nous délivre!...

Demain nous rentrerons dans nos foyers. Nous ne pleurerons point si nous les retrouvons en ruine. Ils renaîtront plus beaux des cendres et des décombres. Nous connaîtrons des jours d'héroïque misère; mais nous avons appris que la misère n'attriste pas les âmes qu'entoure un grand amour et que nourrit une noble pensée. Nous rentrerons, la tête haute, régénérés dans une Europe régénérée, rajeunis par un magnifique malheur, purifiés par la victoire et dépouillés des petitesses qui voilaient les vertus endormies en nous-mêmes et que nous ignorions. Nous aurons perdu tous les biens qui périssent, mais qui renaissent aussi facilement qu'ils périssent. En échange, nous en aurons acquis qui ne mourront plus dans nos cœurs. Nos yeux étaient fermés à bien des choses; ils sont ouverts à des horizons agrandis. Nos regards n'osaient pas quitter nos richesses, notre petit bien-être, nos petites habitudes. Ils se sont détachés de la terre et atteignent à présent des sommes qu'ils n'avaient pas encore aperçus. Nous ne nous connaissions pas nous-mêmes, nous ne nous aimions pas assez les uns les autres; nous avons appris à nous connaître dans l'étonnement de la gloire et à nous aimer dans l'ardeur douloureuse du plus immense sacrifice qu'un peuple ait jamais accompli. Nous allions oublier les vertus héroïques, les pensées sans entraves, les idées éternelles qui mènent l'humanité. Non seulement nous savons aujourd'hui qu'elles existent, mais nous avons enseigné à l'univers qu'elles triomphent toujours, que rien n'est perdu tant que la foi demeure, tant que l'honneur est sauf, tant que l'amour subsiste, tant que l'âme ne cède pas; et que les plus monstrueuses puissances ne prévaudront jamais contre les forces idéales qui sont le bonheur, la gloire et la seule raison d'être de l'homme.

MAETERLINCK.

Below:

Photos from *Excelsior* (Monday 21 December 1914 page 10).

Dimensions: 1247 (H) x 937 (W) mm

Above:
A poster designed by the French-Swiss artist Théophile Alexandre Steinlen helped to promote the work of the Comité Central Franco-Belge.

1. Belgian flag pin made in an embossed yellow metal with a golden fringe around it measuring 20 (H) x 12 (W) mm
2. Celluloid Belgian flag pin - 28 (H) x 19 (W) mm
3. Fabric Belgian flag pin - 24 (H) x 17 (W) mm
4. Paper flag pin - 19 (H) x 11 (W) mm.
   There are numerous varieties of size, colour and widths of colour bands.
5. Metal lapel pin in the shape of a clover leaf in Belgian colours
6. Celluloid flower - black and yellow on two large red petals - 31 mm wide
7. Ribbon bow in Belgian and French colours mounted on a pin
8. An example of the identity cards which would be prominently displayed by all the authorised street collectors

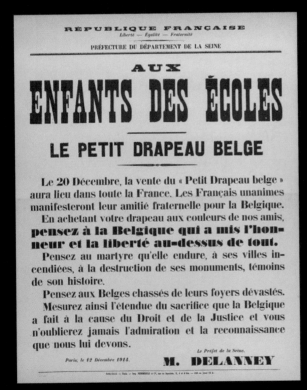

Dimensions: 750 (H) x 560 (W) mm

Above:

Posters were distributed throughout schools giving the date for the fundraising day and urging the children to buy a Belgian flag pin.[9] This particular poster was printed by Imp. Hemmerle et Cie for the Préfecture du Departement de la Seine and is signed at the bottom by Le Préfet - M Delanney.

The German invasion of Belgium caused widespread destruction and the additional demands of the occupying forces led to shortages in many vital materials. The combination of poor harvests along with restricted food supplies and the imposition of a strict martial law resulted in terrible hardships for the Belgian population.

La Cantine du Soldat Prisonnier was one of the most active charity works in occupied Belgium working to save prisoners of war from famine in Germany. The shipment of food and clothing was authorized by the German government, but in fact many parcels could not be shipped and never reached their destination. It was because of this that *La Cantine du Soldat Prisoner* was created in April 1915.

Its main objective was to help prisoners both by sending food directly and by providing families with facilities for children. The Germans, however, were suspicious of the campaign's success and subsequently placed increasing restrictions on the proper operation of 'La Cantine'.

Below:
This pair of medals for *La Cantine du Soldat Prisonnier* was designed by Godefroid Devreese, one of Belgium's most famous medallists. The sale of this design in 'Table Medal' form was initially prohibited by the German occupying authorities because it was felt that the depicted prisoner on the reverse side was represented as unreasonably emaciated and thus a criticism of Germany. These smaller versions, however, were allowed to be sold to the general public.

Below:
One of Théophile Steinlen's most memorable and emotive designs was produced in medal form by Ovide Yencesse and sold to raise awareness of Belgium's brutal invasion by Germany.

Dimension: 50 mm

Dimension: 28 mm

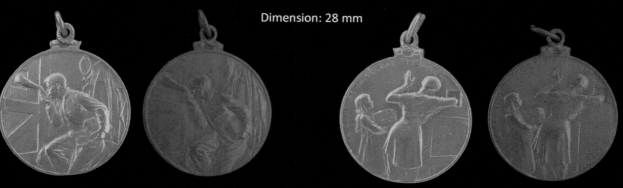

POSTCARDS AND MEDALS

Even before the enormous success of *La Journée du Petit Drapeau Belge*, the Belgian authorities were quick to appreciate that the sale of items such as medals and postcards not only raised funds for the Belgian cause but also served as a means of propaganda, inspiring patriotism and dehumanising the enemy.

Postcards were sold extolling the heroism of the Belgian people. The Royal Family, in particular, was seen as a crucial focal point in the nation's struggle against oppression.

Below:
Some examples of the medals that were sold to the general public to raise additional funds. Many featured King Albert I and Queen Elisabeth.

Journée du 75
7 February 1915

Journée du 75
7 February 1915

The 'Touring Club de France' was created in 1890 with the aim of promoting cycle tourism. The question is often posed: How did the Touring Club come to be involved in the war effort? A major clue can be found in *La Revue du Touring Club*:

"Des Octobre 1914 le TCF, dans l'impossibilité de continuer son oeuvre touristique, a pensé qu'il était de son devoir d'entreprendre une oeuvre patriotique. Pendant que nos jeunes camarades remplissaient leurs devoirs militaires, leurs aînés ont voulu, eux aussi, tenter de se render utiles et contribuer à leur manière à la défense nationale... faire quelque chose pour ceux qui se battent".

At a committee meeting held on 5 December 1914, the decision was taken "d'organiser une grande journée dans toute la France et de faire de cette journée l'occasion d'une manifestation patriotique en honneur de notre glorieux canon sous le nom de Journée du 75".

The French 75 mm field gun was a quick-firing field artillery piece adopted in March 1898. It's official French name was: 'Matériel de 75mm Mle 1897.' It was commonly known as the French 75 or simply the 75 (Soixante-Quinze).

Initially, the French 75 had been designed as an anti-personnel weapon system for delivering large volumes of time-fused shrapnel shells on enemy troops advancing in the open. It soon earned the nickname of the 'Frayeur des Boches' (Dreaded by the Germans) and is almost universally recognised by military historians as the greatest artillery field gun of WW1. It was essential to the success of the French war effort especially at the Battle of the Marne in 1914 and the Battle of Verdun in 1916.

The specific aim of the fundraising day, which was designated to be held on Sunday February 7th 1915, was to raise money for the benefit of the 'Œuvre du Soldat au front' (the work of the soldier at the front). The intention was to use the monies raised to purchase millions of essential items for the frontline soldiers, "everything which is likely to improve their hygiene and help their well-being".

A set of medals, lapel pins and porte bonheurs (lucky charms) were sold to raise monies from the public for the *Journée du 75*. The central motif of all these items was the 75 mm field gun.

The sale of six million items was originally planned but public demand led to more than 22 million being produced. Given the great success of the *Journée du 75*, the decision was taken by the T.C.F. to extend the fundraising during 1915, in particular on three designated days: 14 and 28 February and 7 March. Collections continued throughout 1915 and 1916 with the additional sale of postcards and medals such as those featured below.

The organizers of the *Journée du 75* were able to count on the efforts and goodwill of over 50,000 street collectors throughout France. Nearly two years after the main fundraising days of 1915, the revenue figure of 7,137,562 francs from just 1917 reveals the immense success of the collection.

Below:
This extract taken from *Le Matin* (front page of the 7 February 1915 issue) illustrates the badges and medals for sale to the general public

Dimensions: 1200 (H) x 810 (W) mm

Above:
An official poster for the *Journée du 75*.

Below:
A letter from Henri Defert (Vice President of T.C.F.) pointing out that there was no set price for the insignias and asking the street collectors to simply rely on the generosity of those donating money.

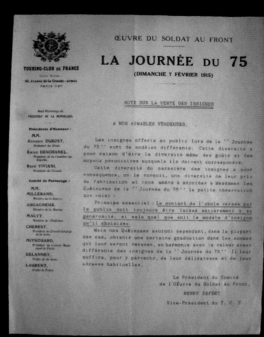

INSIGNIAS

The original items that were sold on 7 February 1915 consisted of:

1. oval lapel/flag pin (with two positions of the '75' and varying colours) made of thick paper
2. a rectangular lapel/flag pin - thick paper
3. a cardboard insignia - gold version
4. a cardboard insignia - multi-coloured version
5. a thin pressed gold gilt brass medal
6. a silvered version of the medal

As the fundraising efforts continued throughout 1916 and 1917, the sale of additional items such as brooches, pendants, charms and porte bonheurs significantly increased public awareness and raised huge amounts of additional money.

1.The oval lapel/flag pin (with two positions of the '75' and varying colours)

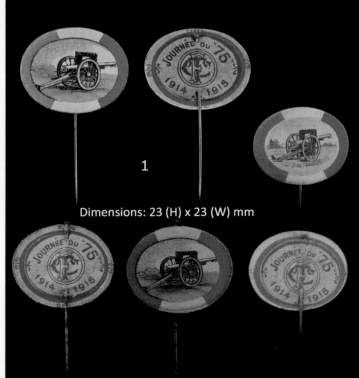

1

Dimensions: 23 (H) x 23 (W) mm

The lapel pin is oval in shape. A tricolour frame encloses the central image of a '75'. In one version the '75' is touching two edges of the frame - in the second version the field gun is centrally set.

The reverse has the legend *Journée du 75* with the monogram T.C.F. and 1914-1915 in blue lettering.

2. The rectangular lapel/flag pin

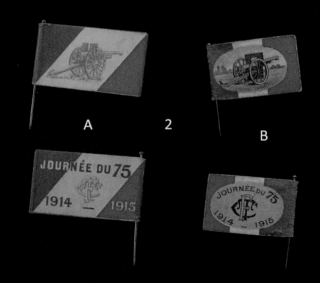

A   2   B

2. Version A measures 33 x 19 mm. The '75' is grey coloured and set centrally on the oblique tricolour colours on the obverse. As with the oval shaped version, the reverse has the legend *Journée du 75*, the T.C.F. monogram and the dates set in blue and white lettering.

Version B measures 25 x 17 mm. The '75' is set in an oval frame across the vertical tricolour colours. A white oval 'frame' with the legend *Journée du 75*, the T.C.F. monogram and the dates set in black lettering is on the reverse.

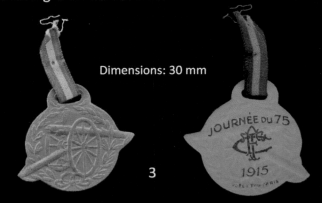

Dimensions: 30 mm

3

3. A rounded gold coloured insignia with the field gun in relief pointing to the right, surrounded by a laurel wreath foliage tied at the bottom by ribbon. Printed on the reverse is the legend *Journée du 75*, the T.C.F. monogram and 1915 date set in grey lettering on a white background. The name of the printer - 'Poyet Fres Paris' - is below the date.

A second 'gold' version was produced which is identical on the obverse. The only difference is that the reverse has no date on it.

4 The multicoloured version is identical in shape and size to the gold version. Set within a gold frame, the grey '75' on a blue background is in relief facing to the right. It is encircled by a green laurel wreath with a red ribbon at the bottom.

Just like the gold version, the reverse has the T.C.F. monogram, the legend *Journée du 75*, and 1915 date set in grey lettering on a white background. The printer's name 'Poyet Fres Paris' is below the date.

Dimensions: 30 mm

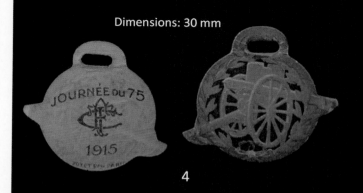

4

5 Just like the Versions 3 and 4 in cardboard, the thin pressed gold gilt brass medal has the '75' as the central feature with the legend *Journée du 75* above it. A rising sun is in the background. The crowned monogram T.F.C. divides the dates 1914-1915 along the bottom rim and the reverse is the obverse incuse. The suspension loop allows for a small tricolour ribbon which would be sold with a pin to allow the medal to be attached.

Dimension: 31 mm

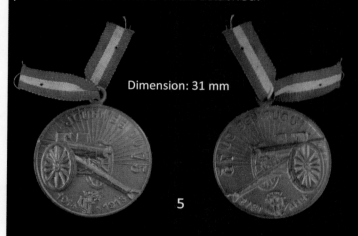

5

6 The silvered version was identical to the pressed gold gilt brass medal.

6

Dimensions: 31 mm

Although the medal has no manufacturer's name on it, it is thought that the medal production was that of J Janvier of Paris.

Further versions of the medal are catalogued by de Bayle des Hermens[10] - the likely explanation for these was that, due to problems of supply to meet the huge demand for the medals, it was necessary to use different manufacturers. Inevitably, this led to the slight variations in design that de Bayle des Hermens refers to.

The design was also used to produce solid medal versions varying in price (5 - 25 francs).

Dimension: 31 mm

Dimension: 31 mm

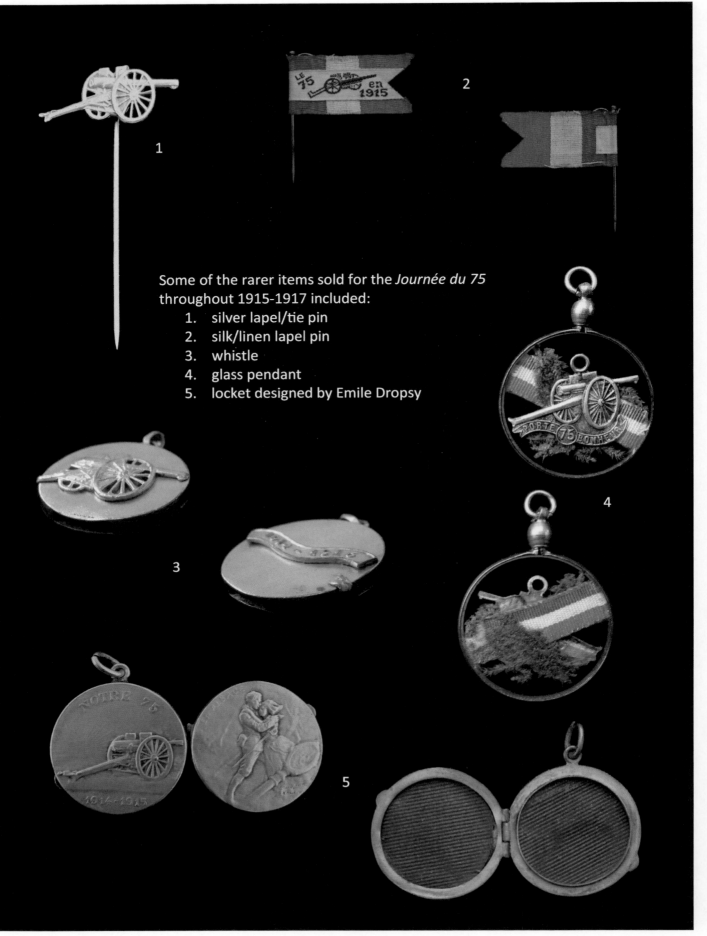

Some of the rarer items sold for the *Journée du 75* throughout 1915-1917 included:
1. silver lapel/tie pin
2. silk/linen lapel pin
3. whistle
4. glass pendant
5. locket designed by Emile Dropsy

PORTE BONHEURS

The number of different models of porte bonheurs produced during the duration of the war is impossible to ascertain. Some versions were designed and produced by specialist medallists and jewellers for their clientele, whereas others were mass produced and sold along with the authorized items on the fundraising days.

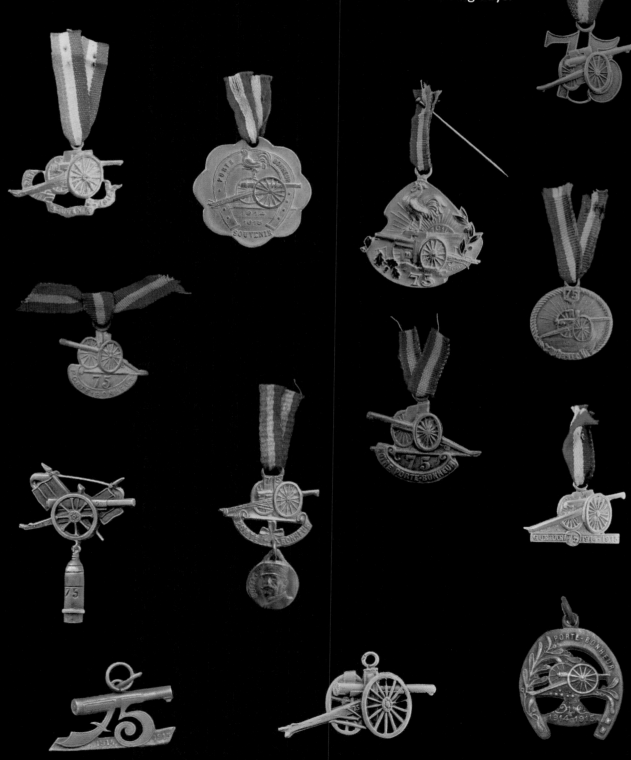

Dimensions: 51 (H) x 33 (W) mm

Dimensions: 80 (H) x 160 (W) mm

Above:

A 'vignette' of *Notre 75* and a rare label that was attached to the packages sent through to the Town Halls which contained the items to be sold on the assigned day.

Below:

An example of one of the labels stuck on the collecting boxes which can also be seen in the photo of the two 'quêteuses' as well as the group photo on page 17. All the collectors, as well as those supervising ('Commissaires'), were asked to clearly display their 'carte d'Identité' to reassure members of the public that they were officially authorized.

Dimensions: 110 (H) x 175 (W) mm

Dimensions: 69 (H) x 59 (W) mm

Dimensions: 68(H) x 59 (W) mm

Below:

As can be seen from the sketch published in the *1918 Almanac Hachette* (page 172), over the course of the war it is clear that the *Journée du 75* was the most successful of all the nationwide fundraising days in terms of the money that was raised.

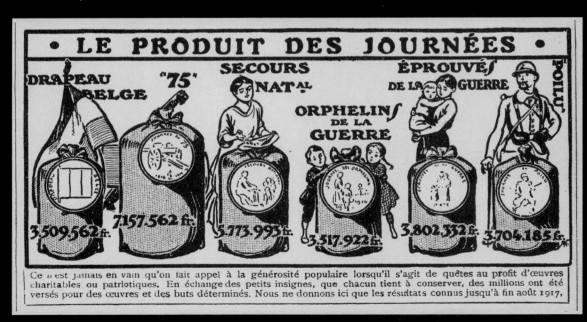

La Journée Française Secours National
23 and 24 May 1915

La Journée Française Secours National
23 and 24 May 1915

Soon after war was declared, the Secours National was created with a central aim to come to the aid of the soldiers, as well as their families "without any distinction of opinions and religious beliefs".

The driving force behind the organisation was the banker and philanthropist Albert Kahn. He had the support of Pope Benedict XV as well as that of the statesman Georges Clemenceau who served as Prime Minister of France on two occasions: from 1906-1909 and again from 1917-1920.

Kahn is better known today for initiating a vast photographical project which spanned 22 years. He assembled a team of photographers and sent them across the continents of the world to record a unique historical record of 50 countries. The 72,000 colour photographs and 183,000 metres of film are assembled in a collection described as 'Les Archives de la Planète'.

Ironically several of Kahn's photographers were engaged in France just a few days before war was declared and subsequently continued work on their project throughout the war years. Through close liaison with the military authorities they managed to record the devastation of war and the struggle to continue everyday life and work.

Below:
Albert Kahn (1860 - 1940)

The Comité du Secours National (C.S.N.) was made up of many influential figures in French society headed by the person chosen to be the President of Secours National - Paul Appell, acknowledged as one of the country's leading mathematicians and Dean of the Faculty of Science at La Sorbonne (below right). Working alongside him was Gabriel Hanotaux of the French Academy, a statesman and eminent historian (below left).

Alongside them was Kahn who, despite being the founder of the C.S.N., preferred to maintain a low profile.

Below:
The Comité's main demand was that everyone should donate generously to the battle "Contre la Misère".

Below:
A letter sent by the Comité to all Mayors set out the dates chosen for the fundraising effort and where the funds would be distributed.

The letter concluded by stating that it was crucial to give the soldiers on the frontline the knowledge that they were cared for and much appreciated.

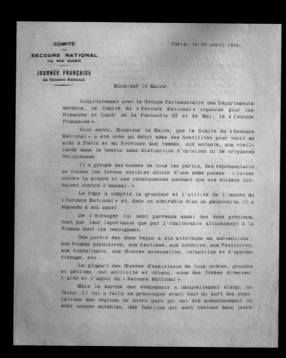

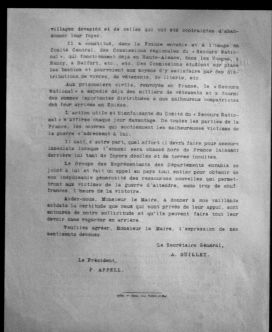

The first initiative organized by the C.S.N. took place on two consecutive days: Sunday May 23 and Monday 24 1915.

La Journée Française was held throughout France with the specific aim to raise funds to help all the victims of the war: refugees, wounded, disabled, convalescents and orphans.

Below:
The front page of *Le Petit Journal* (28 April 1915) illustrates the importance attached to La *Journée Française* which was to be held on two designated days over the Christian festival of Pentecost: Saturday 23 and Sunday 24 May 1915.

The article mentions that the design of the medal was created by Hippolyte-Jules Lefèbvre (1863-1935), a prominent French sculptor and medallist.

It also adds that the numerous street collectors involved in the sale of the medals and insignias would also have sets of postcards created by some of France's and Belgium's most famous artists. These could be used by families to send messages to their loved ones fighting on the front line.

FLAG PINS

As well as the Lefèbvre medal and the series of postcards, a set of flag/lapel pins were also sold to the general public. Attention was focused upon seven regions, all of which were ravaged by the terrible offensives of the Western Front. It was decided to memorialize these regions in a set of flag/lapel pins. The seven regions were:

Alsace, Artois, Champagne, Flandre, Île-de-France, Lorraine and Picardie.

It was decided that a nationwide appeal would be made to the non-invaded parts of the territory to help the misery of the invaded populations. All the flag pins bore the coat of arms of the seven administrative regions on the obverse with the legend on the reverse: *'La Journée Française 1915 Secours National'*. The measurements of the actual paper flag were 17 (H) x 26 (W) mm.

Two versions of the sets were produced:
A. The 'petit blason' version has mantling around the shield - the legend is set on a tricolour reverse background on six horizontal lines;
B. The 'grand blason' version features solely the shield - the legend is set on the tricolour reverse background on five diagonal lines.

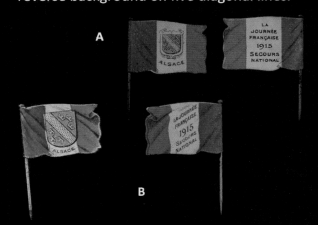

Above:
'ALSACE': (A) features the 'petit blason' with the legend set on a tricolour reverse background on six horizontal lines;
(B) features the 'grand blason' blason' set on the tricolour reverse background on five diagonal lines.

'ARTOIS'

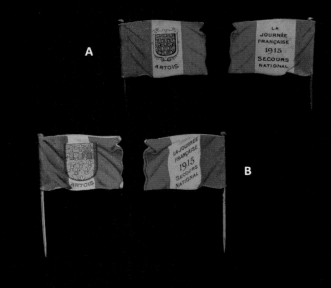

'CHAMPAGNE'

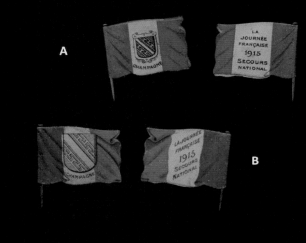

'FLANDRE'

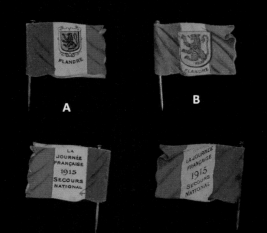

'ÎLE-DE-FRANCE'

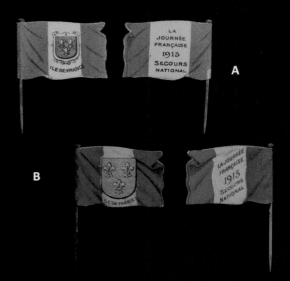

A

B

'LORRAINE'

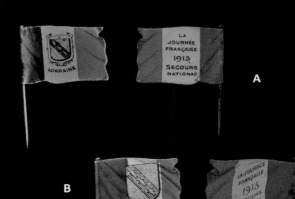

A

B

'PICARDIE'

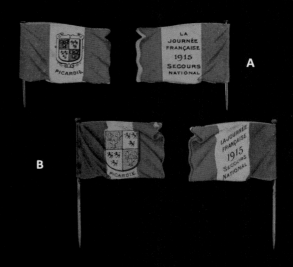

A

B

Below:

In addition to the seven flag pins, a flag pin made of linen/silk was also produced. It was made in two sizes with both of them bearing the legend *La Journée Française du Secours National*.

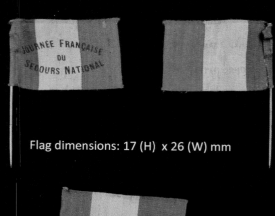

Flag dimensions: 17 (H) x 26 (W) mm

Flag dimensions: 20 (H) x 40 (W) mm

Below:

An example of a national poster used to advertise the fundraising days.

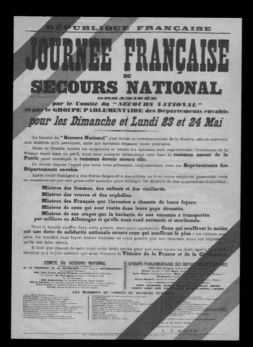

Dimensions: 1210 (H) x 800 (W) mm

Below:

Both of the 'quêteuses' can be seen wearing the identity cards that they were required to wear to reassure members of the general public that they were authorized collectors. The one on the left is carrying sets of postcards and the one on the right has a tray full of insignias.

B

Dimension - 68 (H) x 52 (W) mm

Left and above:

Two examples of the identity cards that were used by authorised sellers (B) and street collectors (A).

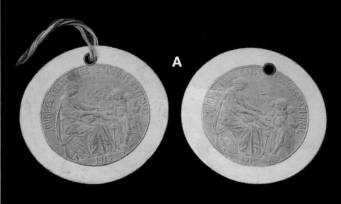

A

Dimension: 65 mm

A (left): A reproduction of Lefèbvre's medal is set on the obverse face. A four line legend is printed on the reverse: *Comité / du / Secours National / Carte d'Identité*. The name of the collector is set below the legend and many of the cards also had an official stamp - in this case that of the 'Mairie du XVIe Arrondissement'. The name of the printer - Marcel Picard Paris - is on the right (3 o'clock).

B: The obverse depicts three French flags amongst branches of foliage, two of which bear the motto: *'Honneur et Patrie'* - all in blue ink. The legend of *La Journée Française* is set at the top with *du Secours National* along the bottom. A 'J Bauzon' signature print in blue is set below the flags. The reverse has: *La Journée Française / du Secours National'* with *Carte d'Identité* below.

One of the cards has the official stamp of the 'Mairie de Saint-Mandé (Seine)' and the signature and the number of the collector.

Below:

An example of an 'étiquette' (the label used for the collecting box).

Dimensions: 80 (H) x 160 (W) mm

Dimensions: 1200 (H) x 810 (W) mm

Above:

An example of a regional poster used to advertise the fundraising days. Unlike the national version (see page 22) emphasis is placed on the religious significance of the two dates clearly associating them with the Festival of Pentecost. It also directly addresses the inhabitants of the City of Antony.

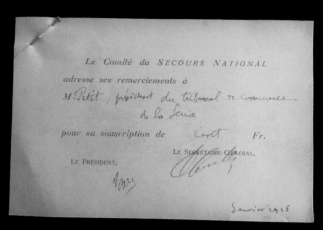

Above:

An acknowledgement/thank you note sent from Le Comité du Secours National - it is dated 'Janvier 1915' and signed by Le Secrétaire Général and Le Président.

Below:

Two examples of the silk/linen 'brassards' worn mainly by the 'Commissaires' who were tasked with supervising the collections.

Dimension: 54 (W)

Dimension: 49 (W) mm

Lefèbvre's design was used in the production of table medals as well as the smaller medals sold on the streets to the general public.

Below:
The two different models of table medals - one was made of solid silver whereas the other version was solid bronze. In the main these were not sold on the streets but rather by subscription. Some were undoubtedly given as presentation pieces to members of the various Department committees throughout France. The blank cartouche on the reverse allowed for the inscription of individual names.

Dimension of both models: 50 mm

Below:
From page 6 of *Excelsior* 24 May 1915 setting out a montage of photos featuring some of the many 'quêteuses' involved on the two days designated to *La Journée Française.*

Right:
The smaller Lefèbvre medals were designed with a suspension hoop which allowed it to be pinned on clothing with a small tricolour ribbon.

Again, these medals came in two versions - one in gold gilt stamped brass and the other in silvered brass.

Dimension: 31mm

POSTCARDS

A series of seven postcards were commissioned by Le Comité du Secours National and these were sold by the street collectors alongside the Lefèbvre medals and the series of flag/lapel pins.

The seven artists involved in this project were Abel Faivre, Gustave Surand, Charles Léandre, Henry de Groux, Théophile Steinlen, Adolphe Willette et Francisque Poulbot.

1. Abel Faivre (1867-1945)

Below:
The reverse of each postcard was entitled *Journée Française Secours National* and at the bottom left had the name of the printer 'Devambez' followed by the series number (Visé No).

2. Gustave Surand (1860-1937)

3. Charles Léandre (1862-1934)

Below:
Abel Faivre (A) and Théophile Steinlen (B)

A   B

4. Henry De Groux (1866-1930)

7. Adolphe Willette (1857-1926)

5. Théophile Steinlen (1859-1923)

Below:
Apart from the Lefèbvre medal (page 25) and the flag pins (pages 21-22) the only other insignia which was sold on the fundraising days was a circular insignia made of cardboard. It featured a seated woman (symbolizing France) cradling a baby in her arms with an elderly person on her right and two infants in the background on her left.

6. Francisque Poulbot (1879-1946)

Dimension: 26 mm

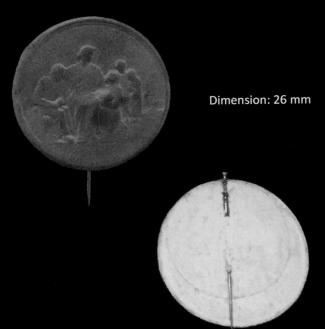

Journée de l'Orphelinat des Armées
20/27 June 1915

Journée de l'Orphelinat des Armées
20/27 June 1915

Tight censorship in France succeeded in concealing the full extent of what had happened since the outbreak of war on 3 August 1914.[11] By early 1915, however, nothing could conceal the fact that 995,000 French troops had been killed, wounded or were missing in action.

A decision was made at the highest Government level to authorise *La Journée de l'Orphelinat des Armées* which was to be held on 20 June 1915. It was organized to help fund orphanages specifically looking after children of soldiers killed fighting for their country. The main individuals charged with the organization of the campaign were Professor Alfred Croiset[12] and Madame Jeanne Paquin.

Jeanne Paquin (1869-1936) was the head of the renowned Paquin Fashion House. Her business and organizational acumen was acknowledged in Government circles and her nomination to head the Orphelinat des Armées campaign reflected the high esteem she was held in. She was able to use her formidable connections to persuade friends and wealthy acquaintances to throw their support behind her. René Lalique, the famous jeweller and glassmaker, employed his superb design skills to create an innovative and brilliant plaquette that would be at the forefront of her campaign.

Early on it became clear that the newly formed Orphelinat campaign was resented by some very prominent organizations and powerful elements of the press. This was due principally to three main reasons:

1. It was felt that the newly formed campaign would detract attention and support from the fundraising efforts of other groups such as the Association Nationale des Orphelins which had been established on 2 August 1914 and had the prominent backing of the immensely influential Roman Catholic Church. Many believed that the general public could be confused when faced with the prospect of two high profile campaigns with similar aims running parallel to each other.

2. In some quarters, the Orphelinat campaign was described as divisive and the two principal organizers were accused of being intransigent (see page 31). Despite the severe criticism that was levelled at her, Paquin was still regarded as a very astute choice to coordinate what turned out to be a very well run campaign.

3. While the plaquette design that Lalique created for the Orphelinat campaign (see page 30) was almost universally accepted as being innovative and highly artistic, it still encountered criticisms related to it being regarded as slightly risqué!

Above:
Jeanne Paquin (1869-1936) and René Lalique (1860-1945)

Below:
La Presse (18 June 1915) gives an insight into how deep the divisions were. The Association Nationale des Orphelins was supported by many prominent charities including the organizations that were to make up La Croix-Rouge française. Importantly, it had the firm support of very influential individuals within the Roman Catholic Church.

> De son côté, le Comité central de la Croix-Rouge française, composé des représentants des trois Sociétés d'assistance reconnues d'utilité publique, à savoir : la Société française de secours aux blessés militaires, l'Union des Femmes de France et l'Association des Dames françaises, a pris, dans sa séance du 15 juin, la décision suivante :
> « La Croix-Rouge française avait été heureuse de promettre son concours à la Journée organisée par l'Orphelinat des Armées, dans la pensée que l'union était faite entre toutes les Associations poursuivant ce même but.
> Elle constate avec regret que des divergences se sont produites entre elles.
> Tout le monde comprendra que, dans ces conditions, la Croix-Rouge s'abstienne, tant que l'accord ne sera pas établi. »

Different versions of Lalique's design were used for the central motif of various small paper flag pins which were sold in huge numbers by street vendors throughout France (see below).

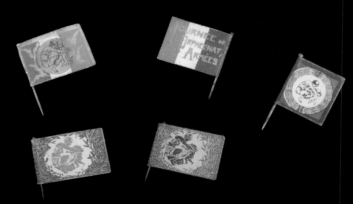

Dimensions varied between - 19/21 (H) mm x 19/30 (W) mm

The rectangular shaped cardboard version of the medal was sold with a tricolour ribbon and pin.

Dimensions: 30 mm (H) x 26 (W) mm

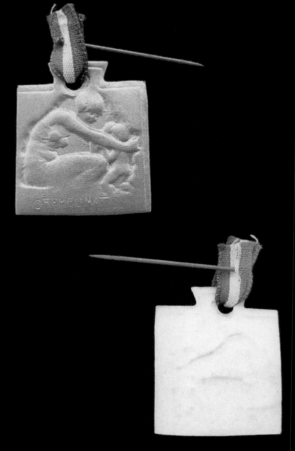

Un de nos confrères, la *Libre-Parole* dit que « l'emblème de distribution pour la « Journée » proposé par Mme Dick May a été formellement refusé par un certain nombre d'associations, qui estiment qu'un tel emblème n'est pas de nature à pouvoir être distribué sur la voie publique par des jeunes filles qui se respectent ».

Nous avons voulu nous procurer cet insigne ou plus exactement la petite plaquette qui devait être vendue au profit des orphelins par les jeunes filles quêteuses. Cette œuvre du graveur Lalique est d'une belle inspiration artistique, mais d'une allure par trop grecque et par trop dépouillée de tout voile ; nos poilus ne peuvent être reçus comme les vainqueurs de Salamine. Ce que l'on peut dire, c'est qu'elle n'est pas de circonstance pour le public auquel elle s'adresse, soit qu'il s'agisse des vendeuses, soit qu'il s'agisse des familles auxquelles on l'offrira. A ce point de vue encore, les dirigeants de l'Ophelinat des Armées nous paraissent avoir été mal inspirés.

Above:
An article from *La Presse* (23 June 1915) reveals that, unlike the medals designed for the Orphelins campaign which were largely conventional in their design (see pages 92 - 93), Lalique's image was deemed by some as being "too Greek and too revealing" and was regarded as unsuitable and embarrassing for the young women and girls who were being asked to sell the Orphelinat medals / plaquettes.

Below:
Le Temps 28 June 1915 - the article reveals that, despite a great deal of criticism being levelled at his design by a largely right wing press, Lalique's plaquettes were the ones that many members of the public chose to wear.

La « Journée des orphelins de la guerre »

De bonne heure, ce matin, commençait la quête pour la « Journée des orphelins ». L'entente réalisée entre les diverses œuvres qui organisent la « Journée » a été largement confirmée par le public, et chacun donne son obole avec un empressement significatif. On voit, à la même boutonnière, non pas un seul des insignes autorisés, mais une véritable brochette, composée de la réduction de la plaquette de Lalique, du petit drapeau de l'Orphelinat des armées, et des fleurs charmantes, roses, pâquerettes, myosotis, qui remplissent les corbeilles — vite dévalisées — des quêteuses. Le soleil aidant, tout fait prévoir qu'à Paris et en province la « Journée des orphelins » réussira aussi brillamment que les précédentes « Journées » dont le souvenir n'est point effacé.

Un détail touchant : les soldats blessés, les invalides de la guerre montrent plus d'empressement encore, s'il est possible, que les « civils » à venir en aide aux orphelins de la guerre. L'union sacrée se continue par le sacrifice et la solidarité dans l'effort. Paris est plein de scènes émouvantes où se révèle la volonté de tous pour assurer le salut de la patrie.

Below:

The article from *La Presse* (18 June 1915) reveals the animosity directed at both Paquin and Croiset. Comment is made about the "intransigence of the political committee of Croiset and Paquin" and the opposition from not just Catholic circles but also from independent bodies.

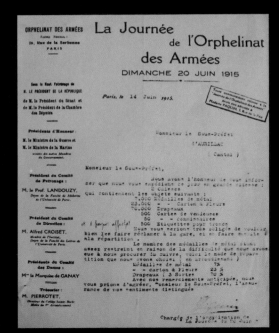

Above:

A more detailed letter (dated 14 June 1915) sent to the Sub-Prefect of Aurillac, detailing the precise number of items being sent through including collection box labels, medals, cardboard insignias, flag pins and collector identity cards. In her own handwriting, Madame Paquin has added a packet of posters to this list. It is interesting to note that she also mentions the difficulties caused by the shortage of copper.

Below:

A copy of the standard letter sent out to all the departments throughout France.

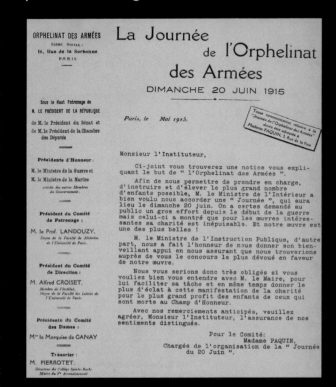

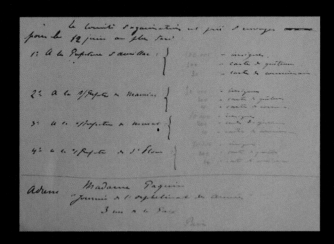

Above:

Madame Paquin's notorious attention to detail can be seen in this handwritten note which details the number of insignias and identity cards, sent to four towns in the department of Cantal in south-central France - Aurillac, Saint-Flour, Mauriac and Murat.

The *Journée de l'Orphelinat des Armées*, which was set initially for Sunday 20 June 1915, was Lalique's first sortie in the fundraising campaigns.

Due to ongoing discussions, related to concerns raised by several influential parties (see page 29), the Journée was postponed for a week and then it was extended on several successive Sundays as well as on a regional basis over the following years.

Lalique's design was strikingly innovative and was synonymous with the creativity, high quality and beauty of his more famous works. The medal came in the form of a stamped bronze cross pattée featuring an embossed crouching female figure whose arms encircle two small unclothed children. A tricolour ribbon was tied through an integral loop at the top and a pin inserted in order to fix to clothing.

Dimensions: 30 (W) mm x 34 (H) mm
Weight: 2.31 gm

Underneath was the inscription 'Orphelinat des Armées' with the engraved name 'R Lalique' which had an unusual double-tailed 'Q'.

There appears to be quite a variation in the weight of the Orphelinat medals (between 1.51 - 2.31 gm) and this is also apparent with some of the other Lalique designs. The reason for this disparity is probably explained by the fact that, as the war progressed, certain metals which were essential for the war effort became increasingly scarce.

Versions that were sold to the general public were generally produced in thin pressed brass and also cardboard. The design was also used for a variety of small paper flag pins which were sold in huge numbers by street vendors throughout France.

La Journée des orphelins de la guerre

Tommy donne pour les petits orphelins de France.   Phot. Matin.

Above:
Le Matin 28 June 1915 page 1
It would appear that no one was immune from the attention of the street collectors, including French soldiers convalescing or British soldiers on leave in Paris!

It is interesting to note that the article headline reveals the confusion, even amongst the media let alone the general public, that was caused by the two different fundraising campaigns for orphans being run almost parallel to each other (see page 85).

The article describes the various areas covered by the street collectors and how all Parisians were quick to show their enthusiasm and patriotism in buying the authorised insignias including Lalique's plaquette design, the little flag pins and blue and red florets.

Right:

Le Gaulois 4 June 1915 page 2

An intriguing and rare interview with Lalique in which he discussed the economies of scale which were involved in the production of the Orphelinat medals, the production process and the difficulties that he encountered.

In the article Lalique explained that his design, of a small golden plaquette measuring 32 mm in the approximate shape of a Maltese cross, would be sold on 20th June. The chosen central motif for the plaquette was the figure of a woman symbolizing the charity with her arms wrapped around two small children.

Lalique then explained how the plaquettes were struck 'au mouton' - using specialised machinery that dropped a huge weight on the selected moulds so that the tiniest details were imprinted on the brass. He pointed out almost with tongue in cheek, that the machines that were being used were French, adding that the German machines were very large, complex and functioned badly.

Lalique asserted that any imperfect plaquettes were "relentlessly eliminated" and added that he personally supervised the whole minting process. In order to illustrate this point, he had brought along three boxes full of rejects to show to the reporter who, not having an 'expert eye', admitted difficulty in trying to identify the faults.

The details that were imparted by Lalique in the interview are fascinating: 22 million plaquettes were struck and the amount of tricolour ribbon that was used for attaching them (allowing three centimetres per insignia) made up a length of 290 kilometres (the distance, for example, between London and Lincoln) and it was estimated that the actual number of insignias produced would fill up five large removal trucks!

It is interesting to note that despite these highly impressive figures, Lalique felt unsure of being able to meet the astonishing demand from the general public for his design.

La " Journée " du 20 Juin

Interview de M. Lalique

Nous avons dit que la journée du 20 juin sera consacrée à l'œuvre, hélas ! si nécessaire, de l'Orphelinat des Armées. Il s'agit d'assurer, dans le présent et dans l'avenir, l'existence des légions de petits enfants que la guerre aura laissés sans parents. En leur faveur, jeunes filles et fillettes vendront sur la voie publique, dans toute la France, un insigne qui restera comme un témoignage de la solidarité nationale.

La population, toujours prête à donner quand il s'agit de nos vaillants soldats, tiendra plus que jamais à honneur de faire acte de générosité envers les innocentes victimes, devenues les pupilles de la nation. Elle fera un accueil enthousiaste au nouveau souvenir qui lui est offert, non seulement à cause de la noble pensée qui l'a inspiré, mais en raison de son caractère artistique.

Cet insigne est en effet une œuvre du célèbre joaillier Lalique, le rénovateur du goût moderne, qui a tenu à le signer.

M. Lalique, que nous avons eu le plaisir de voir en son hôtel des Champs-Elysées, nous a dit :

— Je suis très heureux d'avoir pu contribuer à l'œuvre de l'Orphelinat des Armées. C'est une des plus intéressantes que je connaisse et elle demande à ses organisateurs beaucoup de dévouement, car elle est appelée à se continuer longtemps après la guerre ; aussi ai-je tenu à apporter dans la composition et l'exécution du travail qui m'a été confié toute ma conscience d'artiste et tout mon cœur de Français.

» L'insigne qui sera vendu le 20 juin consiste en une petite plaquette dorée, de trente-deux millimètres de largeur, ayant à peu près la forme d'une croix de Malte. Le centre en est occupé par une figure de femme représentant la Charité et entourant de ses bras deux petits enfants. Ces plaquettes sont frappées au « mouton », c'est-à-dire au moyen de machines qui laissent tomber sur les matrices un poids très lourd, de façon que les moindres détails se gravent dans la matière. Et vous savez, ajouta M. Lalique en souriant, ces machines-là sont bien françaises. Elles n'ont rien des machines allemand, imposantes par leur énormité et leur complication, mais qui fonctionnent mal et font du mauvais travail.

» Je tiens à ce qu'il ne soit mis en circulation aucune plaquette qui ne soit pas parfaite. Je surveille donc moi-même la frappe et j'élimine impitoyablement tous les exemplaires présentant un défaut, si petit soit-il. Voyez plutôt. »

Et M. Lalique nous désigna trois caisses remplies de rebuts, dans lesquelles nous puisâmes à pleines mains ; certes, il fallait l'œil subtil d'un expert pour s'apercevoir qu'elles n'étaient pas toutes au point.

— Du reste, c'est là très peu de chose en comparaison de l'énorme quantité d'insignes que nous frappons : vingt-deux millions, pour tout dire. L'ensemble représente le contenu de cinq grandes voitures de déménagement ; et le ruban tricolore employé pour les attacher, à raison de trois centimètres par insigne, forme la respectable longueur de 290 kilomètres !

» Malgré ces chiffres, je crains que nous en manquions. De toutes parts les demandes affluent, et l'on nous en réclame des quantités considérables. La journée du 20 juin s'annonce donc sous les meilleurs auspices. »

Nous avons pu examiner un exemplaire complètement fini de la plaquette de M. Lalique. C'est vraiment une œuvre d'art. Les creux et les reliefs en sont supérieurement modelés, les draperies ont une exquise finesse et l'ensemble, d'une belle harmonie, dégage une touchante impression de douceur et de grâce.

Ce sera vraiment un succès.

P. C. DE L.

Versions that were sold to the general public were generally produced in thin pressed brass and also cardboard. A small number made of silver can also be found.

Below:
An example of a stamped silver design numbered '693'.

Dimensions: 34 (H) x 30 (W) mm
Weight: 6 gm

Dimensions: 32 (H) x 30 (W) mm
Weight: 14 gm

Other versions of Lalique's design were also made in a variety of finishes including solid bronze, solid silver-plated and solid silver.

Millions of the stamped brass Orphelinat medals were produced from 1915 until the end of the war but medals struck on a solid flan were not mass produced and it is unlikely that they were offered for sale to the general public. Rather these models were produced for the various dignitaries who were closely involved in the campaign.

Silver items produced by Lalique often bear two distinctive symbols - the 'tête de sanglier' (boar's head) silver guarantee mark and the poinçon de fabricant (maker's mark). Lalique's distinctive mark was a diamond lozenge with the initials 'RL' which were separated by an epée.

Right:
A very rare solid bronze cast of the design. It is possibly one of the larger, more detailed models which would have been used to duplicate the smaller medals using the 'tour à réduire' technique employed by Lalique in the production process.

Above:
A solid silver medal using identical dimensions and shape as the hollowed brass version. Despite being tested as solid silver this version bore no marks apart from the stamped number '106'.

Other versions exist with different numbers - '213', '215', '462', '826', '885' and '836'. None of these have the silver symbols of the boar's head or the maker's mark. No explanation has been found for the numbering and there are no records showing that silver Orphelinat medals were ever sold to the general public. It is likely that the numbers were ascribed to a set of specific presentation pieces.

Dimensions: 105 mm x 105 mm x 12 mm
Weight: 236.4 gm

Dimensions: 140 (H) x 136 (W) x 25 (D) mm

Provenance: Accession Number 81.7.74
Bernard Danenberg Former Collection 1981-05-21

Above:
A white plaster plaque with bevelled edges and a smaller raised rectangle which bears the relief of the Orphelinat design. The plaster original was probably duplicated and reduced through the 'tour à réduire' process used by Lalique to generate a master die which would then be used for the mass production of the smaller Orphelinat medals.

Closer scrutiny of the plaque reveals the outline of the shape that was eventually to be chosen for the medal.

Dimensions: 120 (H) x 160 (W) mm

Above:
A label from one of the collecting boxes used for the fundraising day. Note the date of '20 Juin' - due to the problems outlined on page 26 this was later changed to the 27 June.

Dimensions: 600 (H) x 800 (W) mm

Above:
Some French regions, rather than following the set dates for their collections, decided instead to opt for their own fundraising days.

Dimensions: 72 (H) x 61 (W) mm

Above:
All authorised collectors were required to wear an official 'Carte d'Identité'.

Below:
A poster designed by Alfred Philippe Roll

Dimensions: 1190 (H) x 1580 (W) mm

In a similar fashion to the fundraising campaign of *La Journée Française Secours National*, a series of postcards were sold in local shops as well as by the street collectors.

These were sold throughout France and helped to promote the cause as well as raising funds. This particular set of cards was attributed by de Bayle des Hermens to an artist named 'Delgrice' but it appears likely that the artist was named 'Brice'. Despite the illustrator being largely unknown, there is little doubt that the series proved to be very popular, especially with young children.

Further examples of postcards sold for the cause of the *Orphelinat des Armées* included designs by far more famous artists including Alfred Roll (1) Francisque Poulbot (2) Maurice Neumont (3) and Charles Foerster (4).

In addition, some other cards were designed by relatively unknown artists with one card attributed to Jacques Debat-Ponsan who trained at the École Nationale Supérieure des Beaux-Arts but is best known as an architect (5).

1

2

3

4

5

6

7

8

Journée des Éprouvés de la Guerre
26 September 1915

Journée des Éprouvés de la Guerre
26 September 1915

It was mainly at the instigation of 'le Syndicat de la Presse française' that *La Journée des Éprouvés de la Guerre* took place. Details regarding how the Journée would be organized were released in a press statement and published in the national newspapers during the early part of August 1915.

The Press Syndicate was always quick to give its support to all the national authorized charitable works which requested help. On this occasion, however, it was decided that "un acte personnel" would be more appropriate and this decision gave rise to *La Journée des Éprouvés de la Guerre*.

The Syndicate made an application for organizing a national fundraising day and the Minister of the Interior was happy to grant authorization for it. The designated day was the 26 September and the decision was taken to devote the *Journée* to the victims, both military and civil, of the war.

Those involved in the coordination of the event chose to adopt a novel way of fundraising - "dans l'esprit le plus éclectique et le plus libéral".

In order to achieve this goal and wary of the need to generate public interest to distinguish it from the other charitable events that had taken place up until that point, it was decided 'Une Grande Tombola' (a great raffle) would prove to be a new "mécanisme ingénieux". The hope was that the raffle would raise one or two million francs from Parisians as well as those living in the provinces.

A further innovation was the decision to order the design and production of "une petite pochette en papier" (a small paper envelope), the upper side of which was illustrated by Luc-Olivier Merson (1846-1920), a French academic painter and illustrator famous for both his postage stamp and currency designs.

Right:
Luc-Olivier Merson in his Paris studio circa 1890.

LA « JOURNÉE » DU 26 SEPTEMBRE
Une grande tombola pour les éprouvés de la guerre

Le syndicat de la Presse parisienne n'a jamais manqué, dans les circonstances douloureuses que nous traversons, de prêter à toutes les œuvres charitables qui le lui ont demandé son concours le plus actif.

Non content, toutefois, de ce rôle, le syndicat de la Presse a voulu faire mieux encore et marquer, une fois de plus, sa volonté de se manifester par un acte personnel.

C'est ainsi que, devant l'impossibilité de faire un choix parmi tant d'œuvres également intéressantes, il a sollicité du gouvernement l'autorisation d'organiser une « Journée » globale : la « Journée des éprouvés de la guerre » militaires ou civils, qui permît d'alléger les charges des œuvres qui se consacrent à ces glorieuses et intéressantes victimes.

Le ministre de l'Intérieur, entrant dans les vues du syndicat et se rendant compte des résultats qu'on pouvait attendre d'une telle initiative, n'a pas hésité à accorder pour le 26 septembre, la « Journée » demandée : les bénéfices — cela va de soi — devant être répartis, après entente préalable, dans l'esprit le plus éclectique et le plus libéral.

Mais les œuvres de cette nature sont légion et, pour pouvoir faire bénéficier le plus grand nombre d'entre elles du résultat de cette journée, il importe que la recette dépasse les prévisions les plus optimistes. Afin d'atteindre ce but, le syndicat de la Presse, tout en sachant ce qu'on peut attendre de la générosité du public, a estimé nécessaire la création d'un attrait nouveau : il a donc sollicité — et obtenu — la très grande faveur d'une tombola, dont le mécanisme ingénieux permettra tout à la fois de distribuer à de nombreuses œuvres des sommes importantes et de faire circuler dans le commerce, tant à Paris qu'en province, un million au moins et peut-être deux.

Nous aurons sous peu l'occasion de revenir sur ce sujet et de préciser quelques détails complémentaires.

Above:
Article from *Le Petit Parisien* (7th August page 2)

Right:

A letter was sent out to all Departments setting out guiding principles for the event:

1. The chosen date was the 26 September.
2. Money raised by the *Journée* would go to both the military and civilian victims of war.
3. Division of the funds would be determined by the Ministry of the Interior and the Syndicat de la Presse.
4. No flag pins, medals or emblems would be used.
5. Instead small pochettes designed by Luc-Olivier Merson would be sold.
6. Each pochette would contain a reproduction of a military themed design by a famous artist.
7. Instead of images, 100,000 of these pochettes would contain vouchers numbered from 1 to 100,000. To avoid any possible fraud these vouchers would be exactly the same size and weight as the images.
8. Any voucher winner would be entered for a lottery held by the Crédit Foncier - the draw would allocate a prize to each number.

Below:

Advertising posters printed by three imprimeries (printing companies) - Devambez, Crété and Camis

According to de Bayle des Hermens, the pochettes were produced in eighteen different colours. Each one contained one of thirty miniature images of artwork composed by thirty of France's most famous artists including the likes of Auguste Rodin, Abel Faivre, Georges Scott, Lucien Jonas, Auguste Leroux and Marcel-André Baschet.

As stated in the circular sent out by the Syndicat de la Presse (see page 40) one hundred thousand of the envelopes would contain a voucher bearing a number between 1 and 100,000. This would give the owner the right to be entered for a 'Grande Tombola' draw made at the Crédit Foncier de France.

In the Grande Tombola there was one 25,000 franc bon (voucher); one of 10,000 francs; one of 5,000 francs; one of 3,000 francs; one hundred and twenty 1000 franc bons, two hundred and forty bons of 500 francs and so on down to 5 francs. Each of these bons could be presented in any store in Paris or in the provinces, for an exchange of the chosen quantity of goods representing the value of the bon.

Below:
Adverts were placed in many of the leading French newspapers - this particular one was from *Le Petit Parisien* (7th August page 2).

Below:
The front cover of *Les Annales* 26 September 1915.

Below:
Examples of a 5 and a 50 franc voucher (Bon).

GRANDE TOMBOLA
de la Journée des Éprouvés de la Guerre

Prime de la Grande Tombola

AVIS A TOUS LES ACHETEURS

Chaque pochette renferme un dessin, et il y a 30 dessins différents.

L'acheteur qui, le premier, présentera les 30 dessins aura droit à une automobile « Unic », d'une valeur de 12,000 fr.

Le second aura droit à un service d'argenterie, d'une valeur de 4,000 fr.

Enfin, l'acheteur qui, le premier, présentera 29 dessins sur 30 aura droit à un ameublement, d'une valeur de 3,000 fr.

Le second aura droit à un piano Pleyel, d'une valeur de 1,800 fr.

Achetez donc des pochettes et payez-les au moins

25 centimes

Above:

This article from *Le Figaro* dated 25 September (page 2) provides an interesting insight into how the organizers astutely encouraged the potential buyers to purchase multiple numbers of the pochettes. The individual who was the first to come forward with all 30 images would win an 'Unic' car; the second person with all 30 images would win a canteen of silver cutlery valued up to 4000 francs. Similarly, the individual who was first to present 29 images would win furniture up to 3000 francs and the second placed person would be awarded a Pleyel piano valued at 3000 francs.

Right:

Initially, thirty different 'dessins' (images) were chosen to be included in the envelopes and these became collector items especially amongst young children.

It is clear that the press and publicity expertise of those in charge of the event fully appreciated the effect of 'pester power'!

Throughout France, the pochettes were sold in shops and, on the actual day, could be bought from thousands of street sellers mainly composed of young children accompanied with one or two adults. The actual cost of the individual pochette was generally left to the generosity of the buyers - but there was a 25 centimes minimum price.

Dimensions: 85 (H) x 55 (W) mm

Above:

All the collectors were asked to wear individual identity cards to reassure the public that they were officially authorized.

1. Général Pau - P Carrier-Belleuse
2. Le Vieillard et l'Enfant - Alfred Roll
3. Général de Castlenau - Henri-Achille Zo
4. L'Écossais - Georges Scott
5. Lieutenant Warneford - Ed Henry Taudot
6. Chanteclair - Benjamin Rabier
7. Général Joffre - Henri Jacquier
8. Un Blessé le Médecin Major - F Cormon
9. Jean Marie Caujolle - A Calbert
10. L'Infirmière - Henri Gervex
11. M Millerand Ministre de la Guerre - E Friant
12. Zouave en Famille - Jean Béraud
13. Général Dubail - Albert Fourié
14. Au Repos - Abel Faivre
15. Gloria Martirum - J Paul Laurens
16. Maréchal Sir John French - Marcel Clésinger
17. Le Poilu - François Flameng
18. M Poincaré Président - Narcel Baschet
19. Le Grand-Duc Nicolas - Marcel Clésinger
20. Le Turco - Ferdinand Bac
21. La Conquête - Auguste Rodin
22. Général Cadorna - Leonetto Capiello
23. L'Enfant de Troupe - Charles Léandre
24. Général Foch - Albert Leroux
25. Général Gallieni - A F Gorguet
26. Les Victoires Mutilées - Lucien Jonas
27. Sur l'Yser - Maurice Leloir
28. L'Enfant de Troupe - Charles Léandre
29. L'Ambulancière - Albert Laurens
30. Le Senegalais - Abel Truchet

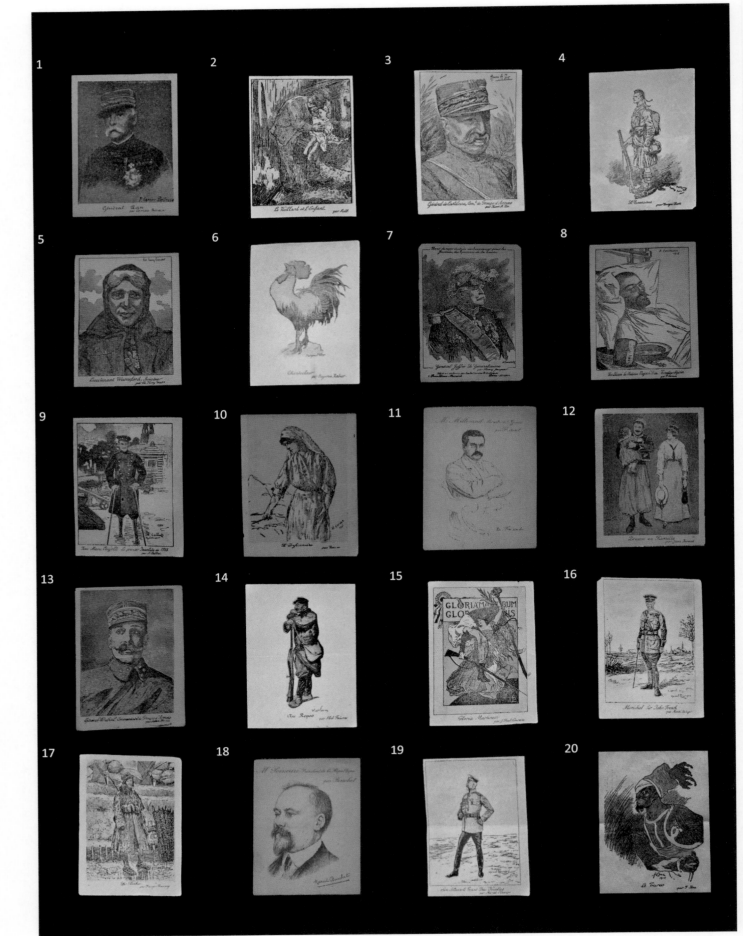

Although all the newspaper articles unanimously refer to 30 different images, de Bayle des Hermens lists 30 designs but he appears to have included duplicate images of Léandre's L'Enfant de Troupe (23 and 28). To further complicate the issue, he added a supplement to his book referring to two further images.

Firstly he illustrated a second version of Gorguet's Général Gallieni (25 and 31).

31

The two versions by Léandre and Gorguet could have a simple explanation - a result of the use of different printing companies.

Secondly he mentions the 'Petit Prince Belge' (32) by Frantz Charlet. This is actually the thirtieth Éprouvé image and the rarest one.

To have an opportunity to win the top prizes in the tombola the public had to collect either 29 or 30 different images. People went to extraordinary lengths to collect their missing Éprouvés, even creating local bourses to trade (see page 45).

Certainly Le Syndicat de la Presse française was faced with many more tombola winners than it had anticipated.

32

Without doubt, the ingenuity and the innovative approach adopted by Le Syndicat de la Presse française, led to this fundraising event being an enormous success which captured the interest of the general public and succeeded in appealing to all age groups.

'La Journée des Éprouvés a été très fructueuse'
Le Journal 27 September page 2

'La Journée de la Pochette'
Le Figaro 27 September page 2

'La Grande Journée des Éprouvés de la Guerre'
Le Temps 28 September page 4

An examination of some of the French national newspapers from the period 26-27 September gives an interesting insight into the coordination and success of the informally named *'La Journée des Pochettes'*.

Le Figaro (outlined in blue) describes the lovely weather on the collecting day after incessant rain in the preceding days. The collectors were made up of young girls and boys as well as scouts and wounded soldiers. Additional thanks were given to owners of cinema and concert venues for allowing the pochettes to be sold within these premises.

Le Journal (outlined in red) - describes the frenzied behaviour of some people buying 200 pochettes in their attempt to win the top prizes. By 3 o'clock in the afternoon many of the street collectors had sold all their 500 pochettes.

Reflecting on the undoubted great success of the *Journée*, *Le Temps* (outlined in green) reports how Le Syndicat de la Presse received telegrams from 20 Préfets informing them that individuals in their regions were claiming the top prizes. In fact, by the end of the day over 1000 individuals possessing all 30 images were recorded and no one could really determine who was first to register the win! The article then goes on to suggest that these 'winners' should now go into a second tombola draw.

No additional information is forthcoming regarding this suggestion and one can only assume that Le Syndicat worked out some form of compromise to satisfy all the claimants.

Voulez-vous venir au secours des éprouvés de la Guerre Civils et Militaires?
(OUI!)
Voulez-vous payer à tous ceux qui ont souffert et qui souffrent encore pour vous, votre dette de reconnaissance?
(OUI!)
ACHETEZ DES PETITES POCHETTES
Vous y trouverez
(QUOI?)
Des dessins admirables signés de nos plus grands Maîtres
C'est tout?
(NON!)

Dans Cent mille pochettes, vous trouverez des Bons pour
DEPUIS 25.000' JUSQU'A 5 FRANCS **UN MILLION** DEPUIS 25.000' JUSQU'A 5 FRANCS
ET AVEC CES BONS ?
Avec chacun de ces Bons, selon votre chance, vous pouvez acheter ce que vous voudrez dans le magasin que vous voudrez comme avec un billet de banque
ACHETEZ LES PETITES POCHETTES
pour le prix que vous voudrez

La « Grande Journée des Eprouvés de la guerre »

La « Journée des éprouvés de la guerre » a obtenu hier, à Paris et en province, le plus franc succès.

Vers quatre heures, quand les premiers numéros des journaux du soir ont paru dans les kiosques, apportant les nouvelles de victoires, Paris a présenté un aspect particulièrement émouvant. Une joie contenue brillait dans tous les yeux; on s'arrêtait en plein boulevard, au milieu de la chaussée, pour lire et relire le communiqué, et la foule, toujours grave et recueillie, sans vaines démonstrations, gardait ce calme admirable et cette dignité dont elle ne s'est pas départie depuis un an. Alors, la vente des pochettes a repris avec un entrain plus grand que jamais, et bientôt la plupart des vendeuses, navrées, étaient obligées de déclarer qu'elles n'avaient plus de munitions.

En province, la « Journée des éprouvés de la guerre » a obtenu un succès dont on mesurera la portée par ce seul fait : le Syndicat de la presse a été avisé hier, télégraphiquement, par vingt préfets, que des collections de 29 et 30 pochettes étaient déjà réunies, en plusieurs exemplaires, dans leurs départements respectifs. Dès huit heures et demie du matin, Mme Daille, de Clermont-Ferrand, avisait le préfet du Puy-de-Dôme qu'elle avait réuni les trente dessins différents répartis dans les pochettes. Mme Daille est une acheteuse « individuelle », c'est-à-dire qu'elle a acheté elle-même les pochettes. Ce détail a son importance, attendu qu'une véritable « Bourse » des dessins s'était constituée hier entre beaucoup de personnes qui achetaient les vignettes manquant afin de compléter leur « collection des trente ».

Dans la matinée d'hier, plus de mille personnes se sont présentées rue Drouot, 2, au bureau de l'œuvre des « Eprouvés de la guerre » afin de faire constater qu'elles se trouvaient bien en possession des trente dessins requis. Mais comment départager tous les possesseurs de la collection des trente dessins qui ont fait leur déclaration à la même seconde? Nous croyons savoir que l'on va ajouter des lots à ceux qui existent, et constituer ainsi une tombola nouvelle à laquelle participeront tous les ayants-droit.

La Journée des Éprouvés a été très fructueuse

De nouveau, les gentils quêteurs, garçons et jeunes filles, ont parcouru Paris, sollicitant les passants « pour les éprouvés de la guerre ».

Cette fois, c'était « la journée des pochettes »; chaque petite enveloppe contenait un dessin et quelquefois un bon donnant droit à un lot important. En outre, le Syndicat de la Presse française, qui organisait cette journée, avait décidé que les souscripteurs qui les premiers présenteraient la collection des trente dessins contenus dans les pochettes bénéficieraient d'une prime. On pouvait gagner une auto, un service d'argenterie, un ameublement de 3.000 francs, un piano, etc. Il s'agissait de réunir les trente dessins un à un. Certains souscripteurs ont acheté cent ou deux cents pochettes pour essayer d'y parvenir et tous n'y ont pas réussi, mais la souscription en a largement profité.

À 3 heures après-midi, certains petits quêteurs avaient écoulé plus de cinq cents pochettes; à 5 heures, les corbeilles étaient vides.

C'est au *Gaulois*, 2, rue Drouot, qu'on devait aller déposer les collections et dès 11 heures des concurrents se présentaient; bientôt les bureaux de notre confrère furent envahis et dans la rue Drouot on dut organiser un service d'ordre, car voici ce qui se produisit.

Parmi les heureux détenteurs de dessins, beaucoup, malgré le nombre considérable de pochettes achetées, n'avaient en leur possession que *vingt-neuf* dessins au lieu de trente, que *vingt-huit* au lieu de *vingt-neuf*.

La Journée de la Pochette

Après les journées de pluie incessantes que nous venions de subir, on n'était pas sans appréhension pour ce dimanche de la Pochette. Le ciel, par bonheur, s'est montré hier plus favorable et, dès sept heures du matin, les vendeuses, jeunes femmes, jeunes filles, fillettes, accompagnées de garçonnets, boy-scouts et soldats blessés, se sont répandues par les rues, les boulevards, les jardins, les bois de Boulogne et de Vincennes. Et partout les promeneurs, les passants répondaient avec empressement à leur appel. Tout le monde, riche comme pauvre, achetait. Il est des personnes qui n'en prenaient qu'une ou deux, mais combien en voulaient dix, vingt, cinquante et quelquefois même davantage.

Il en a été ainsi toute la journée jusqu'à la nuit. Impossible de dire ce que sera la recette, ni même d'émettre une hypothèse. Elle s'annonce magnifique, et tout ce que nous savons c'est qu'elle atteindra et dépassera même les prévisions les plus optimistes.

On doit des félicitations aux directeurs des théâtres, des cinémas, des concerts parisiens, qui ont autorisé la vente de la pochette au cours des matinées d'hier : de grosses sommes ont été recueillies pendant les entr'actes. Car, partout et en tout lieu, Paris a voulu montrer qu'il était toujours sensible à une belle œuvre de charité.

La Journée du Poilu
31 October and 1 November 1915

The first La Journée du Poilu
31 October and 1 November 1915

Encouraged by the success of the *Orphelinat des Armées* campaign, the French Parliament decided to raise funds for front line troops through, what was originally called, a *Journée du Combattant*. Despite a great deal of support for this title, the word 'Combattant' came to be replaced with the term 'Poilu'. This nickname or slang term, which was ironically so disliked by the frontline troops, was to become a prominent feature of this huge campaign.

It is interesting to note that even at that current time, the political climate was strained and the *Journal Des Débats Politiques et Littéraires* in 1915 had to publish an article disclaiming the idea that it was purely a government initiative, and declared that the concept had the support of senators, deputies and town councillors from all political persuasions (see right).

Compared to some of the problems that were to emerge as the arrangements for the *Journée du Poilu* took shape, the need to deny that the fund-raising days concept was solely due to government action and that the word 'Poilu' was a derogatory term, were to prove to be fairly minor issues!

The organising Parliamentary Committee (*Comité parlementaire d'organisation*) invited celebrated French medallists and artists to submit ideas for the various items to be sold to the general public. A deadline was set for 17 September 1915 for the artists to make their submissions.

Not put off by the hostile reaction he encountered from various sections of the Press and public to his Orphelinat plaquette (see page 30), René Lalique was persuaded to submit sketches of his Poilu designs. He was disappointed to discover that his proposed ideas were placed second out of all the submissions because several of the Committee members felt that, like the Orphelinat design, his proposals could be regarded yet again as far too controversial.

Above:
The headline from the *Echo de Paris* 23 September 1915.

Below:
Extract from the *Journal Des Débats Politiques et Littéraires* 19 November 1915.

Dimensions: 30mm

The winning medal design (see above) put forward by Hippolyte-Jules Lefèbvre was based on a far more traditional format than that of Lalique's. It was the one officially adopted to be the centre-piece for the first *Journée du Poilu* campaign . This was originally set to take place on 31 October through to 1 November 1915.

No one could have envisaged the problems that this choice would create, which ended with the Committee and Lalique being embroiled in a rather unsavoury court case, eventually resolved in 1918!

Having won the design competition, Lefèbvre had difficulty in overseeing the actual production of the medal. This was mainly due to his choice of engraver but he also encountered problems in obtaining the necessary raw materials and having them delivered on time. In agreeing a contract with the Committee, Lefèbvre had accepted the request for six million medals to be delivered on a set date but was only able to produce 300,000 just before the deadline. On top of this failure, he also demanded a higher price for the medals than that agreed when the contract had been drawn up.

As a result, the Committee made the decision to intervene in the process. It cancelled the Lefèbvre contract, ordered the production of millions of cardboard insignias and transferred the medal contract to Lalique who promptly decided to make use of his own design at the expense of Lefebvre's.

Angered by the Committee's actions, Lefèbvre was prompted to take out a lawsuit against both the Committee and Lalique. Lalique was charged with failing to supervise the production of Lefèbvre's winning design having opted instead to use his own design. A counterclaim, for the sum of 500,000 francs compensation, was lodged by the Committee for the disruption caused by Lefèbvre's inability to meet the set deadlines. This claim was summarily dismissed and the Court decided to award Lefèbvre the nominal amount of one franc in damages. Lalique was held 'in solidum' - singly liable for the whole amount payment due to Lefèbvre.

Despite being awarded a token amount, Lefèbvre felt that his reputation had been fully restored. His personal victory could be described, however, as a Pyrrhic victory given that it was the name 'Lalique' that appeared on hundreds of thousands of items, and it was Lalique's iconic motif that was forever associated with the 'Poilu Day'.

Below:
Le Matin 30 July - this rather unassuming headline on page 2 was one of the earliest announcements regarding the 31 October/1 November event.

La " Journée du Poilu "

On nous communique la note suivante :
La réunion des parlementaires qui avaient pris l'initiative d'une journée au profit des combattants a eu lieu hier à la Chambre.
Le gouvernement ayant adhéré à ce projet, toutes les mesures seront prises en commun entre les parlementaires des deux Chambres pour l'organisation de cette journée dite du « Poilu ».

Compared with the second Journée du Poilu event, this first one was not so highly profiled but because of the success it achieved, it convinced the French parliament to promote a further event scheduled for December.

Above:
This poster created by by Lucien Jonas, along with one designed by Francisque Poulbot (see page 46), helped to promote the first Journée du Poilu scheduled for 31 October - 1 November 1915.

LAPEL PINS

Préfets/Maires throughout all 86 Departments were contacted and given specific details for the organisation of the fundraising that would take place on these two days. Information had to be supplied about the number of postcards, insignias and medals required. The items selected for the fundraising included lapel pins, medals, cardboard insignias and postcards.

The lapel pins were oval in shape and produced in a variety of colours - de Bayle des Hermens lists 16 in total but it is very likely that there were more than that. It is important to take into account that a number of different printing companies were used in the production process and it is also likely that there were slight differences in the materials and inks that were used. All the lapel pins had the identical legend in blue lettering on white:
Journées/du/Poilu/31Octobre/1er Novembre/1915

In addition to the insignias, four different flag pins were also sold during the first scheduled *Journée du Poilu.*

20 (H) x 23 (W) mm   20 (H) x 23 (W) mm

1. French flag with a golden fringe. The Senate emblem is on the white vertical band of side 1. On the white vertical band of side 2, in black lettering the legend: *Aux/Poilus/Le/Parlement/31 Octobre/ 1er Novembre/1915.*
The printer's name is set on the vertical red band: Lapina Paris.

2. French flag with a golden fringe. The National Assembly emblem is on the white vertical band of side 1. On the white vertical band of side 2, in black lettering: *Aux / Poilus / Le / Parlement / 31 Octobre / 1er Novembre /1915.*

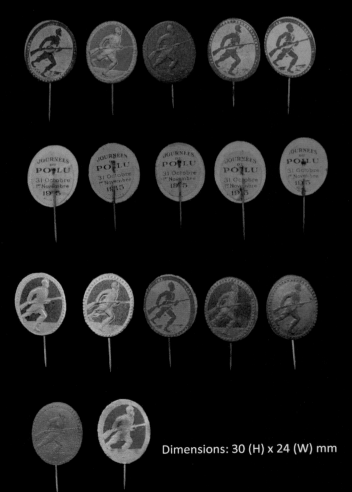

Dimensions: 30 (H) x 24 (W) mm

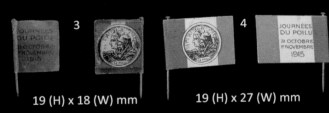

19 (H) x 18 (W) mm   19 (H) x 27 (W) mm

3. French flag with a golden fringe. Side 1 has a reproduction of Lefèbvre's medal (Le Poilu) set in a black rimmed circle. On side 2 in black lettering on the gold background:
Journées/du Poilu/31 Octobre/1^{er}November/1915.

4. Side 1 has the French tricolour flag with a reproduction of Lefèbvre's medal set in a black rimmed circle. On the white vertical band of side 2, in black lettering:
Journées/du Poilu/31 Octobre/1^{er}November/1915.

INSIGNIAS

Initially three insignias were sold along with the lapel pins. Public demand led to a further set of six insignias being produced by Lapina.

Dimensions: 33mm

Dimensions: 37mm

1. An unusual shaped insignia in the shape of a four-leaf clover with a gold colour background on both the obverse and reverse. A poilu wearing a képi and dressed in a horizon blue uniform is the focal point with an allied flag on each of the clover leaves - France, Russia, Great Britain and Italy.

A four line legend in white lettering is set on the reverse:
Journées du Poilu/31 Octobre/1ᵉʳ Novembre/1915.

The printer's name is set immediately below the legend: Devambez Gr. / Paris.

2. A square shaped insignia with cut corners. A gold frame with an array of laurel leaves in each corner forms a frame around a circle measuring 26 mm in diameter.

Inside the circle, against what appears to be a battlefield background, a 'chasseur alpin' (alpine hunter) is charging forward clutching his rifle with bayonet. The 'chasseurs alpins' were trained to operate in mountainous terrain and regarded as an elite infantry force of the French Army.

The reverse is light blue set within a white frame. At the top, a dark blue 'ribbon' has a distinctive white legend: *Journees du Poilu.*
The dates *31 Octobre/1ᵉʳ Novembre/1915* are set in blue ink on a white 'scroll' frame. The printer's italicised name is set in the bottom right corner - Chambrelent Paris .

As with many of the insignias, several 'varieties' exist because of the quality of inks used in the printing process.

Dimensions: 36 (H) x 32 (W) mm

3. An image of a Zouave, wearing the traditional chéchia, taking aim with a rifle is set within an octagonal golden frame.
On the white reverse background a six line legend is set out in blue:
Journées/du/Poilu/31 Octobre/1ᵉʳ Novembre/1915.

No printer's name is on the insignia.

The six insignias produced by Lapina - one of the great Parisian printing companies - were designed in various shapes and sizes but all of them bore the same legend and imagery on the reverse.

The emblems of the Senate and the Chamber of Deputies on each side of a palm are on the reverse white background with a legend in brown lettering *Aux/Poilus/Le/Parlement.* The printer's name is set immediately below the legend: I Lapina, Édit. Paris.

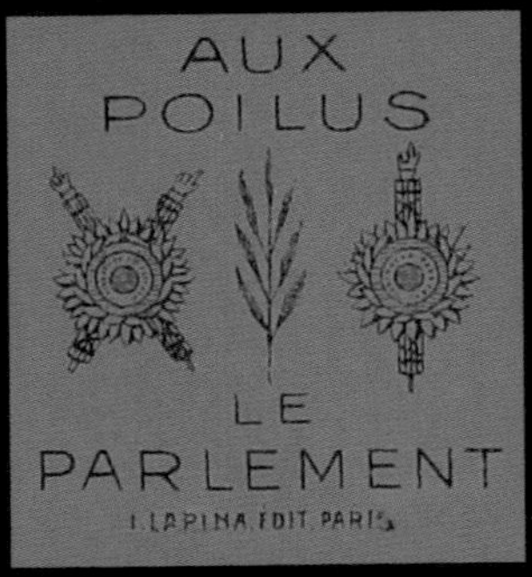

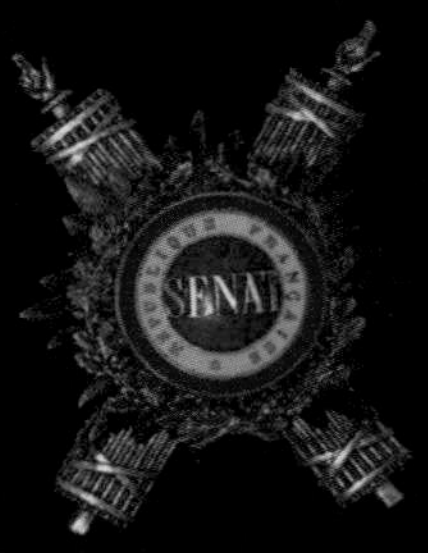

Le Sénat

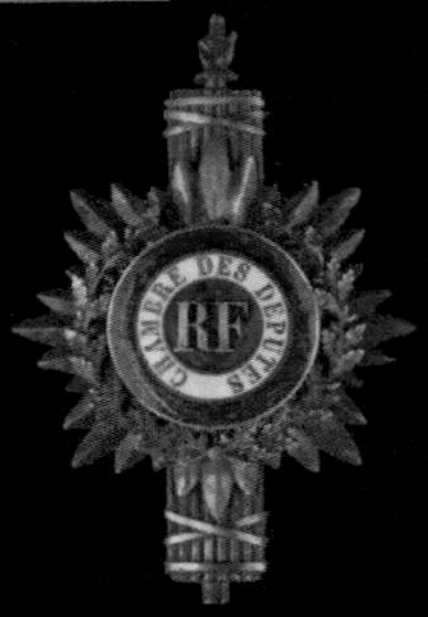

Chambre des Députés

Le Sénat (the Senate) was the name given to the upper house of the French Parliament which, along with the Chambre des Députés (Chamber of Deputies), formed the legislative branch of the government of the French Third Republic.

The French Third Republic was the name given to the republican government of France that ruled from 4 September 1870 to 10 July 1940. During the disastrous Franco-Prussian War (1870-71), the French Emperor Napoleon III was captured and the French army was decimated. At the Hôtel de Ville, the statesman Léon Gambetta[13] publicly declared the founding of the Government of National Defence on 4 September. The provisional government immediately assumed control of all affairs in France.

Dimensions: 35mm

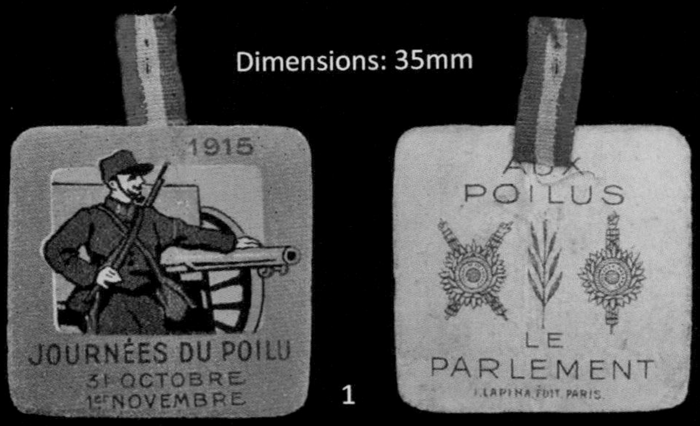

1

1. A square insignia with rounded corners. An image of an 'Artilleur' (Gunner) leaning on a 75 mm field gun on a gold background features on the obverse. The '1915' date is in the top right corner and the legend is below the image in black lettering:

Journées du Poilu / 31 Octobre / 1er Novembre.

Dimensions: 35mm

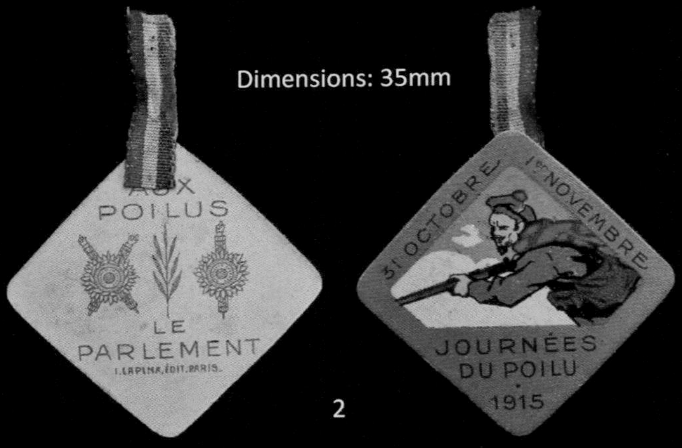

2

2. A square insignia with rounded corners. The obverse features the image of an armed 'Fusilier Marin' (land based naval marines), wearing the distinctive uniform and blue beret with red pom pom, charging forward against a background of a blue sky.

In black lettering in the top left rim is '*31 Octobre*' with '*1er Novembre*' along the top right rim. Set below the image in black lettering:

Journées du Poilu / 1915.

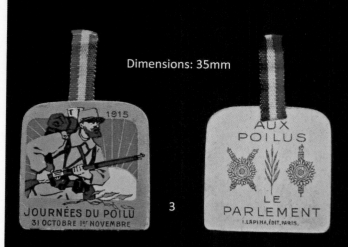

Dimensions: 35mm

3

5. A circular insignia with an image of a 'Zouave', dressed in the traditional colourful uniform, set against a green background, crouched down firing his rifle.

The legend in black lettering is split:
In the top half of the gold surround: *31 Octobre 1915 1er Novembre*. In the lower half - *Journées du Poilu*.

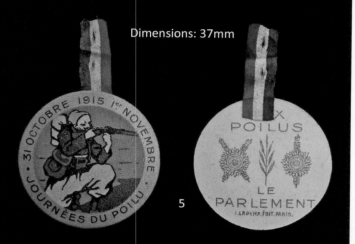

Dimensions: 37mm

5

3. A square shaped insignia with rounded corners. The image is of a 'Poilu', wearing the distinctive horizon blue uniform, charging forward with his rifle against a background of a rising sun.

The '1915' date is in the top right corner and the legend is below the image in black lettering:
Journées du Poilu / 31 Octobre 1er Novembre.

6. A square shaped insignia with concave corners features a 'Tirailleur Algérien' dressed in a light blue jacket and wearing a chéchia, leaning on his rifle, with cartridge belt and a backpack. The image is set against a red background in a golden frame.

The date of *1915* is at the top of the frame and at the bottom *Journées du Poilu*.
The two dates - '*31 Octobre*' and '*1er Novembre*' are set on the two sides.

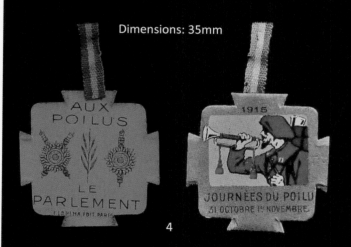

Dimensions: 35mm

4

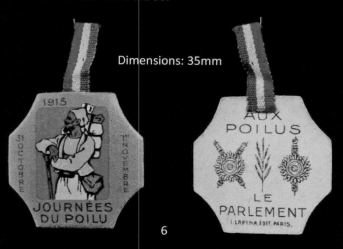

Dimensions: 35mm

4. Insignia cut in the shape of a Maltese cross. Wearing the traditional dark blue wool uniform (called 'Gris de fer bleute') and béret (typically referred to as 'Tarte'), a 'Chasseur Alpin' (elite mountain soldier) is depicted blowing the bugle.

The '1915' date is centred at the top with the two line legend below the image in black lettering:
Journées du Poilu / 31 Octobre 1^{er}Novembre.

6

All monies raised from the sales of the various items were carefully recorded.

Right:
An 'Arrondisement Feuille de Recette' was used to record all the monies collected in a particular 'Quartier'. Paris is made up of 20 administrative districts known as arrondissements and each one is divided into four quartiers. These are not to be confused with the Departmental arrondissements, which subdivided the 86 French Departments that existed in 1914.

Below:
The Bulletin de Recettes was probably recorded by a Commissaire overseeing a group of up to five Quêteuses.

All of the Quêteuses were required to confirm the amounts they had raised individually with their signatures and the total amount raised between them was assessed and signed for by a Comptable (accountant). The Bulletin was then handed in to the Town Hall with the amount raised.

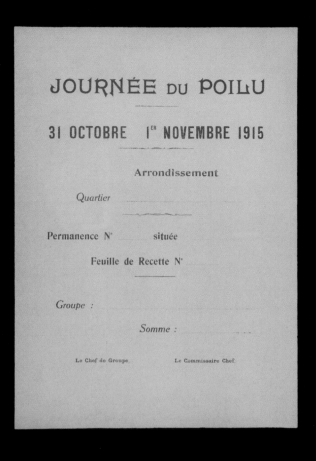

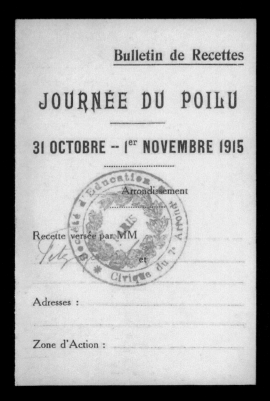

Three postcards were also released to support the event:

Right:
Le Clairon (the bugle) was a design created by Frédéric Regamey. Printed by Lapina, the postcard featured a Zouave soldier with a rifle in one hand and a bugle in the other with other soldiers in the background. The card opened in two and inside was the poem by Paul Déroulède 'Le Clairon', as well as a small portrait of Déroulède.[14]

Below:
Designed by Lucien Jonas, this card features two poilus, one of whom is watching his colleague opening a small parcel (colis) of supplies sent from home.

The words: "Avec vous et par vous nous jurons de sauver la France", were coined by Léon Gambetta, a French politician, statesman and one of the founders of the Third Republic. The phrase was a rallying cry during the Franco-Prussian war of 1870 -1871.

Right:
The third postcard - "Les Aigles Noirs!" This was a famous marching song composed by René de Buxeuil and Maurice Boukay.

All three of the postcards sold for this event bore a unique number on the reverse and all of these were entered into a Tombola prize. Postcards sold for the December *Journée du Poilu* still featured the Lefèbvre medal (outlined in red) but the two symbols of the Chambre des Députés and Sénat were replaced with Lalique's two Poilu designs.

La Journée du Poilu
25 December and 26 December 1915

The second La Journée du Poilu
25 and 26 December

There was little doubt that the two *Journées du Poilu* were immensely successful but it would be fair to say that the second fundraising event totally eclipsed the first one. Any review of the French national newspapers for 1915 will reveal that there was hardly a mention of the first event held on the 31 October / 1 November. The second one, however, enthused the media and this in turn helped to captivate the general public's attention. The reasons for this were largely due to the choice of the Christmas period, nationwide publicity, press support and the incredible array of medals, insignias and postcards that were placed on sale.

Similar to the modus operandi adopted by the *Orphelinat des Armées* campaign, Departments were authorised to continue the 'Poilu' fundraising over the following years on a regional basis and this undoubtedly helped the promotion.

After the bitter court case which involved René Lalique and Hyppolyte Lefèbvre (see page 48), the latter's design was largely sidelined and only sold as table medals or used as presentation pieces (see bottom far right).

The medal designs that took centre stage were those of Lalique and Armand Bargas.

Early on in his career, Lalique gained a reputation for being both a perfectionist and an innovative designer. The Poilu designs he created came to represent everything that the poilus stood for. Unquestionably, the Bargas medals proved to be very popular but it was the Lalique medals, brooches and lapel pins which really caught the imagination of the public and they soon became sought after pieces.

Right:
The article from the front page of *Le Petit Parisien* dated 18 November, illustrates the high profile that the Journée enjoyed.

La « Journée du Poilu »

Elle aura lieu dans toutes les communes de France, les 25 et 26 décembre prochain. L'initiative en revient aux membres du Parlement qui, sans distinction de partis, après avoir apporté

Le bijou de Lalique

leur concours aux œuvres de solidarité nationale et départementale, ont pensé que les « Poilus », eux aussi, devaient avoir leur « journée ». Pourquoi ? Pour donner à ceux d'entre eux qui n'ont pas de famille ou dans la famille est dans le besoin le moyen de profiter à leur tour de leurs permissions. Parce qu'elle était juste, cette simple idée a fait son chemin.

Le bénéfice de la « Journée » sera intégralement distribué aux permissionnaires par l'entremise des chefs de corps. Des médailles, cartes postales, insignes, bijoux, souvenirs seront exposés dans les magasins et débits et vendus publiquement par les soins des organisations régionales et municipales, professionnelles et corporatives. L'achat des cartes postales, toutes numérotées, donnera droit au tirage de la « Tombola du Poilu », qui comprendra les œuvres des maîtres sculpteurs et dessinateurs choisis au concours.

Après la médaille d'*Hippolyte Lefèbvre*, qui symbolise à merveille le « Poilu » tenace et la France invincible, les affiches de la « Journée » ne sont pas moins suggestives. Voici l'admirable fantassin de *Jonas* dans la position du tireur debout, près d'un arbre, regardant une minute son camarade en extase devant sa boîte de médaille et de souvenirs ! Derrière eux, sur un mur éventré par les obus, une vieille affiche parlementaire porte le fier appel de Gambetta : « Avec vous et par vous, nous jurons de sauver la France ! »

Une autre estampe, de *Maurice Neumont*, représente un soldat géant, escaladant les collines champenoises pour lancer dans les tranchées ennemies, parmi les fils de fer barbelés, la grenade vengeresse. Les bombes pleuvent et éclatent autour de lui. Rien ne l'arrête ! Il combattra l'aigle noir jusqu'au bout ! C'est tragique, impressionnant et superbe, comme un colossal défi !

∗∗

Voici la bonne vieille mère, de *Léandre*. Assise au coin de la cheminée, à la lueur du foyer qui flambole, elle vient de lire la lettre de son troupier. Elle songe ! Et dans la fumée du rêve se dessine l'épopée glorieuse. Cavaliers et fantassins s'élancent, sous les plis du drapeau, derrière les clairons, au chant de la *Marseillaise*, clamé à pleins poumons : « Bonne vieille, que fais-tu là ? — J'attends mon gars qui batailla là ? » Déroulède eût applaudi à cette émouvante évocation du bon gîte !

Après la mère, voici la femme de la promise : Jenny l'ouvrière ou Mimi Pinson. Elle a passé combien de nuits à coudre sur sa machine les chemises du paquet du soldat, de son soldat ! C'est aujourd'hui qu'elle l'attend. Il entre ! Elle renverse sa chaise de paille et se jette à son cou ; « Enfin seuls ! » dit la légende. Seuls ? Non, pas tout à fait ! Car le petit chien du poilu contemple de ses yeux écarquillés cette scène de famille où *Willette* a mis toute l'espié-

glerie de son esprit et toute la tendresse de son cœur.

C'est Noël, dans la rue ! *Poulbot* n'a pas craint d'y camper les fines silhouettes de ses deux gosses : la grande « française » en infirmière, tendant à la générosité des promeneurs sa tirelire enrubannée, et le gamin de la « maternelle », coiffé crânement d'un képi de soldat, délaissant la petite guerre pour la grande, offrant aux acheteurs son panier tout

fleuri de drapeaux et d'insignes « pour que papa vienne en permission, s'il vous plaît ! »

Et voici, leurs congés expirés, les deux poilus « costauds » et rustiques, le territorial et « Marie-Louise », le premier avec son regard scrutateur, sa moustache en broussaille, sa pipe et son bâton : l'autre enthousiaste et rêveur, une rose au coin de la bouche ; tous deux retournent à leur gourbi prendre la place des camarades dont c'est bien le tour de partir en permission, là-bas, vers la tiédeur du foyer ami. Cette affiche, signée du maître *Steinlen* est un chef-d'œuvre d'énergie et de sincérité !

Vous admirerez sur les murs toutes ces affiches. Il faut vous rappeler que ces dessins originaux ou lithographiés, en noir ou en couleurs, avant ou après la lettre, constitueront, avec les médailles, les lots de la tombola. Mais, comme en raison des nécessités formidables de l'affichage et de la vente, il n'y en aura que pour un nombre limité de gagnants, le comité de la « Journée du Poilu » a pensé que chacun serait bien aise d'en posséder une image réduite. Il a donc fait tirer ces estampes en cartes postales. Pour deux sous, vous pourrez en expédier une aux poilus du front. Les marraines généreuses joindront à la collection des huit cartes l'envoi d'une épingle sculptée. Et ce sera parfait !

Ainsi les plus humbles conserveront un souvenir artistique de cette journée fraternelle. Et les plus riches, les amateurs, les collectionneurs n'hésiteront pas à payer cent francs la magnifique broche en or de *Lalique* ou la médaille grand module de *Lefèbvre*, à quoi les parlementaires, dont c'est aussi la journée, ne manqueront pas de souscrire. Tous apporteront leur contribution à l'union sacrée, qui relie à ceux qui sont partis ceux qui restent et celles qui n'oublient pas !

Le Président de la République, les présidents du Sénat et de la Chambre, les membres du gouvernement ont accepté

— Pour que papa vienne en permission, s'il vous plaît !

le haut patronage de la « Journée du Poilu ». Nos alliés s'y associeront de même : les Anglais, pour qui le Christmas est une fête quasi-nationale, les Belges, les Italiens, les Russes, les Monténégrins et les Serbes, auxquels nos soldats porteront nos médailles et nos vœux ; les neutres, les Américains en tête, se disputent déjà les bijoux du Poilu ! C'est de bon augure pour le succès !

Chez nous, chaque semaine, les préfets reçoivent du comité, installé à la mairie du quatrième arrondissement, à Paris, les caisses d'affiches, de cartes, d'insignes que les compagnies de chemins de fer transportent gratuitement. Les vendeurs et les vendeuses les auront ; assez tôt dans chaque ville et dans chaque village de France, d'Algérie et des colonies. Les évêques, les pasteurs, les rabbins, les instituteurs, les institutrices, les artistes rivaliseront de zèle. Les directeurs de théâtres, concerts et cinémas, graphes ont promis une journée de recettes. La presse tout entière donnera son concours au Parlement pour que nos magnifiques poilus aient une journée digne d'eux ! Noël ! Noël ! En attendant la victoire finale, la « Journée du Poilu » sera la journée de la France !

Ch.-M. COUYBA,
sénateur, ancien ministre

INSIGNIAS

The six insignias produced by Lapina for the first *Journée du Poilu* held on 31 October/1 November (see pages 51-52) were reproduced for the second *Journée du Poilu* event.

Exactly the same six designs were used as well as the shapes and sizes. Obviously the dates on the obverse were different but the major change was on the reverse where the emblems of the Senate and the Chamber of Deputies were replaced with the Lalique designs. It was felt that there was no longer any need for an additional legend on the reverse. The printer's name (Lapina, Édit) was retained on the new set of insignias.

1. The 'Artilleur' (Gunner) with the Lalique Poilu brooch design.

2. The 'Fusilier Marin' (land based naval marines) with the Lalique lapel pin design.

3. The 'Poilu' with the Lalique Poilu brooch design.

4. The 'Chasseur Alpin' (mountain soldier) with the Lalique Poilu brooch design.

5. The 'Zouave' with the Lalique lapel pin design.

6. The 'Tirailleur Algérien' with the Lalique lapel pin design.

Below:

Two examples of a second version of the insignias.

These combine the reverse 'format' of the Senate and the Chamber of Deputies symbols which were used for the insignias sold on the first *Journée* (see page 51). The plain white background used for the first *Journée,* was replaced with the gold coloured background used for the second *Journée.*

No reference to these insignias is made by de Bayle des Hermens in his book so the assumption can be made that they are rare. It is possible that they were printed by accident or as a sample as there appears to be no evidence of such a set ever having been produced for sale.

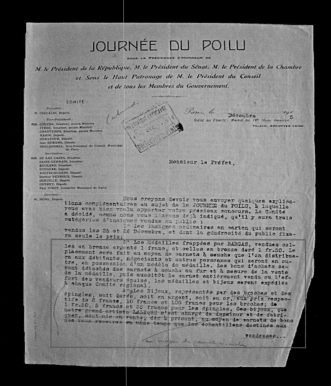

Above:

A letter sent to the Prefecture of Cantal revealed just how much the campaign was meticulously planned. The letter set out the three different categories of insignias being sold to the general public on the 25-26 December 1915. Category 1 related to the flag pins and cardboard badges. The public were encouraged to buy these from the numerous collectors out in force on the two days. The amounts paid for these items were left to the generosity of the members of the public.

Right:

Four different flag pins were also sold during the second scheduled event of the *Journées du Poilu*. The designs for these were identical to those sold on the first fundraising day (for full descriptors see page 49).

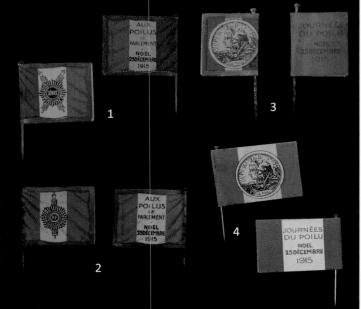

The second category, which was referred to in the letter, related to the medals designed by Armand Bargas - the bronze argenté medals (below right) were to be sold for 1 franc and the bronze doré (below left and middle) for 1 franc 50.

Apart from the '25-26 Décembre' version, Bargas also designed three other versions of the medal which were produced in both bronze argenté and bronze doré :

Dimensions: 34 (H) x 30 (W) mm

A second version exists of the model bearing the names and dates of famous battles. This is likely to be attributable to the use of different manufacturers.

Above:
An extremely rare version of the medal also exists which has a blank reverse.

Above:
Such was the popularity of the Bargas medals that demand quickly exceeded supply and therefore a subscription system had to be introduced (see page 66).

Below:
Le Figaro 25 December 1915
Note the description of the immense popularity of the Bargas and Lalique commemorative pieces and how to reserve them.

LA JOURNÉE DU POILU

Aujourd'hui, Journée du Poilu, qui se prolongera jusqu'à demain soir. Dans toutes les villes et dans tous les villages de France, jeunes femmes et jeunes filles qui ont répondu avec un admirable empressement à l'appel du comité parlementaire, offriront sur la voie publique, les insignes et les médailles du Poilu, dessinés par nos plus illustres artistes. La générosité de l'acheteur, comme on le sait, en fixera le prix.

En raison des demandes de la médaille de Bargas, le jeune prix de Rome, ainsi que des bijoux du grand artiste Lalique, ceux qui veulent posséder ces bijoux et, par cela même, contribuer au succès de l'œuvre de la «Journée du Poilu», devront réclamer dans les préfectures, sous-préfectures, mairies et chez les commerçants, un billet de souscription donnant droit à ces objets.

Below:

Throughout 1916 and 1917, the authorities took the decision to allow the various Bargas designs to be sold in shops and by authorised street vendors.

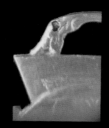

Even the rarer versions of the Bargas medals were sold in this format (see below).

Above:

A close examination of the medal reveals the usual boar's head poinçon on the suspension loop and a maker's hallmark belonging to Albert Bazor and his son Lucien Georges Bazor who later served as the Chief Engraver at the Paris Mint from 1930 to 1958.

As well as the medal, the Bargas design was also produced as a brooch - again in bronze argenté and bronze doré. These were not mass produced on the scale of the medal which, by the end of the war had sold in excess of four million - a testament to the astonishing popularity of the design with the French public.

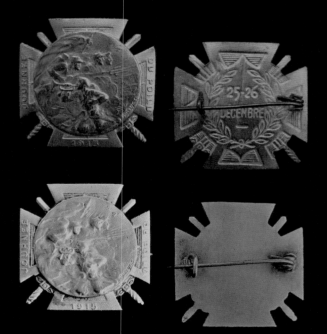

Bargas also produced his Poilu medal in solid silver and in vermeil. The one set out below is a vermeil model - made of gold plated solid sterling silver.

Dimensions: 34 (H) x 30 (W) mm

Dimensions: 30 (H) x 30 (W) mm

As can be seen, the brooches were produced in two different formats - although the obverse was identical the reverse was either blank or bore the identical markings of the traditional medal format with the legend '25-26 Décembre'.

Journée du Poilu brooch

Apart from the cardboard insignias, lapel pins and the Bargas medals, the other items that were sold for the second *Journée du Poilu* fundraising days were those designed by René Lalique.

The brooch that Lalique designed was made in the form of a Maltese Cross and was produced mainly in gilt bronze as well as silver.

The first version sold during December 1915 bore the 'Le Parlement' legend which was the official endorsement of the French Government. At the bottom it also included the legend:
'Journée du Poilu 1915' and *'R Lalique'*.

Dimension: 34 mm
Weight: 10.36 gm

The great success of the Poilu days far exceeded the most optimistic expectations and the demand for the Lalique designed brooches was immense.

A second version which omitted the inscription of *'Le Parlement'* was produced in gilt bronze, silver and gold and continued to be sold during the later years of the war (see above).

All the gilt bronze and silver brooches were sold in a light or dark green cardboard presentation box (see bottom left) which measured 53 mm square and 9 mm in depth.

The box contained a small green cardboard inset which held the brooch firmly in the box.

The attachment was a simple pin made of steel and a 'C' clasp.

Dimension: 34 mm
Weight: 9.68 gm

Gold version: Journée du Poilu brooch

When it was sold to the general public in 1915, the gold brooch cost ten times that of the silver one, and as a result it was only purchased by very wealthy individuals. They were also distributed to a number of Government Ministers and particular individuals who held the prominent positions in the various Departments throughout France or who played major roles in the organization of the fundraising days.

This particular model was stamped with an assay mark on the pin and the eagle's head (indicating 18 karat gold) on the clasp.

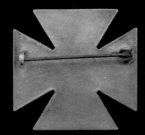

Dimension: 34 mm
Weight: 12.12 gm

Silver version: Journée du Poilu brooch

The silver model was normally stamped with the Lalique silver maker's hallmark on the reverse of the brooch. It can be easily identified - Lalique's initials 'RL' are separated by an épée /sword within a small diamond shaped lozenge. In addition, the mark of the Paris Assay Office - the boar's head - is sometimes found on the side of the 'C' clasp.

Some of the silver brooches that were produced were missing either the 'Lalique' mark and/or the Paris Assay Office silver mark. This was probably simply down to human error as demand exceeded the supply - as a result, the manufacturing process became somewhat rushed!

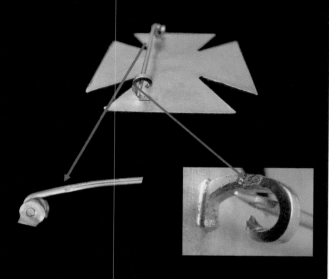

Dimension: 34.5 mm
Weight: 12.71 gm

Journée du Poilu lapel pin

Just like the brooch, the lapel pins were made in gilt bronze, silver and gold. The first version of the pin had the inscription of 'Le Parlement' (see below) - the recognition that these lapel pins were produced for the officially endorsed December 1915 session of the *Journées du Poilu*.

Dimensions: 72 (H) x 17 (W) mm
Weight: 3.03 gm

The second version of the Poilu lapel pin dropped the inscription of 'Le Parlement' replacing it solely with 'Le Poilu 1915'. A third version adjusted the positioning of this inscription to near the top of the rim.

Right:
After the success of the two officially endorsed *Journées du Poilu*, the authorities decided it would be sensible to continue to promote the campaign. To this end, bronze Lalique *Journée du Poilu Bijou-Souvenir* lapel pins, as well as the various Bargas medals, continued to be sold throughout France. The previous subscription processes that had been implemented were no longer used as these items were sold throughout France in shops and through street vendors. Presentation boxes were replaced with highly visible cardboard backing sheets.

The silver model of the pin bears the inscription of 'Le Poilu 1915' and is normally stamped with the Lalique silver maker's mark and the boar's head.

Dimensions of silver pin: 72 (H) x 17 (W) mm
Weight: 3.81 gm

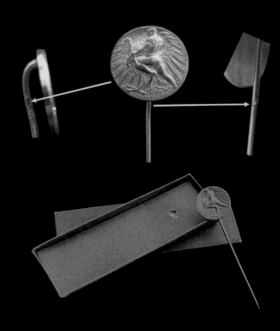

The gold version of the pin was identical to the silver pin and can be easily identified from its bronze counterpart by the mark of the Paris Assay Office (the eagle's head - see page 62), the Lalique maker's mark and a weight difference of about one gram.

Dimensions: 126 (H) x 82 (W) mm

Due to the popularity of the Lalique items, many authorities quickly ran out of them. It was decided to adopt a similar modus operandi to that used with the Bargas designs - problems of supply and high demand were circumvented by implementing a subscription/reservation process. Items could be paid for and reserved to be picked up at a later date from Lalique's boutique or, if purchased in other areas outside the Paris region, at a particular Department Prefecture.

Above right:

A subscription booklet used by vendors to reserve requested Lalique items. Prices for the different versions of the brooch and lapel pin are clearly set out. Costs relating to the Lalique brooches: bronze doré - 2 francs; silver - 10 francs; and gold - 100 francs. The costs of the lapel pins were 1 franc 50 for bronze doré, 5 francs for silver and 35 francs for gold.

Below and right:

Interestingly the Comité d'Organisation decided to encourage the sellers of the items to sell as many as they could by setting out an incentive.

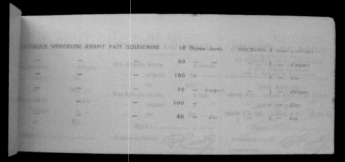

For example, if a seller sold 10 brooches 'Bijoux dorés' they would receive a free brooch; if they sold 150 brooches they qualified for a gold one.

Selling 10 lapel pins 'd'argent' would entitle the seller to a silver lapel pin and if they managed to sell 100 brooches or lapel pins they would receive a free gold equivalent. Selling 40 gold items would be rewarded with a free gold "semblable". All the free items would be uniquely engraved with the seller's initials.

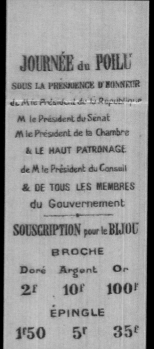

Left:
A ribbon made of silk with gold lettering.

These ribbons were hung over street vendors' stalls and in shops setting out the clear authorization for the collection. In addition it also detailed the prices for reserving the particular Lalique items.

Dimensions: 205 (H) x 55 (W) mm

Right:

These gummed labels were widely distributed and were stuck on the collecting boxes used for the fundraising day.

Dimensions: 80 (H) x 135 (W) mm

Below:

Every collector was given an identity card which was to be prominently worn. Note the warning on the reverse, that it was for the sole use of the named individual.

Below:

A photo was given to each of the eight quêteuses as a souvenir of the fundraising days. It was thanks to the efforts of thousands of individuals like the ones in the photo that led the second *Journée du Poilu* being a resounding success.

Below:

Delivery notes sent from Lalique's residence and workshop to the Prefect of the Cantal Department. The notes set out clearly the number of brooches and lapel pins which had been reserved following a request from the Prefecture.

Below:

A commissaire's identity card and armband .

Dimensions: 75 (H) x 120 (W) mm

A commissaire was the individual appointed to be in charge of the collections taking place in a certain area.

The second note is advising that a further 30 silver lapel pins with presentation boxes and three silver brooches and boxes were being sent out.

Below:

A letter dated 7 January 1916 lists the items sent to the Secretary General of the Bibliothèque et Des Travaux Historiques de la Ville de Paris - Hôtel le Peletier de Saint-Fargeau 29 rue de Sévigné (which is now part of the Musée Carnavalet, Paris).

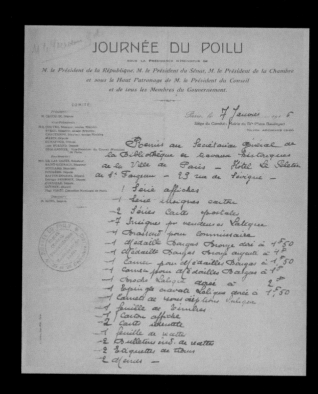

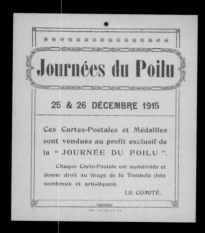

Above:

A display card explaining that the postcards and medals for sale in the shop were exclusively for *La Journée du Poilu 25 & 26 Décembre 1915*. A brief explanation is also given regarding the numbering of the postcards allowing entry into the Tombola.

Below:

A block of 20 'vignettes' (stamps) featuring the Lucien Jonas and Francisque Poulbot postcard and poster designs (see page 69).

Below:

A subscription form which allowed individuals to reserve medals and brooches.

66

Right:

The front page of *Excelsior* (26 December 1915) reveals the importance attached by the media to the *Journées du Poilu*. The fundraising success was described as "un succès qui ne se connut pas de précédent" and to an extent this was undoubtedly true regarding the numbers of insignias, medals, brooches etc that were sold and the publicity given to the event. In terms of the actual net revenues, however, several other *Journées* easily eclipsed *Les Journées du Poilu* (see page 17).

Above:

Further evidence of the high profile given to the *Journées du Poilu*, can be seen with the front page of *Le Pèlerin* 2 January 1916.

Right:

Excelsior Tuesday 21 December: A whole page was used for advertising the various items intended for sale. Comments were made regarding the posters designed specifically for the occasion by some of France's most illustrious artists and concludes with the statement:

"la vente consituera un capital destiné à venir en aide à nos soldats".

The Journée du Poilu table medals

Three table medal versions designed by Hyppolite Lefèbvre and René Lalique were manufactured for the second *Journée du Poilu* event. As they were not mass produced they are difficult to find. Rather than being sold to the general public they were probably distributed to various individuals who were prominently involved in the fundraising activities for the *Journée du Poilu*.

The first table medal to be designed was that of Lefèbvre for the first *Journée du Poilu*. It featured an armed poilu wearing the traditional képi along with Marianne, the symbol of the French Republic, crowned with a laurel wreath. The Republic 'Écu' inscribed 'RF' was positioned on top of three criss-crossed fasces.

Dimensions of silver table medal: 55 mm x 12 mm
Weight: 72.74 gm

Following Lefèbvre's bitter contract termination (see page 48), Lalique was offered the commission to produce the medals and other items.

In an attempt to pacify Lefèbvre, Pascal Ceccaldi[15] (the Committee President) suggested a 'hybrid' medal incorporating the obverse of Lefèbvre's original design (see page 47) and the reverse of Lalique's.

This proposal was rejected but some medals were struck - probably as exemplars to illustrate to the various Committee members and other concerned parties what the 'hybrid' medal would look like.

Below:
Ceccaldi's proposed 'hybrid' medal

Dimensions of 'hybrid' bronze table medal: 55 mm x 12 mm
Weight: 68.1 gm

Looking at the Lalique design, it was easy to see why some commentators speculated that he was heavily influenced by Greek mythology, which some critics felt had been inappropriate for the Orphelinat design earlier that year (see page 30).

The obverse of the medal depicts a naked warrior strangling the German eagle with the inscription '*Journée du Poilu 1915*'. The eagle is incused and the warrior is in relief which gives the medal a striking effect. It bears the signature 'R Lalique' (8 o'clock).

The reverse side depicts a laurel branch with the embossed inscription '25-26 Décembre 1915'.

Dimensions of silver table medal: 55 mm x 10mm
Weight: 71.1 gm

Six posters designed by some of France's most famous 'affichistes' - including Francisque Poulbot, Charles Léandre, Théophile Steinlen, Lucien Jonas, Maurice Neumont and Adolphe Willette - were used to promote these events.

Apart from the Jonas design, the posters used a similar format of wording: The words 'La Journée du Poilu' are at the top and at the bottom '25-26 Décembre 1915 - Organisée par le Parlement'.

Right - Clockwise from top right:
Lucien Jonas (1880-1947) - Amongst the ruins of a house one poilu stands on guard watching his seated colleague opening up a supply parcel. The words *'La Journée du Poilu'* are set between an image of the Lefèbvre medal and the dates *'25-26 Décembre 1915 Le Poilu'*. The Gambetta phrase figures prominently on the card (see page 54).

Francisque Poulbot (1879-1946) - Two figures - a girl dressed as a Croix Rouge française nurse with a small gift and a young boy wearing a képi and holding a tray of Journée insignias - feature very prominently with the words beneath them: "Pour que papa vienne en permission, s'il vous plait".

Charles Léandre (1862-1934) - A woman, sat near a chimney place with a blanket over her knees, dreams of the soldiers, bearing the standard and regimental flags, alongside the cavaliers mounting an attack.

Maurice Neumont (1868-1930) - Holding a rifle in one hand a poilu, amongst the explosions of the battlefield, is depicted throwing a grenade.

Théophile Steinlen (1859-1923) - The veteran with his pipe in hand and a young conscript with a rose in his mouth are profiled against a landscape of fields with a tree and a farm in the background.

Adolphe Willette (1857-1926) - The soldier on leave embraces his wife. To their left a little dog shows off; a sewing machine and upturned chair can be seen on their right with the words "Enfin seuls...!" beneath them.

POSTCARDS

As with the first *Journée du Poilu* event, all five of the postcards had a unique number on the reverse which was automatically entered into a Tombola prize draw.

Three of the designs - those of Willette, Steinlen and Neumont - retained a sole image of the Lefèbvre medal on the reverse of the cards. The Poulbot and Léandre designs replaced the Sénat and Chambre des Députés symbols which had appeared on the three postcards sold during the first Journée du Poilu event and instead used two of Lalique's Poilu designs.

Below:
Charles Léandre

Below:
Maurice Neumont

Below:
Théophile Steinlen

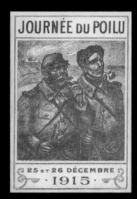

Above:
Francisque Poulbot

Above:
Adolphe Willette

Above:
Posters surround the statue of Joan of Arc in the Place des Pyramides outside the entrance to the Louvre Museum

Below:
Faced with appalling weather, collectors for the *Journée du Poilu* thronged the Paris streets.

Journée Serbe
25 June 1916

Journée Serbe
25 June 1916

Exactly one month after the Sarajevo assassination of Archduke Franz Ferdinand, who was the heir to the Austro-Hungarian throne, and having secured the unconditional support of Germany, Austria-Hungary declared war on Serbia. This act was to effectively signal the beginning of World War One.

The decision was taken for the Austrian army to invade Serbia on the 12 August 1914. The belief was that it would be a short, punitive campaign. This view quickly evaporated as the invasion was repeatedly repelled by the Serbian forces. The campaign was attritional and brutal. The Austrians lost 227,000 men, more than half the invading force. Despite arguments regarding the accuracy of the recorded casualty figures, there is little doubt that Serbia suffered enormous losses. By the end of 1915, it was estimated that one sixth of Serbia's entire population was dead and, despite the initial great successes in repelling the invasion, the ill equipped Serbian army was being pushed back by the Austro-Hungarian forces which had been joined by Bulgarian troops. By early 1916, out of 400,000 of Serbia's army, all that remained was 100,000 soldiers.

Unwilling to surrender in the face of the 'Triple Invasion', Serbian troops were forced to retreat through Albania and were then evacuated to Corfu where they managed to rest, regroup and rearm. Along with their French allies and troops from Montenegro and Albania, the Serbian army played a critical role in the war in the Balkans.

The bravery of the Serb nation was much admired by the allied powers. In late March 1915, schools throughout France organised fundraising days for the Serbian cause. Following this highly successful campaign, the National Relief Committee (*Comité du Secours National*) took the decision to organise the *Journée Serbe* to be held nationwide on the 25th June 1916 to raise funds to help the Serbian struggle. Not surprisingly, there was a tremendous response from the general public.

Having orchestrated the highly successful *Journée Française Secours National* in 1915, the Comité felt confident that it could match the success of the previous event.

Informations

La Journée Serbe

Pour répondre aux vues du gouvernement, le Comité du Secours national a accepté d'organiser une « Journée Serbe » pour le dimanche 25 juin.

L'éminent ministre de Serbie, M. Vesnitch, vient d'adresser, à ce sujet, à M. Paul Appell, président du Comité du Secours national, une lettre dont nous extrayons ce passage :

La Journée Serbe que le Comité du Secours national a accepté d'organiser, en vue de venir en aide à nos familles en détresse, marquera une nouvelle dette de notre gratitude envers votre noble pays. Dans la plus retirée des chaumières serbes, elle apportera, avec le réconfort de l'espérance, la certitude de la victoire commune ; elle sera, à notre égard, une manifestation éclatante de l'amitié et de la générosité françaises qu'aucun Serbe n'oubliera jamais.

C'est pour tous les Serbes que le Secours national s'adresse aujourd'hui au cœur de tous les hommes et de toutes les femmes de notre pays.

Above:
Le Figaro 24 June 1916 page 2. It is clear from the comments of Dr. Milenko Vesnitch (Vesnić), the Minister of Serbia in France, that the generosity and help of the French people would never be forgotten.

Below:
Two Serbian soldiers on leave recovering from their wounds.

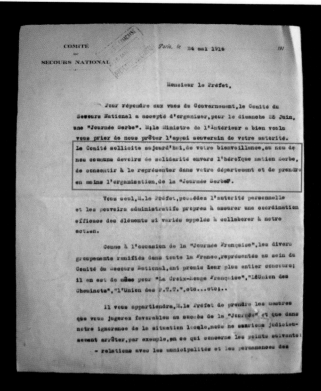

Above:

A letter (dated 24 May 1916) from the National Relief Committee to the Préfet of Cantal gives a fascinating insight into the preparation needed to organize a nationwide event for "l'héroïque nation Serbe".

The letter explains that his cooperation, authority and local knowledge would be essential for the success of the day. Sadly, the letter also highlights the need for the Police to protect the numerous quêteuses and to be on the alert for the possible activities of unauthorized individuals who might be involved in the sales of counterfeit items!

Below:

An information letter sent by the organizing body details the items that were going to be sent to the Prefecture. It also refers to a possible shortage of metal and states that if this causes a shortfall in the Prud'homme medals, surplus medals from the 1915 *Journée Française du Secours National* could serve as replacements.

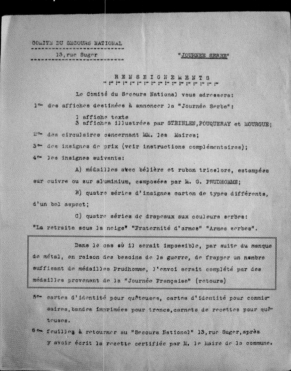

Right:
Four different models of small paper flag pins were produced, all of them featuring the background of the Serbian flag of red, blue and white colours. The flag pins were based on three significant themes: *'Armées Serbes'*, *'Fraternité d'armes'* and *'La retraite sous la neige'*.

Dimensions: 18 (H) x 28 (W) mm

1 A gold circle inside of which is the Serbian coat-of-arms. Reverse: The four line legend - *Journée/Serbe/25 Juin/1916* - is set within a white circle.

Dimensions: 17 (H) x 27 (W) mm

2 The Serbian coat-of-arms in a shield feature on the obverse. Both sides of the flag are gold fringed with the Serbian colours and on the reverse the French flag with *Journée Serbe/25 Juin 1916*

Dimensions: 21 (H) x 24 (W) mm

3 A winter landscape scene, featuring a column of Serbian soldiers, is depicted on an inner frame which extends to the reverse. The four line legend - *Journée/Serbe/25 Juin/1916* - is set on the flag. On the reverse, a dead soldier lies on the snow.

Dimensions: 21 (H) x 28 (W) mm

4 Divided with a diagonal line with the French flag colours on the left and Serbian colours below with a yellow border. A circle in the centre depicts two soldiers shaking hands - a French poilu on the left with a Serbian soldier on the right. A yellow circle with *Journée / Serbe / 25 Juin / 1916* on four lines is on the reverse.

POUR LES HÉROS ET MARTYRS

La " Journée serbe "

Les secours affluent

La « Journée serbe » a été comme l'apothéose de la solidarité française et du souvenir. C'est que le peuple de France a la claire vision du gigantesque rôle joué par la Grande petite Serbie dans cette guerre atroce. Il sait que ces glorieux vaincus qui n'ont cédé qu'écrasés sous le nombre et traîtreusement surpris par les Bulgares, supportent courageusement, fièrement, les plus grandes misères pour être demeurés fidèles à l'honneur et à la foi jurée. Et l'amitié séculaire qui unit la Serbie et la France, cimentée par le sang versé en commun pour la plus noble cause, s'est encore accrue de toutes les infortunes des familles serbes exilées, ou pleurant sur les ruines de leurs foyers détruits.

Dès la première heure, des jeunes filles, des fillettes vêtues de robes claires, cheminant par les rues, guettant aux gares de chemins de fer ou du Métro l'arrivée des trains, tendaient à tous et à toutes, la corbeille tricolore joliment garnie d'insignes et de médailles. Et les sébiles s'emplissaient vite de sous et de pièces blanches, et tous les Parisiens se décoraient aux couleurs serbes. D'ores et déjà, bien que les résultats ne soient pas encore connus, on peut affirmer que la « Journée serbe » sera un grand succès.

Le comité du Secours national, à qui avait été confiée l'organisation de cette belle manifestation, avait d'ailleurs fait les choses avec ingéniosité. Les affiches, qui ont parlé au cœur des Parisiens, étaient signées : Fonqueray, Mourgue, Steinlen, et les médailles, de purs chefs-d'œuvre : Prud'homme, Bargas, Lordonnois, Lalique. La médaille Prud'homme représente la Serbie accablée par le nombre et par la force et revendiquant son droit : *Meum jus.* M. Bargas a gravé une mère qui fuit, éperdue, emportant son enfant, avenir de la Serbie, sous la garde d'un veillard s'éloignant d'un foyer aimé que peut-être, il ne reverra plus. L'épingle de M. Lalique montre le génie de la Serbie déployant la devise de la dynastie régnante : *Spes mihi prima Deus. Gloire aux intrépides héros serbes !* a écrit M. Lordonnois sur son insigne.

La Ligue française pour le droit des femmes, avait, de son côté, fait, au profit du comité organisateur, une vente spéciale de jouets et articles fabriqués dans ses ouvroirs.

Le conseil municipal de Paris s'était fait inscrire pour une somme de 10.000 francs.

Above:
Le Matin 26 June page 2
Four of France's most famous medallists - Armand Bargas, Georges-Henri Prud'homme, René Lalique and Marcel Lordonnois - designed the medals for this cause.

INSIGNIAS

A set of four insignias, three of which were issued with fixing ribbons in the colours of the Serbian flag, were issued for the *Journée Serbe* which was set for the 25 June 1916:

1 On a golden mosaic background with a border made up of two interwoven ribbons in Serbian and French colours, the portrait of King Peter I dressed in the khaki uniform of the Serbian army and wearing a calot (cap), is central to the insignia. The reverse features a plain gold background with a legend in white letters:

Journée Serbe / 25 Juin 1916 / Comité du Secours National.

Dimensions: 36 mm

Printed by Lapina, Paris

2 The profiles of the Prince Regent Alexander and King Peter I, both in military uniform and wearing calots, are featured on a background colour of aqua marine with a gold border. To the left of the profiles are the words 'Journée Serbe'. A legend in white letters on a gold background made up the reverse:

Comité/du/Secours National/25 Juin 1916.

Dimensions: 36 mm

Printed by Devambez G, Paris

3 The shape of the insignia is that of a cross. All four arms are composed of a striped frame in gold and brown, surrounded by white dots. An oval shape containing the portrait of Prince Regent Alexander in full military uniform with all honours, is at the centre. The reverse features a plain gold background with a legend in white letters:

Comité / du / Secours National / Journée Serbe / 25 Juin 1916.

Dimensions: 32 (H) x 28 (W) mm

Printed by Devambez G, Paris

4 The insignia is designed in the form of a medal - a six-pointed star with a gold crown at the top which is suspended from a printed ribbon in the colours of the Serbian flag. In the centre of the star is a circle with the Serbian coat of arms. A golden crown of laurels encircles the outer ring.

The reverse features a plain white background with a legend in blue letters set in a blue circle:

Journée Serbe / 25 Juin / 1916.

Dimensions: 60 (H) x 37 (W) mm

Printer: Unknown

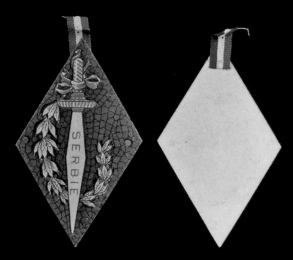

Dimensions : 70 (H) x 40 (W) mm

Above:

In addition to the official set of four insignias issued for the Journée Serbe, a fifth insignia was also produced. This very rare insignia is a striking design and an unusual shape - a vertical lozenge. A sword is set on a blue mosaic background with a red ribbon bow on the hilt and a curved oak branch on the blade. The word 'Serbia' in red is set on the blade. The reverse is blank.

As no mention is made of this particular item in any newspaper article covering the *Journée Serbe* it is highly unlikely that it was sold on the actual fundraising day. The fact that the insignia was also issued with a French tricolour ribbon as opposed to the Serbian national colours, adds credence to this presumption.

Below:

The collecting box label (étiquette) was designed in the Serbian colours with the coat of arms and fundraising date.

Dimensions: 82 (H) x 64 (W) mm

Above:

To avoid any possibility of fraudulent behaviour authorised identity cards for both the collectors and commissioners were issued.

Below:

The vast majority of collectors who were involved in organising the sales on the *Journée Serbe* were made up mainly of young women and children. The étiquette (bottom left) is clearly visible in the photo below on the collector's box as is the official identity card on her lapel .

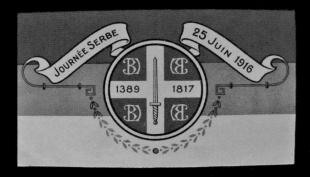

Dimensions: 74 (H) x 132 (W) mm

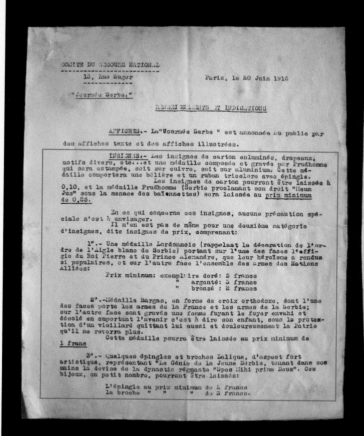

Above:

The National Relief Committee sent out a standard two page letter to all local authorities dated 20 June 1916, setting out various 'Renseignements et Indications' (Information and Directions).

The cost of the cardboard insignias was set at 10 centimes and the set minimum price for the Prud'homme medals was 25 centimes.

Categories included Lordonnois's medal portraying the King and Prince-Regent which was to be sold for 2-5 francs and the Bargas medal "Gloire aux Serbes" which was to be sold for a minimum price of 1 franc.

The final category - that of Lalique's "bijoux" - was recommended to be sold at a price of 2 francs for the lapel pin and 3 francs for the brooch.

Referring to Lalique's items, the letter commented on the "aspect fort artistique" and describes:

"Le Génie de la Jeune Serbie, tenant dans ses mains la devise de la dynastie reignante 'Spes Mihi Primā Deus'."

It was emphasised that these items were limited in number.

Interestingly, clear advice was given regarding the sale of the items designed by Lordonnois, Bargas and Lalique. As these were regarded as being too valuable to be 'trusted' to the younger collectors, the Committee devised a system where the more senior collectors were involved in selling them at a minimum fixed price.

Other observations included the need for accurate recording of the insignia sales, advice on the best places for the collectors to sell to members of the general public and the need to ensure that all the donation funds were transferred to branches of the Banque de France.

MEDALS

The designers for the three medals that were sold for the *Journée Serbe* were Armand Bargas, Marcel Lordonnois and Georges-Henri Prud'homme.

Below:
The Prud'homme medals were made out from brass and aluminium. Due to the huge demand for the medals, different manufacturers were used in the production process leading to a great variety in the quality and finish of the medals. Many were badly stamped as can be seen in two of the medals (below top) and were often produced in different hues depending on the constituent alloys used.

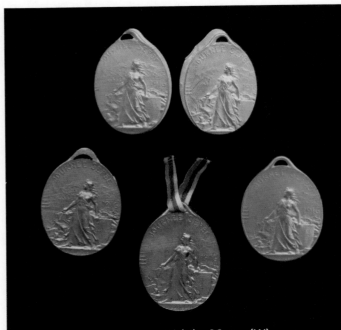

Dimensions: 36 (H) x 26 mm (W)

The uniface medal features a woman, hair blowing in the wind, with a long robe which has slipped over the shoulder leaving her left breast exposed. She is leaning with her left hand on a shield which bears the Serbian coat of arms. She holds a sword in her right hand facing four rifle bayonets aimed at her. A German Pickelhaube lies near her right foot and the background is one of a battlefield and ruined buildings. The legend *'Journée Serbe'* is located at the top, the G Prud'homme signature is on the left (9 o'clock) and *'Meum Jus'* (My Right) is below her feet.

Armand Bargas (1880 - 1920) designed a circular medal giving the impression of being imposed on a cross, with a loop for ribbon suspension in the form of two cranes; the obverse depicts a full length figure of a mother carrying a child in a blanket with a Serbian soldier holding a rifle just behind her, presumably depicting a scene from the Serb retreat through the mountains of Albania in the winter of 1915-1916. The inscription 'Gloire aux Serbes' is set below the two figures with the Bargas signature on the left (9 o'clock).

Dimensions: 28 mm in diameter

The reverse features the nations' respective coat of arms - French on the left, Serbian on the right - above two intertwining branches, one of which is oak and the other is laurel. The date '1916' is set just below the suspension loop.

The Maison Bargas was in sole command of the production of the medals but the increasing need for metals which were needed for the war effort resulted in some of the medals containing a varied alloy composition which in turn gave a different appearance in tone. Two different versions were produced: 'en métal argenté' (see above) and 'en metal doré' (see below).

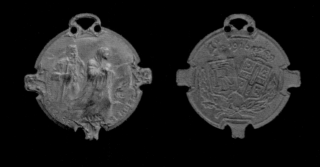

Marcel Lordonnois had been badly wounded in the war and on his return from the frontline he helped the war effort through the use of his skills as a medallist , designing some of the most well known medals of WW1 which included this medal.

The ovoid shape design was striking. The obverse face depicted a Serbian double-headed eagle with outstretched wings supporting in the centre a crowned circle with the conjoined busts of King Peter I and Prince-Regent Alexander circumscribed 'Pierre I - Alexandre'.

The medal is inscribed *'Journée Serbe'* with the bilingual six-line French and Serbian inscription:
Glorieux / Défenseurs de la / Liberté Serbe
СЛАВНИ ЗАТОЧНИЦИ / СРПСКЕ СЛОБОДЕ /
1914 - 1915

It is signed 'T S M Lordonnois Graveur Edit' along the lower medallion edge.

The Serbian double-headed eagle is portrayed again on the reverse with the inscription '1916' and below is a circular crowned medallion with the arms of the Allied nations within a ring inscribed 'Gloire Aux Intrépides Héros Serbes'. Alongside the crown is the inscription 'Secours National'.

Three different medal finishes were produced: in bronze, silvered and gold gilt (see above right).

Dimensions: 45 (H) x 32 (W) mm

LA " JOURNÉE SERBE "
Les médailles qui seront mises en vente

Après la journée du 75, celle de la Ville de Paris, celle des Orphelinats des armées, la Journée des Réfugiés, les Journées du Poilu, voici bientôt la « Journée Serbe », sous les auspices du Secours national.

Plusieurs souvenirs seront offerts, dimanche, à la générosité des passants : une médaille de M. Bargas, une de M. Prud'homme, une épingle de cravate et une

La composition des deux faces en est des plus heureuse. A l'avers, sur un médaillon timbré de la couronne royale, se détachent les profils géminés du roi Pierre Ier et de son fils Alexandre, brochant sur les aigles de Serbie et surmontant un cartouche, où on lit leurs titres de gloire (en français et en serbe) « défenseurs de la liberté serbe ». Au premier plan, le profil énergique du roi Pierre. Le support de la médaille représente l'aigle blanc de Serbie, au cœur duquel se détache, dans une jarretière, timbrée de la couronne royale, l'inscription : « Gloire aux intrépides héros serbes ». Le coq gaulois se dresse, passant, sur les écussons des huit alliés.

Bien peu de Parisiens se priveront de cet insigne, qui est agréé par le roi de Serbie. L'auteur, qui est récompensé de la Société des Artistes français, est aussi un courageux enfant de Paris. Après deux blessures reçues, dès les premières hostilités, à Hirson et à Reims, il a été réformé et a quitté le fusil pour le poinçon.

Voici les prix minima fixés pour chacune des médailles qui seront mises en vente dimanche : Médailles Prud'homme : 0 fr. 25 ; Bargas : 1 fr. ; Lordonnois : 2 fr., 3 fr. ou 5 fr., selon qu'il s'agit d'un exemplaire bronzé, argenté ou doré ; Lalique : en épingle, 2 fr. ; en broche, 3 fr.

La médaille de M. Lordonnois

broche de M. Lalique, enfin une médaille de M. Marcel Lordonnois, ancien élève des maîtres graveurs Ponscarme, Vernon et Mouchon. C'est celle que nous reproduisons aujourd'hui.

Above:

Le Petit Journal 22 June 1916 page 2
The article illustrates the importance and profile attached to the *Journée Serbe*. Specific details are given about the various medals that will be offered for sale on the day, with particular emphasis on the Lordonnois medal.

The bravery of Lordonnois is also lauded - finally invalided out of the army after being wounded in action at Hirson and then again at Reims.

Brooch and lapel pin

When the National Relief Committee organized the Journée Serbe, René Lalique was approached and asked to design a commemorative brooch and lapel pin.

He produced a memorable Art Nouveau design which featured a radiant star with an angelic-like figure holding a banner bearing the motto of the Serbian Royal family: "Spes Mihi Primā Deus" (My first hope is in God).

The brooch has a simple 'C' clasp with the pin extending past the body of the brooch itself .

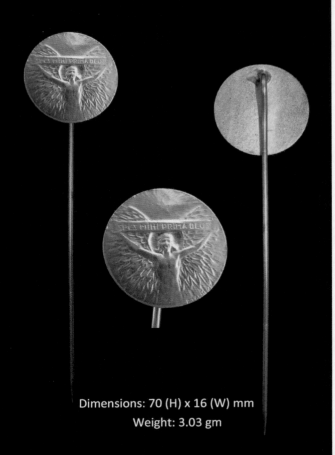

Dimensions: 70 (H) x 16 (W) mm
Weight: 3.03 gm

Dimensions: 28 mm x 3 mm
Weight: 7.2 gm

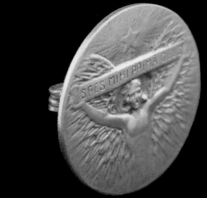

For the lapel pin, Lalique used exactly the same design as the brooch. Unlike all the other Lalique designs for sale on the various *Journées*, the brooch and lapel pin appear to have been made only in gilt-bronze.

As the correspondence from the National Relief Committee so clearly reveals (see page 74), Lalique like all the other medallists and manufacturers, would have been aware of the problems regarding the metal shortages throughout France. Almost certainly it is this specific factor which explains why Lalique produced only a limited number of the *Journée Serbe* brooches and lapel pins and why he did not make use of precious metals such as gold or silver which had featured with his earlier designs for *Les Journées du Poilu*.

It is likely that the views of Paul Appell (President of the Secours National) who strongly disapproved of commissioning famous designers (see page 87), also influenced Lalique.

Right:

Journal Des Débats Politiques et Littéraires
23 June 1916 - An extract from an article extolling the "perfect taste and great style" of the Lalique designs for the commemorative pieces sold for the *Journée Serbe*. As can be seen from the extract, particular items were set at a minimum price.

Other medals were also produced for the Serbian cause but these do not appear to have been sold on the specific fundraising day on the 25 June.

Below:

The table medal design created by Ovide Yencesse (1869 - 1947) was based closely on one of several disturbing sketches made by Théophile Steinlen. The haunting imagery drew on the horrors that were experienced by the Serbian civilians.

Une médaille d'un goût parfait et de haut style, ce qui n'a rien de surprenant puisqu'elle est signée Lalique, montée en broche ou en épingle, où l'on voit le génie de la Serbie déployant la devise de la dynastie régnante : *Spes Mihi prima Deus*, complète cette première catégorie.

Enfin, des insignes divers en carton enluminé, d'un agréable aspect, constituent une série riche par la variété, et aussi par les soins attentifs apportés à l'impression.

Voici les prix minimum fixés : Médaille Prud'homme, o fr. 25 ; Bargas, 1 fr. ; Lordonnois, 2 fr., 3 fr. ou 5 fr. (selon qu'il s'agit d'un exemplaire bronzé, argenté ou doré) ; Lalique, en épingle, 2 fr.; en broche, 3 fr.

***

Below:

Excelsior Monday 26 June 1916
The front page with an array of photos depicting the numerous collectors on the Parisian streets.

Comments were made on the success of the event which was put down mainly due to the excellent weather, the sound organization of the campaign by the National Relief Committee and the terrific efforts of the numerous street collectors. It is interesting to note that the collector in the bottom left photo also featured in the photo on page 77.

Above:

An example of one of several medals designed by Tony Szirmai which were sold to raise funds for the relief of Serbian children. The reverse features jugate busts of King Peter I of Serbia and Crown Prince Alexander. The two members of the Serbian royal family were also depicted on many of the fundraising cardboard insignias (see page 76).

POSTERS

Right:
Designed by Charles Fouqueray (1869-1956) and printed by Imp. Devambez, Paris 1916

The poster commemorated the Battle of Kosovo and depicts King Peter I, civilian refugees and the remnants of the Serbian army crossing the River Drina. Thousands died during the winter of 1915-16 from lack of food and the freezing conditions.

Below:
The poster designed by Théophile Steinlen shows a group of Serbian civilian refugees and soldiers as they head into the mountain regions of Albania and Montenegro, fleeing from the invading forces of Germany and Austria-Hungary.

Printed by I Lapina Imprimerie, Paris.

Dimensions : 1210 (H) x 810 (W) mm

Dimensions : 1140 (H) x 800 (W) mm

Below:
Poster designed by French artist Pierre Mourgue and printed by Chambrelent, 11 rue de l'Hôpital St Louis, Paris.

The scene, which bears a certain similarity with that of Fouqueray's image, depicted the haunting winter landscape and the journey of the Serbian civilians and military retreating across the Mostar bridge over the River Drina into Albania[16].

Dimensions : 1200 (H) x 800 (W) mm

Journée Nationale des Orphelins
1 and 2 November 1916

Journée Nationale des Orphelins
1 and 2 November 1916

"Everyone will give what they can afford, so that the children of those who have so nobly shed their blood in defence of our country can live despite the dangers and that they can be brought up as their fathers would have wanted to raise them themselves". Paul Appell

A conservative estimate of the number of French orphans at the end of the war placed the number at a staggering 1,100,000. In early 1917 President Theodore Roosevelt stated that over half a million French children had lost their fathers. In the same year, a special status that was to be unique in Europe, was introduced specifically for French war orphans - *'Pupilles de la Nation'* (see page 181). Having the status of 'Ward of the Nation' entitled a child to receive assistance until they reached the age of majority. Children who were left parentless lived in orphanages created to protect them and provide for all their basic needs. The orphanages required constant funding from outside donations.

The debt contracted by the state on behalf of the orphans who were rightly regarded as 'victims', met with some resistance from various conflicting interests and harsh financial realities. As a result, various organizations and individuals instigated campaigns to raise support for the war orphans.

In France there had been a very successful, albeit controversial, nationwide campaign - *Journée de l'Orphelinat des Armées* held on 27 June 1915. It was now felt that another fundraising day should be organized - this time with the authority of the Ministry of the Interior under the auspices of Le Secours National which had already played a key role in organising *La Journée Française Secours National* and the *Journée Serbe*.

Paul Appell, the President of Le Secours National and heading the Comité de la Journée Nationale des Orphelins, made it clear that the methods that would be employed by the Committee would be, for want of a better term, 'back to basics'.

In other words, the main thrust of the Journée would be to raise as much money as possible by keeping the overhead costs very low. The medals and insignias produced for the day would be of simple design and low value, allowing them to be affordable for everyone rather than just an 'elite'.

Dimensions : 1200 (H) x 800 (W) mm

Above:
Poster used to inform the public about the event.

Below:
A letter sent by the Committee setting out details of the items being sold on the day, refers to nine differently designed insignias in addition to a set of insignias made from cardboard in a faux metallic and ivory finish. Two of the set of nine insignias have the name of the artist but the majority of them are unnamed.

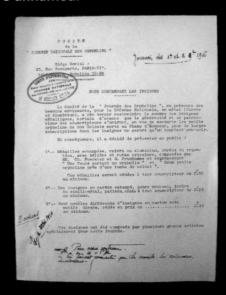

L'AVENIR DE LA RACE

Pour les orphelins de la guerre

LES 1er ET 2 NOVEMBRE : QUÊTE NATIONALE

JOURNÉE NATIONALE
DES ORPHELINS Guerre 1914-15-16
Petits Français et petites Françaises, pour les enfants dont les papas ne sont plus, donnez ce que vous pouvez, donnez un peu de votre joie donnez un peu de votre bien-être et beaucoup de votre âme ! Les Orphelins de la guerre sont vos petits frères et vos petites sœurs
Ne les oubliez pas –

Le 1er et le 2 novembre prochain, à la Toussaint et au Jour des Morts, une quête nationale sera faite pour les enfants dont les pères sont tombés au champ d'honneur, pour ces innocentes victimes d'une guerre que l'agression des deux empires du centre de l'Europe a imposée à l'humanité civilisée. En ces journées consacrées au culte des morts, tous les Français et toutes les Françaises se rappelleront le sublime sacrifice de ceux qui offrirent leurs poitrines pour barrer la route aux envahisseurs, pour sauver la patrie et la civilisation. Leurs cœurs se rempliront d'un sentiment d'affectueuse et tendre solidarité à l'égard des enfants de ces héros. Chacun donnera tout ce qu'il peut donner, afin que les enfants de ceux qui ont noblement versé leur sang pour la défense de notre pays en danger puissent vivre, et qu'ils soient élevés comme leurs pères eussent voulu les élever eux-mêmes. Tous voudront que l'union, réalisée dans la lutte contre l'ennemi, se réalise aussi pour la protection des orphelins de la guerre.

Mais le devoir du comité, qui recueillera les fonds, est d'expliquer au public ce qu'il est, ce qu'il fait, comment il procède, quelles garanties d'impartialité, d'efficacité, d'économie et de méthode il offre pour la distribution des secours qui lui sont confiés.

On se rappelle qu'une première Journée des orphelins a eu lieu le 25 juin 1915 et a produit un bénéfice net de 3.100.000 francs. Pour assurer la distribution de ces fonds, le ministre de l'intérieur, dans un sentiment élevé d'impartialité et de justice, a demandé au Secours national de faire l'union entre les diverses œuvres secourant les orphelins de la guerre, en vue d'aider ces enfants, sans distinction de croyances religieuses ni d'opinions politiques. Le Secours national a répondu à cet appel en contribuant à constituer, à son image, un comité qui comprend vingt membres représentant toutes les croyances, tous les partis, tous les milieux sociaux.

Ce comité, dont le siège est 33, rue Bonaparte, a pris le titre de Comité d'attribution des fonds de la Journée nationale des orphelins. Il a employé les méthodes du Secours national en prenant comme base de la répartition l'orphelin dans le besoin, âgé de moins de seize ans et ayant perdu son soutien habituel du fait de la guerre. Il secourt l'orphelin par l'intermédiaire des œuvres, sous la réserve que chaque œuvre doit fournir les garanties de moralité, de bonne tenue et de bonne gestion financière qui sont indispensables partout, mais qui doivent être exigées avec une sévérité particulière lorsqu'il s'agit d'enfants qui formeront la France de demain.

Quand une demande de secours est faite pour un enfant isolé, le secrétariat du comité envoie à la famille une liste des œuvres subventionnées, parmi lesquelles elle choisit librement celle qui convient à ses croyances, à ses opinions, à son milieu social.

Eu égard au grand nombre de demandes, le comité a dû limiter la subvention mensuelle à un maximum de 10 francs par enfant. Le dossier de chaque enfant doit contenir une demande de secours signée de la personne qui a la charge de l'enfant, la preuve du décès du père ou du soutien habituel par le fait de la guerre, une pièce donnant la date de naissance de l'enfant, une déclaration du président de l'œuvre établissant qu'une enquête a été faite sur la situation de la famille, enquête dont le rapporteur peut demander communication. Les demandes de subvention sont soumises par le comité à l'examen d'un rapporteur responsable, qui vérifie les dossiers des enfants et la justification des dépenses, qui s'assure de la bonne tenue de l'œuvre et qui présente au comité un rapport écrit et signé. Le travail exigé par ces rapports étant devenu très considérable, le comité s'est adjoint une vingtaine de rapporteurs présentés par les divers groupements qui le constituent. Afin d'éviter les doubles emplois, des fiches nominatives, par familles d'orphelins, sont établies par l'œuvre demanderesse elle-même et sont centralisées au secrétariat. Ce système a fonctionné pendant les dix-huit mois qui nous séparent de la première Journée avec une régularité et une efficacité qui ont donné satisfaction à tous. Le nombre des œuvres subventionnées est à ce jour de 111 ; celui des enfants dépasse 60.000. Les secours ont été donnés dans toute la France. Une partie de ces œuvres ont leur siège social en province ; d'autres ont leur siège à Paris, mais elles assistent néanmoins des enfants dans tous les départements. C'est ainsi que des œuvres corporatives et mutualistes, au nombre de 43, ont touché 1.390.000 francs ; parmi ces œuvres nous citerons en particulier : l'Orphelinat des chemins de fer français ; l'Orphelinat des sous-agents des P. T. T. ; celui de la Fédération des tabacs ; celui des employés de la Banque de France ; la Fédération des amicales d'instituteurs et institutrices publics ; la Saint-Cyrienne ; l'Orphelinat de l'enseignement primaire de France et celui de l'enseignement secondaire ; la Fédération du personnel des Douanes ; la Caisse centrale mutualiste de la Franche-Comté ; la Fédération nationale des coopératives de consommation ; les Pupilles de l'école publique ; l'Œuvre de la mairie de Lyon, etc.

Des œuvres philanthropiques (religieuses ou laïques), au nombre de 688, ont touché 1.975.000 francs. Nous citerons notamment : l'Œuvre des orphelins de la mer ; l'Aide aux veuves des militaires de la grande guerre ; la société la Bretagne ; l'Œuvre nationale de protection des femmes et enfants victimes de la guerre ; l'Association nationale pour la protection des veuves et orphelins de la guerre ; la Délégation générale des diaconats réformés ; l'Action sociale de Seine-et-Oise ; l'Union des familles françaises et alliées ; l'Association nationale pour la protection des familles des morts pour la patrie ; le Comité de bienfaisance israélite ; l'Alliance catholique savoisienne ; l'Orphelinat des armées (sections de Paris, Nice, Rouen, le Havre, Bordeaux, Dieppe, Fécamp) ; les Pupilles corses ; les Unions provinciales (aveyronnaise et lozérienne), de l'Ouest, de Guyenne, de Bourgogne, de Lorraine, des dames limousines et creusoises, de la Nièvre ; la Compagnie des filles de la charité ; l'Œuvre de l'assistance aux orphelins de la guerre ; la Société dauphinoise de sauvetage de l'enfance ; le Comité d'aide et d'assistance coloniale, etc.

Aussi le comité est-il vraiment un comité national d'attribution, puisque toutes les œuvres, de quelque département

2

qu'elles soient, peuvent participer aux secours, du moment qu'elles envoient une demande basée sur des dossiers régulièrement établis.

Le comité est assisté, dans son œuvre, par le comité de secours de l'American Clearing House, qui a bien voulu se faire représenter par deux de ses délégués et qui a déjà versé d'importantes subventions. Je saisis cette occasion d'exprimer publiquement les remerciements des orphelins français aux généreux donateurs américains, citoyens libres d'une république sœur qui a le même idéal de liberté et de justice que notre patrie.

Les distributions de fonds, qui ont été pendant le mois de juillet 1915 de 35.000 francs, se montent maintenant à près de 500.000 francs par mois. Aussi la caisse du comité est-elle vide depuis le 1er octobre. Pour que les secours ne soient pas interrompus, le comité a fait appel au Secours national qui lui a consenti généreusement une avance de 500.000 francs. Les Journées des 1er et 2 novembre étaient donc indispensables pour la continuation des subventions.

Certaines journées précédentes ont multiplié les insignes de luxe offerts sur la voie publique et sont devenues presque des ventes de bijoux. L'expérience a montré qu'il est résulté de cette méthode des frais considérables dans l'établissement des insignes et pour des raisons faciles à comprendre une diminution notable dans le pourcentage des sommes utilisables pour les secours.

Le comité est revenu à la véritable conception d'une journée nationale. Il a estimé, comme l'avaient fait le Touring-Club pour la « Journée du 75 » et le Secours national pour la « Journée française », que l'insigne est un souvenir de la journée et non un objet de vente ; que chacun doit donner tout ce qu'il peut donner, sans s'attacher à la valeur marchande de l'insigne, et que la journée doit être la journée des « Orphelins de la guerre » et non celle des fabricants de médailles et de bijoux.

Toutes les œuvres qui secourent des orphelins s'unissent pour faire appel à la bonté, à la générosité, à la reconnaissance des Français et des Françaises, à l'affection et à la pitié des enfants qui ont le bonheur et la joie de posséder encore leurs parents. Nous sommes certain que cet appel sera entendu. Pour sauver des existences indispensables à l'avenir de la race française, pour assurer le nécessaire aux petits orphelins de nos soldats, que le cœur de chacun s'émeuve et comprenne le grand devoir de la fraternelle solidarité.

P. Appell,
de l'Académie des sciences, Président du Comité.

Left and above:

Le Matin 28 October 1916 Pages 1 and 2.
The article is written by Paul Appell who was the President of the Secours National (see page 19). He was asked to oversee the smooth running of the *Journée Nationale des Orphelins* and he gives an interesting insight into the approaches adopted by other nationwide *Journées.*

It is an informative piece but there is one section in particular which is controversial. Although he mentions no particular examples, it is clear that Appell is singling out *La Journée de l'Orphelinat des Armées, Les Journées du Poilu* and possibly to a certain extent the *Journée Serbe*. Very pointedly, he singles out the *Journée du 75* and *La Journée Française Secours National* as examples of sound practices which were able to achieve great success without having to resort to commissioning famous jewellers and designers such as René Lalique and Armand Bargas.

Appell opposed the methods employed by the likes of Jeanne Paquin and was supportive of the Association Nationale des Orphelins (see page 29). He was critical of the 'luxury' items that had been offered for sale on previous *Journées* which, in his words, amounted to nothing more than 'jewellery sales'. Undoubtedly the involvement of famous artists and medallists increased interest in the event but often led to an increase in the overhead costs, thereby reducing the funds raised for the particular cause. Appell felt strongly that the items sold should be mere souvenirs of the actual day not prestigious high value items of jewellery!

His scathing assessment would also have taken into consideration the unsavoury Lalique-Lefèbvre court case (see page 48) and rumours circulating regarding the profits made by Maison Bargas and, to a lesser extent Lalique, for their production cost charges for *Les Journées du Poilu*.

Below:

A report in *La Croix* from 8 November 1917 page 7 made comparisons between the small amount charged for administration costs for the *Journée du 75* compared to the "vraiment étonnants" expenses of the likes of Lalique and Bargas.

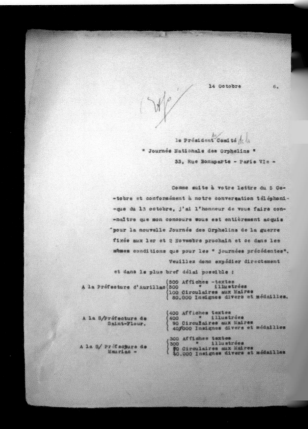

Above:

A note confirming the number of items being through to the Prefectures of Aurillac, Saint and Mauriac.

Below:

A letter informing the Préfet of possible de problems with one of the manufacturers.

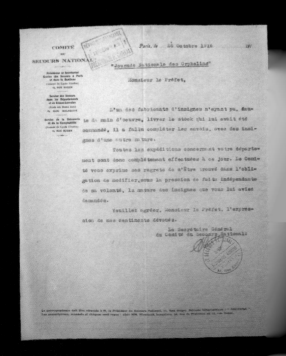

INSIGNIAS

Dimensions: 38 (H) x 42 (W) mm

1. The insignia has a golden frame with a relief motif in the form of two crossed swords, foliage and palms. A circle measuring 23 mm in diameter, features two young boys in each other's arms sitting on the steps of a ruined house. The reverse bears a six line legend set in white letters on a bronze coloured background:

Journée/Nationale/des/Orphelins/de la/Guerre

The printer's name 'Chambrelent - Paris' is located at the bottom.

Dimensions: 48 (H) x 40 (W) mm

2. The oval insignia has an orange rectangular shape in the centre which measures 37 x 29 mm. Marianne, the national personification of the French Republic, is wearing a winged helmet and pink robes and cradling an orphaned baby. The reverse is white with the legend in blue:

Journée / Nationale / des Orphelins / de la Guerre

The printer's name is set at the bottom.

Dimensions: 44 (H) x 31 (W) mm

3. The ovoid shape has a gilded frame of laurels tied at the bottom by a tricolour ribbon. An oval shape in the centre portrays an orphaned boy and girl embracing each other and kneeling in front of a grave with white crosses in the background. The reverse is plain white with the legend in blue on four lines - *Journée/Nationale/des Orphelins/de la Guerre*. The printer's name is set at the bottom.

Another version, using the identical imagery and dimensions, was also produced. This may have been deliberate or just a regional variance as different manufacturers were commissioned to produce the items. This version differed in that it has gold lettering on the reverse.

Below:
Made of thick paper - a French tricolour flag has a circle (18mm) at the centre with the same design as the insignias above. The reverse maintains the French colours with the printer's name located at the bottom.

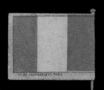

Dimensions: 22 (H) x 30 (W) mm

Right:

4. In the general shape of a cross, a golden frame which creates a 'niche' in which a woman holds out her arms to a young boy and girl. The three figures are depicted in grey and black standing out against a burgundy red background. Reverse - on a gold background in white lettering on six lines: *Journée/Nationale/des/Orphelins/de la/Guerre.*

Two further versions exist with exactly the same form, dimensions and imagery. Roger de Bayle des Hermens suggests that five versions existed as he felt there was a significant difference in the red background on the obverse face - the burgundy red being replaced with bright red. That said, the variations in colour are far more likely to be due to changes in the inks that Chambrelent was using.

Left:

Version 2 has a white reverse face with the legend in blue lettering

Bottom left:

Version 3 has a gold reverse face with the legend in white lettering

Below:

5. Bordered with a gold frame, the symbolic figure of Marianne, draped with a French tricolour and wearing a phrygian cap, consoles a weeping girl dressed in white. The reverse is plain white - other versions are recorded as being dark green and salmon red.

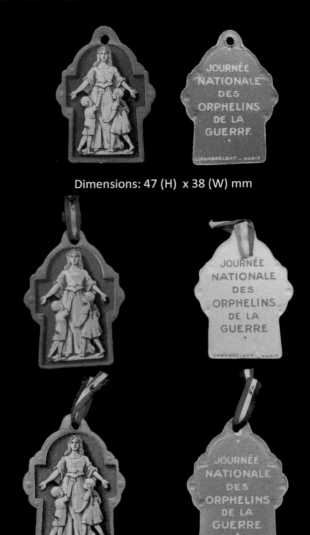

Dimensions: 47 (H) x 38 (W) mm

Below:

6. The oval shaped insignia is bordered with a gold frame. Amongst the ruined buildings a woman is sitting and hugging a young girl who is wearing a red chequered apron. 'Chambrelent Paris' can be seen on the left (7 o'clock). The reverse is plain salmon red although another version is recorded as being dark green.

Dimensions:
42 (H) x 36 (W) mm

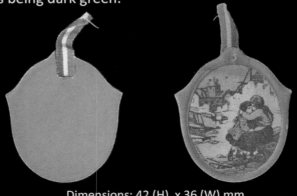

Dimensions: 42 (H) x 36 (W) mm

Dimensions: 40 (H) x 35 (W) mm

7. Oval shaped insignia with an inner oval outlined in blue. A seated woman holds a small child in her arms and a little girl, obviously crying, cuddles into her. The ruins of houses can be seen behind them. The artist's name, possibly J Jegondalou, is at the bottom right. Reverse - the italicised legend in blue on a white background: *Journée/Nationale/ des/ Orphelins/Guerre/1914-15-16*. The name of the printer - 'Devambez Paris' -is set at the bottom.

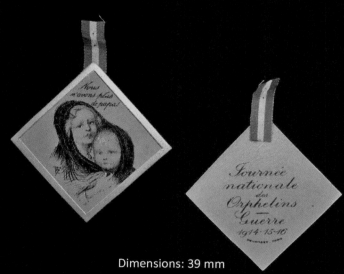

Dimensions: 39 mm

8. On a grey background with a silver frame, a young girl is wearing a scarf which also covers the head of the baby in her arms. The inscription above their heads reads: *'Nous n'avons plus de papa!'* The reverse has the italicised legend on a silver background:
Journée/Nationale/des/Orphelins/Guerre/1914-15-16. 'Devambez Paris' is set at the bottom.

A second version was also produced which was identical to the first version (grey background within a silver frame) except that the colour in the background behind the two children is cream not grey. Again, this might be quite deliberate but could be due solely to the different quality of inks being used by the printer.

9. On a rose pink background, a young boy who is wearing clogs and blue and white striped overalls, is holding a large French flag in his right hand with the legend *Journée des Orphelins 1916* on a white background. The words along the perimeter are from La Marseillaise:
"Nous entrerons dans la carrière quand nos aînés n'y seront plus".

On the reverse on a white background in black print is the legend:
Journée/Nationale/des/Orphelins/de la/Guerre.
A second legend is set around the edge of the insignia - *Guerre 1914-15-16.*

Dimensions: 38 mm

The letter on page 85 refers to three categories of insignias and, of the three, the second category is often overlooked. These were made from stamped cardboard and according to many commentators they were produced in two forms - faux metallic and ivory finish. There does, however, appear to be a variety of other finishes.

Very few survive in good condition. Over a period of time the vast majority of the millions made just simply deteriorated. This stems from the materials that were used in the production process. The cardboard was quite crude and flimsy and the 'finishes' easily flaked off when the insignia was 'mishandled' in any way.

The two artists whose designs were used for these three insignias were Charles Foerster and Marcel Pautot. Foerster also designed one of the medals and he replicated this design for one of the two insignias he produced.

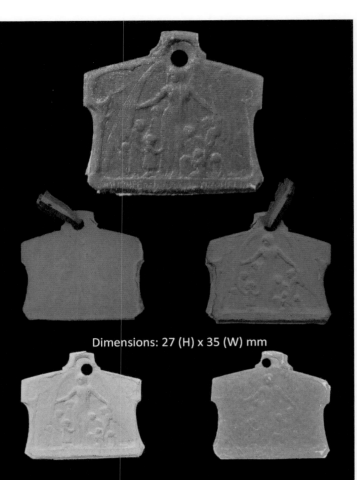

Dimensions: 27 (H) x 35 (W) mm

Below:
Foerster's insignia is rectangular in shape with the upper side rounded to give the impression of a stained glass window. It features a seated woman with a baby on her knees. The legend *'Journée des Orphelins'* is at the top with '1916' on the left and the artist's signature 'Ch Foerster' (9 o'clock).

Above:
Pautot's design in relief features a winged angelic figure protecting a group of children. The legend *'Journée des Orphelins'* is at the base with the artist's name - 'M Pautot' on the right.

Below:
Foerster's second design, rectangular in shape, features a woman holding a flag in her right hand, welcoming three little children stretching out their arms to her. The legend *'Journée des Orphelins'* is located in the top right with 'Ch Foerster' on the left (9 o'clock).

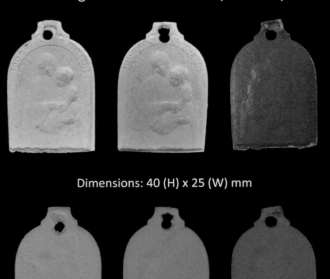

Dimensions: 40 (H) x 25 (W) mm

Dimensions:
35(H) x 22 (W) mm

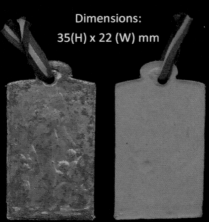

MEDALS

Charles Foerster and Georges Prud'homme were commissioned to produce two medal designs for *La Journée Nationale des Orphelins*.

Prud'homme's design was manufactured in three different stamped metal versions and with two different suspension loops probably as a result of the use of different manufacturers rather than any need to slightly alter the design.

The manufacturers were encountering problems due to the increasing shortage of metals and the additional problem of retaining a skilled work-force. As the French army was suffering appalling losses, many individuals previously exempt from military service as they were regarded as being 'essential' workers, were now being recruited to fight on the frontline. As a result many factories were finding themselves short staffed.

Below:
The Prud'homme design in 'métal jaune' features a young girl with her right hand on a little boy's shoulder standing in front of a grave with a cross bearing the képi of a poilu.

The legend *Journée des Orphelins* is around the perimeter at the top of the medal with the date '1916' towards the bottom right. A small cartouche at the base of the medal has the signature stamp of the designer 'G Prud'homme'.

Dimensions: 31 mm

Above:
Two more of the listed three metal finishes used for this version : on the left - 'cuivre bronzé' and on the right - 'métal blanc'.

Below:
These Prud'homme designs feature a more robust suspension hoop and illustrate the variation in metal finishes.

Charles Foerster's design was produced in several different versions and unlike Prud'homme's design it was also manufactured not only in a stamped metal finish but also as a solid medal/plaquette.

All the medals had the exact same obverse design. In relief, a seated woman cradles a baby in her arms. The rectangular shaped medal is rectangular with the upper side deliberately rounded, giving an impression of a stained glass window. The legend *'Journée des Orphelins'* is stencilled along the rim with the artist's signature 'Ch Foerster' (9 o'clock).

Dimensions: 32 (H) x 20 (W) mm

Despite variation in the alloys used in the metal, and slight differences in the suspension loop, the three finishes appear to have been 'métal blanc', 'cuivre bronzé' and 'métal jaune'.

Dimensions: 37 (H) x 24 (W) mm

Above:
Larger versions were also produced again in the silvered metal, bronzed copper and gilt bronze.

Sold medal versions, as seen below, in bronze, gilt bronze and white metal were also made available to the general public for the fundraising efforts. The relief design is nearly identical to the stamped versions but the engraving is more detailed and in stronger relief. The reverse has a laurel branch with the legend: *Guerre / 1914 / 1915-1916*.

Dimensions: 35 (H) x 24 (W) mm

Below:
A table medal was also produced but was used as a presentation piece rather than for general sales.

Dimensions: 50 (H) x 32(W) mm

Below:

An authorized identity card for a street collector. In the upper part, a dark blue section is framed in red and gold with a legend in white letters on four lines:

Guerre 1914-15-16 / Journée Nationale / des Orphelins / 1 & 2 Novembre 1916

The lower part, framed in gold is made up of two bands in French colours.

Dimensions: 100 (H) x 83 (W) mm

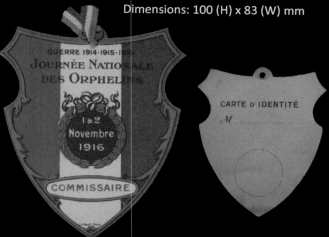

Dimensions: 75 (H) x 78 (W) ⅠⅠⅠⅠⅠ

Above:

A Commissaire's identity card. The French colours are framed in gold in the shape of a shield with the legend at the top on three lines: *Guerre 1914-15-16/Journée Nationale/des Orphelins*.

In the centre of the identity card there is a laurel wreath which is bordered in gold interwoven with tricolour ribbons at the top. In the centre on a brown background: *1 & 2/Novembre/1916*.

Set below is a white oval shape with 'Commissaire' in blue letters. At the bottom near the point: 'Le Papier, Paris'.

Dimensions: 86 (H) x 145 (W) mm

Above:

An étiquette used on the collecting boxes - in nine tricolour bands. A white frame with a tricolour border contains the legend in red letters:

Guerre 1914-15-16 / Journée Nationale / des Orphelins / 1 & 2 Novembre 1916.

Left:

A postcard sent by the mayor of Rochefort-en-Yvelines to each of the four collectors as a "Souvenir de la Journée Nationale des Orphelins". Their ID cards are all clearly visible.

POSTERS

Dimensions: 1070 (H) x 660 (W) mm

Above:

Poster designed by French artist Charles Foerster (1860-1925) and printed by Specialité d'Affiches 'Le Papier' 10 et 12, Avenue du Pont-de-Flandre, Paris .

The poster features a young girl and small boy standing in front of a grave. The girl is holding a bouquet of flowers in her left hand. A village lies in ruins in the background.

The legend: *Guerre 1914-15-16 Journée Nationale des Orphelins.*

At the bottom of the poster:
"Les dons et Souscriptions doivent étre adressés au Siège Social du Comité, 33 Rue Bonaparte, Paris VIᵉ."

Below:

Designed by the French artist and war illustrator Bernard Étienne Naudin (1876-1946), the poster was printed by Specialité d'Affiches 'Le Papier' 10 et 12, Avenue du Pont-de-Flandre, Paris .

Set against a plain white background, the image occupies the upper half, with the title below in red. The image features an orphaned girl and two boys holding hands. The girl is seated right, with her hand resting on the shoulder of one of the boys. The second boy is wearing a sailor's uniform.

The legend: *Journée Nationale des Orphelins - Guerre 1914-15-16* is followed by the text:
"Children of France, for the children who no longer have fathers, give what you can, give a little of your joy, give a little of your well-being and a lot of your soul! The Orphans of the war are your little brothers and sisters - do not forget them".

At the bottom of the poster:
"Donations and Subscriptions should be addressed to Siège Social du Comité, 33 Rue Bonaparte, Paris VIᵉ."

Dimensions: 1200 (H) x 800 (W) mm

La Journée Nationale des Tuberculeux (Anciens Militaires) 4 and 17 February 1917

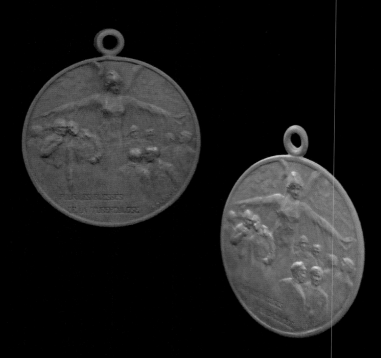

La Journée Nationale des Tuberculeux (Anciens Militaires) 4 and 17 February 1917

Up to the start of the war, control of tuberculosis in France was relatively secure. It is estimated that between the period 1894 and 1902, out of four million soldiers, there were only 36,000 recorded cases of the disease and these were nearly always treated in hospitals or sanatoriums. Mobilisation of the French army in August 1914, however, was to involve over a sixth of the French population and inevitably the squalid and cramped conditions of trench life, combined with the very inadequate medical facilities, contributed to the rampant spread of the disease in the French army.

Early on in the war it became abundantly clear that the French medical authorities were not well prepared to deal with such a large number of infective secondary tuberculosis cases. What to do with soldiers with active tuberculosis was not an easy problem to solve. First, the infected soldiers had to be hospitalized in special sanatoriums and kept away from other hospital patients. Second, with no hope of cure in the immediate future and judged unable to fight, they were often compelled to return home which undoubtedly spread the infection among their families and friends thereby causing a public health disaster.

In 1916 and largely as a result of the paucity of sanatorium facilities, over 100,000 of the 160,000 French soldiers who had contracted the disease were discharged and sent home. By 1917 it was further estimated that there were 450,000 soldiers in France incapacitated by wounds suffered in the theatre of war and another 450,000 incapacitated by active tuberculosis. By 1918 the disease was responsible for one in six of all deaths in France.

Several fundraising days were organized by the 'Comité central d'assistance aux anciens militaires tuberculeux'. The intention was to raise money to help provide assistance for tuberculosis sufferers, to improve hospital facilities and to raise public awareness of the crucial importance of hygiene in order to combat the spread of the disease.

Reports reveal that the freezing weather caused some regions to postpone the first authorized day and resulted in the Comité declaring that a second day would be held in March. Despite this setback the *Journées* set aside for this cause received an incredible response from the general public.

La journée des tuberculeux

Paris a revu une fois de plus la charmante armée des gracieuses vendeuses d'insignes. La « Journée des tuberculeux » comme il était à prévoir et en dépit du temps maussade et glacial, a fait très bonne recette dans tous les quartiers de la capitale. Le cœur des Parisiens qui ne se lasse pas de témoigner de sa générosité pour toutes les victimes et pour toutes les misères de la guerre, ne pouvait rester indifférent alors qu'on le sollicitait pour le bien de ces infortunés fils de France : blessés obscurs, mais non moins glorieux de la grande lutte, les blessés de la tuberculose.

Dans tout Paris, dans le brouillard gris et froid du matin, les passants sollicités par les jeunes quêteuses dont la bise glaciale n'arrêtait en rien la courageuse activité faisaient l'emplette de l'insigne du jour, médaille de carton ou d'argent, nouée aux couleurs nationales. Dans le Métro, dans les tramways, sur les boulevards, autour des gares, des places et des églises, partout, jeunes femmes et enfants ont quêté durant toute la journée pour les tuberculeux et partout on leur a fait le meilleur accueil.

En Seine-et-Oise, M. Autrand, préfet, a autorisé les maires du département à remettre les quêtes à une date ultérieure, à cause du froid.

Above:
An extract from *Le Petit Parisien* (dated 5 February 1917) reveals that the street collectors were faced with snow, fog and freezing weather. In Seine-et-Oise, M. Autrand (the Prefect), authorised the Mayors to actually postpone the Journée date.

Below:
Le Petit Parisien (dated 5 March 1917) reveals that the second authorised day met with far better weather conditions.

La Journée des Tuberculeux

La Journée des Tuberculeux, qui n'avait pu avoir lieu à cause des grands froids le mois dernier, avait été reportée à hier dimanche. Elle fut favorisée par un temps splendide. Les fillettes et les femmes qui se dévouèrent à cette œuvre pieuse et charitable furent récompensées de leur zèle par le bon cœur des Parisiens.

Right:

Excelsior (dated Friday 2 February 1917) page 6
A set of photos highlighted in *Excelsior* revealed the effect of the freezing temperatures in Paris. The appalling weather caused a huge amount of disruption and had an adverse impact on the first fundraising day.

La neige et le verglas ont entravé hier la circulation à Paris

Bien que la température se soit légèrement relevée dans la journée d'hier, le neige qui est tombée à peu près partout n'a pas fondu et, à Paris, le verglas a considérablement gêné la circulation : 1° Voitures arrêtées et dételées sur les grands boulevards; 2° Un cheval vient de s'abattre sur la chaussée; 3° Une scène qui s'est répétée des centaines de fois dans la matinée; 4° Un cocher conduit à pied son fiacre chargé; 5° Beaucoup de chevaux avaient les pieds garnis de chiffons.

Journée du **4 FÉVRIER**

Dimanche prochain

par toute la France

on quêtera

pour les Anciens Militaires

TUBERCULEUX

Donnez votre Obole

En les sauvant vous préserverez la race de la contagion

Left:

The *Journée Nationale des Tuberculeux (pour les Anciens Militaires)* was well publicised in many of the national newspapers including *Le Gaulois* (2 February 1917) page 3

Below:

The poster was designed and distributed by the American Committee for Tuberculosis Prevention throughout France in 1917. It warned of the need to defeat two plagues:

'The German eagle will be defeated.
Tuberculosis must be as well'.

Aujourd'hui, dimanche, dans toute la France on quêtera pour les anciens militaires tuberculeux

LES INSIGNES QUI SERONT VENDUS AUJOURD'HUI

Voici l'ensemble des insignes de la Journée des Tuberculeux, qui seront vendus dans toute la France et que vous pouvons reproduire grâce à l'obligeance du graveur Deicambez, Celui du centre au bas et le dernier, à droite, reproduisent respectivement les affiches de MM. Lévy-Dhurmer et Abel Faivre.

Above:

Excelsior (dated 4 February 1917) page 10
A half page advert of the different examples of the insignias/pendants being sold for the cause.

Mainly due to these fundraising campaigns and the support of the Rockefeller Foundation[17], the number of dispensaries in France grew from 22 to 600. In addition, the number of hospital beds that were available to tuberculosis patients rose from 8,000 to 30,000.

When the war ended, the French Parliament was to pass a law that required every Department in France to build a tuberculosis sanatorium or, if this proved impossible, to arrange to have its patients sent to another Department for treatment.

Dimensions - 87 mm

Above and below:

A rare novelty envelope. It originally contained 'surprise' insignias/medals and were designed to attract purchases from children. The envelopes were sold in shops and by street vendors for 2 francs.

The images on the front of the *pochette* bore a certain similarity to those used by Lalique for one of his most evocative designs (see page 107).

Details about the envelope and the contents were set out on the back along with the price.

L'ORGANISATION DES SECOURS

— *Les insignes de la « Journée des tuberculeux ».* —
Le comité central d'assistance aux tuberculeux anciens militaires, réuni sous la présidence de M. Léon Bourgeois, vient de décider que les insignes suivants seraient offerts au public à l'occasion de la « Journée des tuberculeux », qui aura lieu le 4 février prochain.

1° Broche ou breloque Lalique, offerte au prix de 3 francs; 2° épingle de cravate Lalique, 2 fr.; 3° nœud tricolore comportant une médaille de forme carrée, offerte au prix de 1 franc; 4° une petite enveloppe contenant une collection d'insignes de la journée au prix de 2 francs. A noter que beaucoup de ces enveloppes renferment un bon gracieux pour un insigne artistique supplémentaire; 5° des insignes métalliques estampés, au prix de 0 fr. 50; 6° des insignes en ca carton production des affiches d'Abel Faivre et de Lé Lévy Dhurmer prix de 0 fr. 20; 7° des insignes en carton ioinm artistiques, à 0 fr. 10; 8° des autographes relatifs à la tuberculose, émanant hommes illustres ou de personnalités en vue. Ces autographes seront vendus à partir de 0 fr. 50.

Above:

Le Temps (2 February 1917) set out details relating to the 4th February fundraising day. Eight different categories of articles were described which were to be sold on the day. These included:

1. Lalique brooches and pendants
2. Lalique lapel pins
3. a small lozenge shaped pendant designed by Lalique tied to a tricolour bow
4. a novelty envelope (see right)
5. stamped brass medals
6. miniature cardboard insignias of the Lucien Lévy-Dhurmer and Abel Faivre posters (see page 105)
7. cardboard insignias
8. autographs of famous individuals connected to the tuberculosis cause.

INSIGNIAS

Three printing firms - Chambrelent, Devambez and Lapina - were awarded contracts to manufacture nine individual cardboard insignias/badges which were sold in markets and shops throughout France as well as by street collectors.

Dimensions : 40 mm

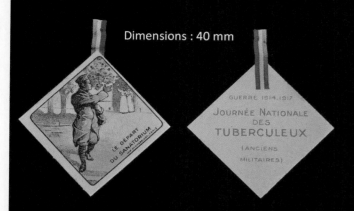

1. This lozenge shaped insignia features a soldier in a blue horizon uniform turning to wave his hand at two nurses who are watching him leave. Two background colours are described: ocher and olive.

On the right hand side is the legend:
'Le Départ du Sanitorium' with 'Imp. Chambrelent Paris'.
The reverse is a white background with the legend set in brown lettering: *Guerre 1914-1917 Journée Nationale des Tuberculeux (Anciens Militaires).*

Another version was produced which is identical regarding the imagery, however, the lettering of the legend is blue.

Above:
A further version was also produced where the lozenge corners were rounded and the legend lettering was more refined.

Below:
2. Based on a famous poster design by Jules Abel Faivre, the rectangular shaped insignia with a light green or pink rounded frame depicts a patient recovering from tuberculosis seated by the sea with the arms/hands of a nurse on his shoulders.

The legend is set in blue italic lettering on a white background *Guerre 1914-1917 Journée Nationale des Tuberculeux (Anciens Militaires)* with 'Dessin d'Abel Faivre/Devambez Imp' set below.

Dimensions : 51 (H) x 16 (W) mm

3. A rectangular shaped insignia with cut off corners and a gold coloured background. The image is of a soldier, in his blue horizon uniform carrying a brown musette bag, returning home and being greeted by his two children. At the bottom is the legend: *Retour du Sanitorium*.

The reverse is a white background with the legend set in blue lettering: *Guerre/1914-1917/Journée Nationale/des/Tuberculeux/Anciens/Militaires*.
The printer's name is set along the bottom rim: 'Imp Chambrelent, Paris'.

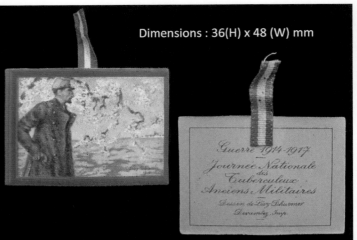

Dimensions : 36(H) x 48 (W) mm

Above:
4. This insignia is basically a miniature of a famous poster design by Jules Lucien Lévy-Dhurmer.

Set within a brown rectangular frame, a soldier recovering from tuberculosis is depicted with his cane, underneath an apple tree in blossom, gazing out across the countryside. The legend is set in blue italic lettering on a white background:
   Guerre 1914-1917 - Journée Nationale / des / Tuberculeux / Anciens Militaires
Set below the legend: 'Dessin de Lévy-Dhurmer/ Devambez, Imp'

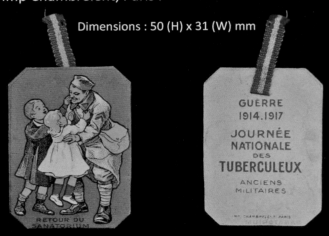

Dimensions : 50 (H) x 31 (W) mm

Another version was produced which is identical regarding the imagery, however, the lettering of the legend is brown. The variations of quality and finish which could occur in the printing process can be seen below.

Below:
5. This oval shaped insignia set in a brown frame, features a soldier sat near a pine tree looking at the mountains in the distance.

The legend is set in blue italic lettering on a white background: *Guerre 1914-1917 Journée Nationale des Tuberculeux Anciens Militaires* with 'Dessin d'Abel Faivre / Devambez Imp'.

Dimensions : 51 (H) x 41 (W) mm

6. A vertical oval insignia set in a gold frame. The image is of a patient seated in a lounge chair on a terrace, stretching out his hands towards the sun shining in the sky. A nurse in white stands to his left.

The bronze reverse bears the legend in white lettering:

Guerre / 1914.1917 / Journée / Nationale / des /Tuberculeux / Anciens / Militaires

The printer's name 'Chambrelent Paris' is below.

As can be seen with the two examples below, the colours of the sun, trees and balustrade vary in colour largely due to the inks being used.

Dimensions : 45 (H) x 33 (W) mm

The photos above reveal the variations of quality and finish which could occur in the manufacturing process.

Dimensions : 39(H) x 43 (W) mm

Above:

7. The gold bordered circular insignia is topped with a bouquet of five roses. A scene is of a terrace overlooking a lake with a backdrop of mountains - a soldier standing against a barrier is talking with another soldier reclining in a lounge chair.

The legend is the same as the other Chambrelent insignias with the printer's name set along the bottom rim.

A second version has the same image with slightly different colouring - the roses are white instead of pink, the mountain range is light blue rather than pinkish grey and the terrace is a lighter brown.

8. Printed in black on cream-coloured cardboard; the foreground features two women looking at a group of tuberculosis patients with a rising sun in the background. A circular legend reads: *"Aidez-nous à sauver les tuberculeux réformés"*.

The signature of Maurice Chabas is near the rim at the bottom (5 o'clock). The reverse features pine branches with a 'handwritten' three line legend: *"Journée Nationale des Tuberculeux"*. Set below this, in small letters - *"Anciens Militaires"*. Around the rim: *"Guerre 1914-1917"* and also 'Dessin de Maurice Chabas, Devambez Gr'.

Dimensions : 43 mm

Below:

9. A circular insignia which features a recuperating seated Senegalese tirailleur with a large white scarf around his neck, wearing a dark blue Zouave style tunic and red chechia fez. A legend is set on a countryside background: *"La France soigne tousses soldats"*. The reverse has a legend set in white lettering on a gold background: *Guerre/1914-1917 Journée Nationale/des/Tuberculeux*.

The printer's name is set below: 'Lapina. Imp Paris'.

Dimensions : 38 mm

Dimensions : 45 (H) x 33 (W) mm

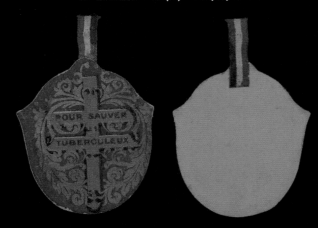

Above:

Vertical oval badge on a blue background with gilded stylized foliage patterns supporting a red Lorraine cross. On the two crossbars: "Pour Sauver Les Tuberculeux".

The reverse is plain cream white in colour.

Dimensions : 20 (H) x 30 (W) mm

Above:

Only one flag pin design was released for sale. Both sides depict the French flag colours.

The obverse features Marianne, the embodiment of the French Republic, who is helping a soldier with tuberculosis. On the reverse, in a double lined circle:

Journée Nationale / des / Tuberculeux / Anciens Militaires / Guerre 1914-1917.

Right:

An authorised identity card for a street collector. A vertical oval shaped design with the French colours positioned horizontally in a golden frame. A laurel wreath bordering a blue circle is in the centre with the legend in light blue: *Journée Nationale des Tuberculeux Anciens Militaires*. Around the rim at the top is the word 'Guerre' with the two dates '1914 / 1917' positioned at the bottom on the left and right. The reverse has a white background with the identical legend as the obverse with 'Carte d'Identité' and the printer's name at the bottom.

Dimensions: 81 (H) x 74 (W) mm

Below and bottom right:

A Commissaire's identity card. A vertical rectangle in shape with French horizontal colours within a golden frame. The fasces symbol, representing the authority of the State, is discretely positioned at the top; on each side two branches of holly, which border a cream coloured oval shape on which the legend is clearly set out in green lettering.

The reverse has a white background with the same legend as the obverse with 'Carte de Commissaire' and the printer's name at the bottom - all set out in blue lettering.

Below:

One of the official stickers (étiquettes) which were used on the collecting boxes. A tricolour frame encloses a blue rectangle dotted with stars and a badge/shield with two heads of chimeras at the tips dominate the centre with the legend in red lettering.

Dimensions: 98 (H) x 160(W) mm

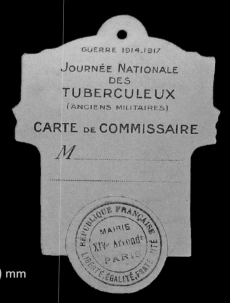

Dimensions: 90 (H) x 44 (W) mm

POSTERS

Right:
This poster was designed by Jules Abel Faivre (1867-1945) and printed by Devambez Imp Paris.

Set against a plain white background, the image totally dominates, with the title above in red and black lettering. The phrase *"Sauvons-les"* (save them) is set below the image in italicised lettering. The phrase would be used again by René Lalique in one of his medal designs (see page 106).

The image features a profile of a soldier with tuberculosis, sitting near the sea with a hopeful expression and his head raised to the skies. He is wearing a brown army coat and the hands of a nurse rest on his shoulders.

The legend is set in red block letters at the top of the poster: *Journée Nationale des Tuberculeux Anciens Militaires* with 'Devambez Imp Paris' in the bottom left corner. Faivre's signature is in the bottom right of the image and near the left hand corner of the image is an official stamp forbidding any other use apart from being displayed:
> *"Cette affiche, destinée à être apposée, ne peut être ni cédée, ni vendue; il est formellement interdit de la détourner de son objet".*

Dimensions: 1190 (H) x 800 (W) mm

Dimensions: 1200 (H) x 800 (W) mm

Left:
The poster was designed by Lucien Lévy-Dhurmer (1865-1953) and produced by Devambez.

The poster features a convalescent French soldier leaning on a walking stick stands in profile beneath the branches of an apple tree in blossom. Green fields are in the background with a small village on the horizon.

The legend: *Journée Nationale des Tuberculeux* is set in brown lettering at the top and at the bottom left of the image - *Anciens Militaires.*

MEDALS

Right:

The article in *Le Temps* (1 February 1917) focused on the various insignia that were to be sold and urged the general public to be generous. It also mentioned that the small number of the Lalique items that were for sale was due to the limited supply of metal brought about by the war.

Lalique was the only individual who was chosen to design a range of pendants, medals, brooches and lapel pins for this fundraising event. All the designs he proposed were far more conventional than the other designs he created during the war period.

One of his designs, produced as a uniface medal and as a brooch, had a clear connection with the poster (page 105) created by Jules Abel Faivre with the words *"Sauvons Les"*. Exactly who influenced who in the actual design and wording is largely conjecture but there is little doubt that Lalique's design met with full public approval.

Dimensions: 28 mm x 31 mm

Below:

Lalique's design of a pendant made from pressed brass again features an image depicting a seated convalescing poilu with his nurse behind him. They appear to be looking out over the countryside. It bears the legend - *"Aidez-Nous à les Sauver"* (Help us to save them) and the Lalique name (5 o'clock).

Dimensions: 31 mm x 36 mm

Dimensions: 28 mm

Lalique also created a smaller lozenge shaped design normally sold with a tricolour bow which was sown through the suspension ring and attached to clothing with a pin. It was produced in hollow pressed brass and also a silvered version.

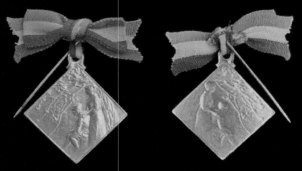

Dimensions: 27 mm x 31 mm

Three different versions of this design were sold for the benefit of those soldiers struck down by tuberculosis in World War One.

The design is regarded as the most evocative and iconic of all those that Lalique created for the *Journée*. Made of thin pressed brass, the central motif depicted an angelic figure with outstretched wings over a group of almost ghost-like poilus. All three versions bear the legend: *Pour les blessés de la tuberculose.*

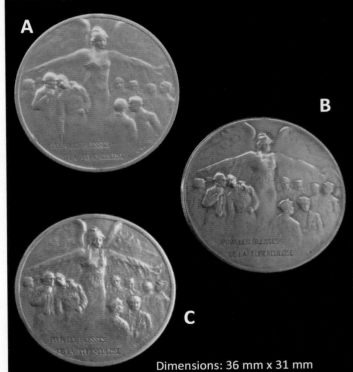

Dimensions: 36 mm x 31 mm

Silvered versions of this pendant were also sold - they are rarer to find, especially in good condition.

These two silvered pendants, just like the pressed brass versions, bore the same image. The slight differences relating to the brass versions can be seen again with these two versions.

In **A**, the position of the heads of the two soldiers (4 o'clock) are looking inwards whereas in **B** and **C** they are looking in the opposite direction. Rather than wearing képis, the two are bare headed.

Although **B** and **C** had exactly the same image they carried different stamps/signatures of 'Lalique'.

In **B**, 'Lalique' was engraved and was placed in a slightly different position than the embossed ones seen in **A** and **C**. In addition the legend *Pour les blessés de la tuberculose* is set higher up and there appears to be a different spacing between two of the soldiers (3 o'clock and 9 o'clock) and the rim of the pendant.

With the version (above), the image appeared to be slightly more detailed and bore an embossed raised signature.

The second version (below) bore an engraved rather than embossed signature.

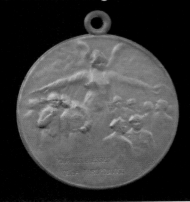

LAPEL PINS

Lalique produced two variations of lapel pins for the *Journée Nationale des Tuberculeux*. Both of them have as their central motif a nurse with her hands on the shoulders of a soldier recuperating from the deadly illness.

The imagery of the first version (1) is less refined than that of the second version (see 2 and 3).

In the first design which appeared to be quite crude, the nurse's stance is far more upright, the soldier's face is turned rather than in profile and his facial features appear to be almost blurred.

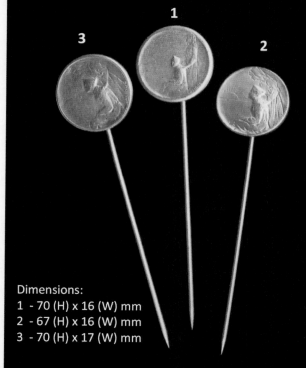

Dimensions:
1 - 70 (H) x 16 (W) mm
2 - 67 (H) x 16 (W) mm
3 - 70 (H) x 17 (W) mm

The nurse and soldier in the other version appear to be closer up and much more clearly defined.

Even with the second version there were slight variations in the design with Version 3 having a slightly more pronounced rim edge.

BROOCHES

Dimensions: 33 mm

The brooch design is clearly based on the imagery used in the second version of the lapel pin.

The brooch was produced in gilt bronze. The metal quality varied a great deal with some brooches having a far greater copper content, giving rise to a variation in colour. It was fastened with a 'C' clasp and the pin, made from steel, was attached by a round hinge.

With the brooch design, some were produced with the pin extending beyond the main body of the brooch but others were produced with a shorter pin. The Lalique stamp is embossed rather than engraved.

Le Devoir - Social Reconstitution des Foyers Détruits par la Guerre 21-22 May 1917

Le Devoir Social - Reconstitution des Foyers Détruits par la Guerre 21-22 May 1917

The two individuals regarded as the driving forces behind Le Devoir Social were Paul Deschanel and Henri Viet.

Deschanel was a politician and statesman. During the war he served as the President of the lower house of the French Parliament ('La Chambre des députés') and then in 1920, he was appointed President of France. Viet was an architect who also served as the Mayor of the XIe arrondissement - one of the 20 arrondissements of Paris.

Le Devoir Social was founded with one principal aim in mind and that was to bring relief to those inhabitants of the French and Allied countries who had suffered devastating damage caused by the war.

The listed 'Haut Patronage' reveals that Le Devoir Social movement received support from the very highest offices of the country including Raymond Poincaré (the President of France), Jean-Baptiste Bienvenu-Martin (the Minister of Justice), Antonin Dubost (the President of the French Senate), Leon Bourgeois (a former Prime Minister of France) and Émile Loubet (a former French President).

The movement was receiving subscriptions and donations as early as 1915 but the *Reconstitution des Foyers Détruits par la Guerre* set for the 21-22 May 1917 was the first time that monies were raised through the sale of insignias to the public.

Henri Viet
(1872-1960)

Paul Deschanel
(1855-1922)

Below:

A letter, addressed 'Aux Français', from the ten individuals heading the campaign, set out the laudable aim of reconstructing the devastated communities and concluded by stating:

"Nous avons confiance que tous les Français voudront, selon leurs moyens, participer à cette oeuvre qui est, en même temps qu'un acte de légitime réparation, une haute manifestation de la fraternité et de la solidarité françaises".

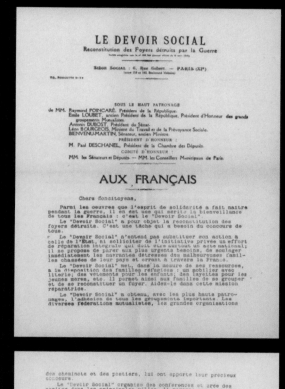

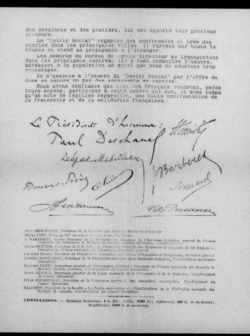

Ten specific historical towns/cities that had been decimated by the German bombardments were chosen to be the subjects for a set of ten insignias. Manufactured by the Ehrmann printing company of Paris, the insignias were sold to the general public on the two designated collecting days of Monday 21 May and Tuesday 22 May 1917.

All the insignias were identical in size and shape - a vertical rectangle with a rounded upper side. The images were all bordered with a yellow frame and bore the same legend on the reverse:
Devoir Social / Reconstitution / des Foyers Détruits / par la Guerre / 1914-1917

Set below the legend:
6 Rue Gobert, Paris XIe/ Journées/des 21 et 22 Mai *1917* and the printer's name - Ehrmann Paris.

ARRAS:
Hôtel de Ville / détruit par les Allemands / Janvier 1915

Dimensions: 46 (H) x 35 (W) mm

Arras Hôtel de Ville 1917

BAPAUME:
Hôtel de Ville / détruit par les Allemands / Mars 1917

Bapaume Hôtel de Ville 1917

FURNES:
Hôtel de Ville / détruit par les Allemands / 1914

111

NOYON:
Hôtel de Ville / détruit par les Allemands / Mars 1917

Noyon Hôtel de Ville 1917

PERONNE:
Hôtel de Ville / détruit par les Allemands / Mars 1917

ST QUENTIN:
Hôtel de Ville / détruit par les Allemands / Avril 1917

REIMS:
Hôtel de Ville / détruit par les Allemands / Septembre 1914

SOISSONS:
Hôtel de Ville / détruit par les Allemands / Octobre 1914

VERDUN:
Hôtel de Ville / détruit par les Allemands / Février 1916

YPRES:
Hôtel de Ville / détruit par les Allemands / Juillet 1915

Above right:
An example of a 'Carte de Sociétaire' for Le Devoir Social dating from 1915.

Right:
Individuals who made significant contributions to Le Devoir Social through volunteering their time to the movement or by making donations or regular subscriptions were given a certificate - 'Hommage de Gratitude'.

This particular certificate was designed by the renowned artist and illustrator Charles Fouqueray.

Dimensions: 295 (H) x 210 (W) mm

Journée de l'Armée d'Afrique et des Troupes Coloniales 10 June 1917

Journée de l'Armée d'Afrique et des Troupes Coloniales
10 June 1917

Soldiers from the colonies played a considerable role for the allied forces on the European fronts and in the Balkans. France deployed more than 480,000 troops in Europe from French colonies and some overseas territories during the war. This included 134,300 from West Africa, 172,800 from Algeria, over 60,000 from Tunisia, 37,300 from Morocco, 34,400 from Madagascar, 2,100 from the coast of Somalia and 44,000 from Indochina. Originally the majority of the colonial troops were volunteers but as the war dragged on and losses increased at an appalling rate, French authorities increasingly relied on conscription in to mobilize Arab and West African soldiers.

The majority of men in the colonies did not want to fight for France, and forced recruitment met with great resistance. In West Africa, local chiefs provided France with potential recruits, often young men from lower social strata. Many of these recruits, however, escaped conscription by taking refuge in Liberia or in some neighbouring British and Portuguese colonies.

In 1916 'La Commission des Affaires Musulmanes' proposed the idea of a *'Journée'* to raise funds for African soldiers who were prisoners of war and for their families in need. The idea was considered and authorization for the fundraising day - set for Sunday 10 June 1917 - was given by the Ministry of the Interior.

The concept which underpinned *'La Journée de l'Armée d'Afrique et des Troupes Coloniales'* was to sell insignias at an individual price of 0.50 francs and also to promote subscriptions to a nationwide tombola. All the proceeds were deposited at the Crédit Algérien, 10 Place Vendôme in Paris ready for redistribution to the relief organisations. The insignias proved to be a resounding success and it seems likely that ticket sales for the tombola were not limited to one day but were extended through June.

La « Journée » de l'armée d'Afrique et des troupes coloniales

La « Journée » des troupes coloniales et noires, ce qui maintenant est presque la même chose, puisqu'on a incorporé dans nos régiments coloniaux de nombreux soldats de couleur, a, malgré un temps douteux, obtenu un accueil des plus favorables. Les insignes étaient au nombre de huit, représentant les types divers de notre armée coloniale : marsouins, zouaves, chasseurs d'Afrique, spahis, tirailleurs algériens et marocains, soudanais et annamites. Les passants avaient le choix, mais beaucoup prenaient la série complète.

En même temps les quêteurs, jeunes filles et fillettes, voire même garçonnets, offraient, au prix de 50 centimes des billets de la tombola autorisée pour le même objet par le ministre de l'intérieur, et pour laquelle des lots représentant une valeur de 300,000 francs sont déposés au Crédit foncier.

Above:
An extract from *Le Figaro* 11 June page 2 details the great success of the day despite the inclement weather and lists the different insignias that were sold.

Below:
Le Petit Journal Supplément Illustré dated 1 June 1919 pays homage to the collective heroism of the Tirailleurs Sénégalais. Sent to the front in France from the first weeks of the war, the tirailleurs saw a great deal of combat as they were frequently deployed as attacking 'shock troops'.

INSIGNIAS

Three printing companies - Lapina, Chambrelent and Devambez - produced the insignias. As a result, it is apparent that there are slight variations in the typesets used for the legends on both the obverse and reverse of the insignias. In addition, there are also differences in the dimensions, the colours, the shapes and even the images used. It would be impossible to accurately record all these variations - instead, the Lapina versions are set out with other examples from Chambrelent and Devambez. Even within the Lapina collection, there are still some interesting variations in size, imagery and colours. The size of the insignias vary between 65-70 mm in height x 55-60 mm in width.

The one area which is consistent throughout all the insignias, no matter which printing company manufactured them, is the wording of the legends set out below:

Obverse:
Journée de l'Armée d'Afrique et des Troupes Coloniales 1917

Reverse:
1914 / La Marne, L'Yser / 1915 / Batailles d'Artois et de Champagne / 1916 / Verdun, La Somme / Campagne d'Orient

The complete set consists of eight images:
1 Soldat annamite
2 Soldat de l'Infanterie Coloniale
3 Chasseur d'Afrique
4 Tirailleur Sénégalais
5 Spahi Algérien
6 Tirailleur Marocain
7 Tirailleur Algérien - Turco
8 Zouave

1 SOLDAT ANNAMITE: Between 1914 - 1918, the French deployed approximately 43,430 Annamese from Indochina (present-day Vietnam). In addition, 48,981 Indochinese workers were sent to French factories replacing workers who left for the front lines.

The left profile of an Annamite soldier is set in a circle held up by two golden dragons; the legend in red is set against a blue dotted background. Both the insignias are Lapina produced and yet there are quite pronounced changes: the legend colours are slightly different and there are marked variations in the profile.

Above:
An Annamite regiment on parade - 14 July 1916

116

2 *SOLDAT DE L'INFANTERIE COLONIALE:* The title 'Troupes de Marine' was used to identify French troops stationed permanently in France's various overseas territories as well as the indigenous troops recruited in the French colonies (excluding North Africa). Until 1900, both services came under the administration of the 'Ministère de la Marine'.

The title 'Troupes Coloniales' was adopted after 1900 when all the Marine Infantry and Artillery troops, previously under the Ministry of the Navy were transferred to come under the command of the War Department. As a reminder of the past history, the anchor badge was retained.

3 *CHASSEUR D'AFRIQUE:* The Chasseurs d'Afrique were a light cavalry corps of chasseurs in the French Armée d'Afrique (Army of Africa), recruited from either French volunteers or French settlers in North Africa doing their military service.

Along with the Spahis (see page 118), they formed the cavalry elements of the Armée d'Afrique.

During WW1, seven regiments of Chasseurs were transferred to France and fought with distinction during the Gallipoli campaign, in the Middle East fighting against the Turks and they also served in the Balkans.

The portrait of the colonial infantry soldier is set in a circle resting on an anchor and laurel branches.

The portrait of the chasseur is set within a circle supported with laurels; a blue sky and a silhouette of a mosque form the background.

Below:
Both the insignias are Chambrelent products but there are several differences: the quality of the cardboard, image colours are slightly different and there are subtle variations in the profile.

Below:
Apart from depth of the ink colours, the Devambez version has more enhanced facial features and far more detail than its Lapina counterpart.

4 *TIRAILLEUR SÉNÉGALAIS:* The word 'tirailleur' is translated as 'rifleman', or 'sharpshooter' and was used to describe the indigenous infantry recruited predominantly from eight French African colonies. Despite recruitment not being limited to Senegal, the infantry units took on the adjective 'sénégalais' because that was where the first black African Tirailleur regiment had been formed.

During World War 1, the Senegalese Tirailleurs provided around 200,000 troops - more than 135,000 fought in Europe and 30,000 were killed.

At least four versions of the Senegalese Tirailleur were produced by Lapina. His profile is centred in a gold framed rectangle which is surrounded by geometrical motifs.

5 *SPAHI ALGÉRIEN:* The Spahis were light cavalry regiments of the French army recruited primarily from indigenous populations drawn from Algeria, Morocco and Tunisia.

All seven Spahi regiments saw service on the Western Front but it was inevitable, as with the Chasseurs d'Afrique, that their role diminished with the advent of trench warfare.

The insignia depicts the profile of a Spahi in front of an oriental window with a dotted dark blue background surrounded with two palms with white ribbons, wearing the traditional high Arab headdress called a 'guenour', short red jacket and distinctive white burnous.

In the Devambez version, the facial features are quite different; in addition, apart from the insignia having larger dimensions, the blue background is noticeably paler and the ribbons are distinctly French tricolours.

6 *TIRAILLEUR MAROCAIN:* Formed in 1915, the Moroccan tirailleurs was one of the most feared as well as decorated units of the French Army. Throughout the war they were deployed in some of the most attritional fighting on the Western Front. Their resilience and courage drew universal admiration and prompted the Minister of War M. Millerand to report in a note to General Lyautey:
"Disciplined under fire just as in manoeuvres, fierce in attack, tenacious in defending their positions including personal sacrifice and enduring beyond all expectation harsh climate conditions, they give indisputable proof of their value".

Wearing the traditional rezza and khaki uniform, the semi profile of the tirailleur is set within an oriental window which is framed in gold with two palm leaves intertwined with white ribbons. A dark blue dotted sky and fortress make up the background.

The Devambez version is larger in dimensions and has greater intensity of colours; the skyline is a simple pale blue and the tirailleur's features are far more clearly defined.

7 *TIRAILLEUR ALGÉRIEN:* The Algerian tirailleurs served with distinction in the Crimean War and the Franco-Prussian War as well as in many French colonial campaigns. Along with the Zouaves (see page 120) they were among the most decorated units of the French Army during World War One.

The tirailleurs acquired the nickname of 'Turcos' during the Crimean War - a name that reportedly arose because the Russian enemy had difficulty in distinguishing them from the Turkish soldiers serving alongside the French and British forces at the Siege of Sevastopol.

The tirailleur, wearing the traditional chechia, is positioned in front of an oriental window which is set in a gold frame with white ribbons and a dotted dark blue background.

In the second Lapina version (see below) the blue sky is dark an d the facial features are different. In addition the second version is over 5 mm wider and the legend 'plate' is yellow as opposed to light brown.

8 *ZOUAVE*: The French term 'Zouave' derived from the fact that the Zouaves were originally drawn from the Zwawa group of tribes in Algeria. From the very beginning of the First World War, the four Zouave light infantry regiments saw extensive service on the Western Front. Initially the Zouaves wore their traditional colourful uniform but the deadly use of machine guns and rapid-fire artillery forced them to adopt a plain khaki uniform from 1915 onwards.

Many press reports relating to the *Journée de l'Armée d'Afrique et des Troupes Coloniales*, refer to eight insignia designs but two versions of the 'Zouave' design were produced.

A Lapina version portrays a clean shaven Zouave in profile, set in a circle held up with laurel branches with a dark blue sky background and a silhouette of a mosque without a minaret.

The Devambez insignia below portrays a bearded Zouave in profile against a light blue sky and the silhouette of a mosque with the distinct minaret.

Dimensions: 1225 (H) x 780 (W) mm

Above:
A poster designed by Henry de Waroquier[18] that served the purpose of publicizing the event as well as giving the general public detailed information about the fundraising day. In particular it lists the numerous battles where the 'Armée d'Afrique' and the 'Troupes Coloniales' had served with such distinction.

Below:
A group of soldiers from the 4th Spahi Regiment wearing their distinctive 'guenours'.

POSTERS

Right:
Designed by Charles Fouqueray (1869-1956) and printed by Lapina, Paris 1917

The image is bordered with a narrow hand-drawn brown border. In the foreground right, Fouqueray depicts French colonial infantrymen, made up of a group of Moroccan and Algerian tirailleurs and Zouaves charging forward. In the background, a mounted Spahi is riding in support alongside other troops. The title is placed separately across the bottom dark brown: *Journée de l'Armée d'Afrique et des Troupes Coloniales.*

At the top, there is an Arabic inscription and just below this there is an official 'stamp':
"Cette affiche ne peut être vendue: des épreuves spéciales sont vente au bénéfice de la 'Journée' à l'Office de l'Algérie 5, Galerie d'Orleans Paris Charles Fouqueray 1917 Lapina, Paris".
[This poster cannot be sold. Special proofs are on sale for the benefit of the 'Day' at the Algerian Office [address].

JOURNÉE DE L'ARMÉE D'AFRIQUE ET DES TROUPES COLONIALES

Dimensions - 1200 (H) x 800 (W) mm

Left:
Poster designed by French artist Lucien Jonas and printed by Devambez, 43, Bd Malesherbes, Paris.

A narrow hand-drawn black border encloses the image of a Senegalese tirailleur, with his rifle held aloft, charging into battle. Two French poilus and an Indo-Chinese soldier stand on his left, beside a tree in blossom. Another Senegalese soldier stands to his right. The title is placed separately across the bottom in red outlined in black: *Journée de l'Armée d'Afrique et des Troupes Coloniales.*

An official 'stamp' is just above the title on the left:
"Cette affiche ne peut être vendue: Des épreuves spéciales sont en vente au bénéfice de la 'Journée' à la Maison Devambez 43, Bd Malesherbes Paris".
[This poster may not be sold: special proofs are on sale for the benefit of the 'Day' at the offices of Devambez [address].

JOURNÉE DE L'ARMÉE D'AFRIQUE ET DES TROUPES COLONIALES

Dimensions - 1200 (H) x 800 (W) mm

TOMBOLA

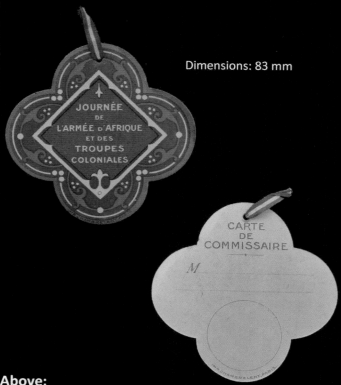

Dimensions: 83 mm

CARTE DE COMMISSAIRE

Dimensions: 170 (W) x 110 (H) mm

Above:
Étiquette - these were stuck on all the collecting boxes as proof of authorization. It featured the distinctive blue and red colours and stylized foliage patterns which were a common theme on all the insignias, identity cards and the Tombola tickets.

Above:
As with all the other nationwide *'Journées'*, any person who was authorized to sell the insignias and Tombola tickets had to wear an official 'Carte d'Identité'. This particular version was a 'Carte de Commissaire' - for the individuals placed in charge of supervising the street collectors.

Below:
All subscribers who contributed between 50 to 99 francs were awarded a bronze plaquette designed by Pierre Roche. Those who donated more than 100 francs received the silver version.

Dimensions: 70 (H) x 47 (W) mm

Below:
A Tombola ticket printed in green and blue with the Series number in green and the unique ticket holder number in red. The legend is positioned between stylized foliage patterns:

Tombola/Autorisée par le Ministre de l'Intérieur/ au profit des Œuvres d'Assistance/de l'Armée d'Afrique/et des Troupes Coloniales.

The printer's name can be seen in the bottom right corner: Gamichon et Maignas, Paris.

Dimensions: 102 (W) x 70 (H) mm

Le Devoir Social - Reconstitution des Foyers Détruits par la Guerre 27-28 May 1918

Le Devoir Social. Reconstitution des Foyers Détruits par la Guerre 27-28 May 1918

Two insignias were produced for sale on these two designated days.

1: This unusually shaped insignia features an allegorical female figure dressed in white against a background of blue sky. She is holding a white banner with the legend *'Le Devoir Social'* above a house with an ornate gate opening onto the street.

On the reverse, set within an orange frame: *Le/DevoirSocial/Reconstitution/des/Foyers Détruits /par la Guerre/1914-1918/6 Rue Gobert, Paris XIᵉ/ Journées/des/27-28 Mai/1918.*

The printer's name - Imp. Minot Paris - is set along the bottom rim.

2. The second insignia is identical in shape and has exactly the same reverse.

The image on the obverse is of a woman holding a model of a house. The red background has a series of the letters *'DS'* and above her head the legend: *'Le Devoir Social'* with a small star set just below.

1

Dimensions: 51 (H) x 32 (W) mm

2

Dimensions: 210 (H) x 140(W) mm

Left:
This 'Souvenir de Reconnaissance' certificate was given to individuals who were regarded as having made a significant contribution to Le Devoir Social.

Although the quote by Deschanel dates from early 1917 it is highly likely that this particular design was distributed in 1918 as the Fouqueray design was the one that was used in 1917 (see page 113).

Le Devoir Social - Reconstitution des Foyers Détruits par la Guerre 1914-1919

Le Devoir Social. Reconstitution des Foyers Détruits par la Guerre 1914-1919

1. The head and shoulders portrait of President Paul Deschanel in formal dress, set between two laurel branches, features on the obverse. Above the portrait, set on a background of various brown tones, is the legend *'Le Devoir Social'* positioned between two tricolour cockades. Set below the portrait in a pale blue/grey frame:

Paul Deschanel / Président de la République

On the reverse in a light blue frame:
Le Devoir Social / Paul Deschanel / Président d'Honneur / Reconstitution / des Foyers Détruits / par la Guerre / 1914-1919 / 37 B^d Voltaire Paris XIe / Ste Imp. Minot Paris.

2. The obverse features the head and shoulders portrait of Maréchal Foch in full uniform and bicorne hat. The portrait is set between two laurel branches on a background of yellow/brown tones. Above the portrait is the legend *'Le Devoir Social'* positioned between two tricolour cockades. Set below the portrait in a pale red frame:

Maréchal Foch

The reverse is identical to the Deschanel insignia.

Dimensions: 210 (H) x 140 (W) mm

Dimensions: 52 (H) x 42 (W) mm

1

2

Left:
The 'Souvenir de Reconnaissance' was given to the individuals who made regular subscriptions to Le Devoir Social. This particular certificate design was the work of Francisque Poulbot.

Journée des Régions Libérées
13-14 July 1919

Journée des Régions Libérées
13-14 July 1919

The devastation caused by the war in France was the subject of a general report commissioned by the French Government. According to the report, approximately 410,000 buildings were destroyed or seriously damaged - 170,000 partially damaged and 240,000 totally destroyed. It was estimated that the cost, just for rebuilding these houses and factories, would be over 21 billion francs and at least an additional 2.5 billion francs would be needed to cover the cost of just clearing the ruins.

It was observed that in some regions one could travel up to 50 - 100 km without finding a single standing or intact building. Some examples were cited in the report: between Soissons and Saint-Quentin (60 km) and between Armentières and Peronne via Arras (95 km).

As the war proceeded, the photos and newsreel footage taken of the ruins on the Western Front conveyed the apocalyptic power of the constant bombardments. The terrible devastation wrought by the invading German forces resulted in many cities, such as Bapaume, Armentières, Verdun and Saint-Quentin, no longer existing. The razing of these cities made ideal visual copy for the rapidly expanding news media.

Seven medieval cathedrals were laid to waste: Reims 1914, Mechelen (Malines) 1914, Ypres 1914 -1915, Cambrai 1917, Saint-Quentin 1917, Arras 1918 and Noyon 1918. Even the national Cathedral of Nôtre Dame in Paris suffered damage following an isolated Zeppelin raid in January 1916.

At the end of the war, the French government was determined that all these historic landmarks were to be returned to their pre-war condition. Within a few months work began, funded initially by the German reparation payments and using German prisoners-of-war as labour. The work to restore the cathedrals was used explicitly to advance the case for German war guilt - *'le crime allemande'*.

Above:
One of the main streets in Armentières in 1918

Below:
Destruction of the town of Lens in April 1919

It was clear that the reconstruction of these areas and cities/towns was naturally one of the greatest concerns of the public authorities in France. At the request of the Government, Le Secours National organized two national fundraising days known as *Journée des Régions Libérées.*

All proceeds were to be distributed among the various organisations which were in charge of the relief sectors. It was decided that the majority of the street collections would be placed under the supervision of the Croix Rouge française.

It is likely that the sale of the insignias was not limited to the two designated dates because some French Departments took the decision to extend the collection dates.

INSIGNIAS

The commission for the production of the insignias appears to have been shared yet again between the three Parisian printing companies: Devambez (1-4), Lapina (5-7) and Chambrelent (9-12).

One of the insignias (8) does not appear to have any printer's name.

1. The image depicts an evacuated family looking back on their ruined home. The signature of the artist (J Thil) is at the bottom left.

All four Devambez insignias, had identical legends in brown lettering on the reverse set on a white background:

Journée/des/Régions/Libérées

Dimensions: 42 mm

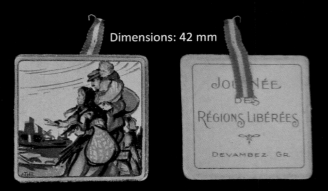

2. A stonemason is walking across a construction site carrying a slab. The artist's signature (J Thil) is at the bottom left.

Dimensions: 53 (H) x 37 (W) mm

Dimensions: 51 (H) x 41 (W) mm

3. Set in a gold tricolour frame, a workman with a cockerel on his shoulder is standing out against a background of factories and smoking chimneys. The legend *Journée des Régions/Libérées* is set above his head and along the bottom rim a second legend reads: *'Après la Victoire au Travail'*.

Dimensions: 51 (H) x 41 (W) mm

4. In a gold and black tricolour frame, a homeless family stands out against a background of ruined and burning buildings.

Set above their heads is the legend *'Journée au profit des Régions Libérées'* and along the bottom rim there is a second legend which states: *'Après la Victoire au Travail'*. The reverse has the identical legend as the other insignias. In the bottom right corner of the image the name of artist can be clearly seen - Charles Fouqueray.

This image was also used on a poster as well as the 'Carte de Commissaire' (see pages 132 and 133).

5. Set in a gold frame, the image depicts a solitary grave marked with a wooden cross - a withered wreath hangs around the cross, and flowers grow at the base amongst the discarded barbed wire. Against a background of the sun rising over an abandoned battlefield, a small bird is perched on the top of the cross.

The title and text are integrated and positioned across the bottom edge, in brown against a white background: *Journée des Régions Libérées / que votre aide à nos frères malheureux soit généreuse!* On the reverse in brown lettering: *Journée / des / Régions / Libérées* - the printer's name of Lapina Imp. is set below.

Dimensions: 52 (H) x 38 (W) mm

6. In a gold frame, the French colours serve as a background with a gold fasces and axe supported by ivy leaves. An escutcheon bears the monogram 'RF' (République française).

The legend is on the reverse on a gold background in white lettering: *Journée/des/Régions Libérées*

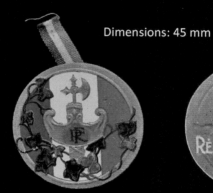

Dimensions: 45 mm

Dimensions: 45 mm

7. Set in a gold tricolour frame, the dove of peace carrying an olive branch in its beak flies above the ruins of a house.

The legend is on the reverse on a gold background in white lettering:
Journée / des / Régions Libérées

Dimensions: 45 mm

8. A composition in blue camaïeu depicts the ruins of a village. The image is set in a gold frame with two sets of intertwining tricolour ribbons.

The legend is on the reverse in black lettering on a white background:
Journée/des/Régions/Libérées

It is interesting to note that there is no printer's name or that of the artist.

Dimensions: 51 (H) x 46 (W) mm

9. A vertical insignia which has two convex sides at the top and bottom and two concave sides on the right and on the left. The image of ruined houses is set in a golden frame with a legend in the top left corner: *Verdun/Rue des Rouyers* and *Journée des Régions Libérées* at the bottom.

A printer's name is visible along the gold frame rim at the bottom: Imp. Chambrelent Paris.

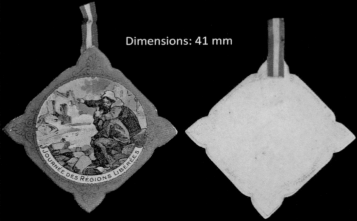

Dimensions: 41 mm

10. The insignia is square in shape with cut angles. In a circle set within a gold frame, a man and a woman are seated on a pile of stones looking at the ruins of surrounding houses in a village square.

The legend set in black lettering on a white band:
Journée des Régions Libérées.

The name of Chambrelent is below left on the rim.

11. In the shape of an eight pointed star, a map of France with the liberated regions in black is in the centre surrounded by a golden frame with a laurel wreath; angled across is a tricolour ribbon with a legend in blue lettering: *Journée des Régions Libérées*. The printer's name is set out just above the bottom point: Imp. Chambrelent Paris.

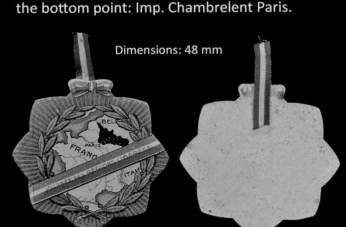

Dimensions: 48 mm

12. The insignia is an unusual shield-like shape. Within a golden frame a helmeted figure, clearly representing France, holds a flag. The legend, in brown lettering on the reverse:
Journée des Régions Libérées.

Dimensions: 55 (H) x 47 (W) mm

MEDALS

Three medals were also issued for sale on the two designated fundraising days. All three of them were produced in two finishes: bronze gilt and a silvered version.

Dimensions: 32 mm

1. Made of stamped metal the image depicts a winged figure symbolising victory extending a palm with the left hand and protecting with the right arm two children, one of whom is leaning on a marine anchor with the other hand resting on a fasces. The three figures are watching numerous workers busy reconstructing a building. The legend *Journée des Régions Libérées* is along the bottom rim.

Dimensions: 32 mm

2. The symbolic figure, who represents France, comforts a young woman wearing the traditional Lorraine headdress. A circular legend along the rim reads: *Journée des Régions Libérées* with *1919* at the bottom.
The medallist's name of Emmanuel Hannaux (1855-1934) is visible (9 o'clock).

Dimensions: 32 mm

3. An identical medal to the Lorraine version (below left), with the only difference being that the young woman is wearing a traditional Alsatian headdress.

Dimensions: 85 (H) x 75 (W) mm

Dimensions: 91 (H) x 70 (W) mm

Above:
Identity cards distributed to the authorised street collectors (left) and the Commissaires (right).

Below:
An étiquette used on the collecting boxes

Dimensions: 86 (H) x 145 (W) mm

POSTERS

Three posters were used to promote the *Journée des Régions Libérées*.

Dimensions: 1200 (H) x 790 (W) mm

Dimensions: 1200 (H) x 790 (W) mm

Above:

1. Auguste Leroux: The image occupies the whole poster, with the legend integrated and positioned upper left, in black. The text, in brown and in black, is integrated and positioned across the bottom edge. The image depicts a demobilized French soldier in civilian clothes but still wearing his army helmet, carrying a sledgehammer in his right hand and an oversized cockerel on his left shoulder. In the background, a pickaxe and a spade lean against a ruined wall. Signed on the plate with the artist's name and lettered with title and caption. Printed by Devambez, Paris.

Right:

2. Théophile Steinlen: The image is held within a black border, with the title and text in brown lettering, integrated and positioned along the bottom edge. Set against a background of the sun rising over an abandoned battlefield, a small song bird is perched on a wooden grave. A withered wreath hangs around the cross and flowers grow at the base amongst the discarded barbed wire. Printed by Lapina, Paris.

Above:

3. Charles Fouqueray: The legend is placed at the top of the poster in red outlined in black. The text is integrated and positioned across the bottom edge again in red and black. The image is set against a background of burning buildings with a family group in the foreground. A mother holds a younger child on her lap and the father comforts their daughter. In the background, another man stands before the rubble with his head bowed. Printed by Devambez, Paris.

Dimensions: 1160 (H) x 770 (W) mm

Fête de la Reconnaissance Nationale aux Poilus de la Grande Guerre 2 - 3 August 1919

Fête de la Reconnaissance Nationale aux Poilus de la Grande Guerre
2 - 3 August 1919

This event was organized by l'Union des Grandes Associations Françaises under the chairmanship of Paul Deschanel and Ernest Lavisse. The goal was to organize a *'Fête de la Reconnaissance des Enfants de France aux Poilus de la Grande Guerre'* in every French commune.

A circular was sent to all municipalities. It included a pre-stamped response card which was to be returned to Monsieur le Délégué Général de l'Union des Grandes Associations Françaises (3 Rue Récamier, Paris VIIe) indicating whether this event was going to be organized by the municipality.

The 'Diplôme aux Morts pour la Patrie' (see above right) were to be distributed to the families of soldiers who had lost their lives in the conflict. In Paris, a ceremony took place at the Sorbonne in front of 1200 children who had been selected to attend (see page 136).

Raymond Poincaré, the President of the Republic, paid homage to the 'glorious soldiers' of the Great War, ending his speech with these words:

"Il n'y a que les morts qui ont le droit de se reposer. Hier la France a trouvé des soldats, il faut aujourd'hui qu'elle trouve des citoyens".

The press, on Saturday 2 August 1919, published a call from Ernest Lavisse, the Directeur de l'École Normale Supérieure de l'Académie Française who gave an address to the children:

"Vos pères ont eu leur jour de gloire, a vous est échu le jour de travail".

Chambrelent produced three cardboard insignias. Rather than being sold on the streets these were distributed as gifts to all French school children. They all bear the same phrase: *'Offert par l'Union des Grandes Associations Françaises'*. Exactly the same phrase was also printed on the insignias that

Dimensions - 50 (H) x 40 (W) mm

were distributed to children on the *'Jour de Deuil National'* held on 2 November 1919 (see pages 139-140).

Dimensions: 38 (H) x 68 (W) mm

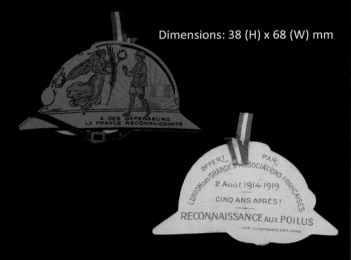

1. An unusual insignia shaped like a Poilu helmet. On a pale blue background, a winged figure, who symbolizes Victory, holds out a palm and a crown to a Poilu who advances towards her. A rising sun which lights up a French flag is in the background. A legend is set along the helmet rim:

À Ses Défenseurs La France Reconnaissante

Reverse: legend in blue lettering:

Offert par / l'Union des Grandes Associations Françaises /2 Août 1914-1919/ Cinq ans après! /Reconnaissance aux Poilus

2. A vertical oval badge - the head and shoulder portrait of a poilu in his horizon blue uniform and Adrien helmet is set within a laurel frame. A substantial tricolour ribbon is intertwined with the wreath and bears the legend:

'*À Ses Défenseurs / La France Reconnaissante*'

The reverse bears the identical legends to the other two insignias.

Dimensions: 49 (H) x 35(W) mm

3. A rectangular insignia which is an outline of the Arc de Triomphe which is printed in light grey. In the background, the Allied troops march past with the various allied flags. In the foreground, a poilu stands out carrying three palm leaves on his left shoulder.

The legend reads:

'*À Ses Défenseurs / La France Reconnaissante*'

The reverse bears the identical legends to the other two insignias.

Dimensions: 49 (H) x 38 (W) mm

A repoussé medal made in white metal which is in the shape of the Arc de Triomphe. In the centre, a poilu brandishes a rifle in his right hand and holds a Prussian pickelhaube helmet in his left hand.

The head and shoulders of two women - one from Lorraine and the other from Alsace - can be seen in the two lower angles of the medal. Unlike the three insignias, it is likely that this medal may have been sold during the two day period.

Dimensions: 33 (H) x 22 (W) mm

Below:

Headlines from *Excelsior* 4 August 1919 and *Le Miroir* 10 August 1919 reporting on the *Fête de la Reconnaissance Nationale*.

Jour de Deuil National
2 November 1919

Jour de Deuil National
2 November 1919

Following the publication of a law set out in the Journal Officiel de la République Française (Lois et Decrets), a day of national mourning which was named the *'Jour de Deuil National'*, was organized to take place in all the French Departments on the 2 November 1919.

This event was to be organized in all communes of France with the assistance of the civil and religious authorities. The following year, a new law stated that this ceremony would in future take place on 11 November and would be known as the *'Fête de l'Armistice'*.

Throughout France, for the *Jour de Deuil National* in 1919, commemorations took place in front of war memorials and cemeteries as well as in places of worship. The families of those 1,500,000 soldiers who sacrificed their lives for their country were given diplomas as a recognition of their loss.

In addition, all school children were given insignias commemorating this day - like the insignias that were distributed on the *Fête de la Reconnaissance Nationale aux Poilus* (held on 2 - 3 August 1919), these were free and not sold to the general public.

Below:
Journal Officiel de la République Française (Lois et Décrets) 26 October 1919 No 291 page 2

LOI relative à la commémoration et à la glorification des morts pour la France au cours de la grande guerre.

Le Sénat et la Chambre des députés ont adopté,

Le Président de la République promulgue la loi dont la teneur suit :

Art. 1er. — Les noms des combattants des armées de terre et de mer ayant servi sous les plis du drapeau français et morts pour la France, au cours de la guerre de 1914-1918, seront inscrits sur des registres déposés au Panthéon.

Art. 2. — Sur ces registres figureront, en outre, les noms des non combattants qui auront succombé à la suite d'actes de violence commis par l'ennemi, soit dans l'exercice de fonctions publiques, soit dans l'accomplissement de leur devoir de citoyen.

Art. 3. — L'Etat remettra à chaque commune un livre d'or sur lequel seront inscrits les noms des combattants des armées, de terre et de mer, morts pour la France, nés ou résidant dans la commune.

Ce livre d'or sera déposé dans une des salles de la mairie et tenu à la disposition des habitants de la commune.

Pour les français nés ou résidant à l'étranger, le livre d'or sera déposé au consulat dont la juridiction s'étend sur la commune où est né, ou a résidé le combattant mort pour la patrie.

Art. 4. — Un monument national commémoratif des héros de la grande guerre, tombés au champ d'honneur, sera élevé à Paris ou dans les environs immédiats de la capitale.

Art. 5. — Des subventions seront accordées par l'Etat aux communes, en proportion de l'effort et des sacrifices qu'elles feront en vue de glorifier les héros morts pour la patrie.

La loi de finances ouvrant le crédit sur lequel les subventions seront imputées réglera les conditions de leur attribution.

Art. 6. — Tous les ans, le 1er ou le 2 novembre, une cérémonie sera consacrée dans chaque commune à la mémoire et à la glorification des héros morts pour la patrie. Elle sera organisée par la municipalité avec le concours des autorités civiles et militaires.

Art. 7. — La présente loi est applicable à l'Algérie et aux colonies.

La présente loi, délibérée et adoptée par le Sénat et par la Chambre des députés, sera exécutée comme loi de l'Etat.

Fait à Paris, le 25 octobre 1919.

R. POINCARÉ.

Par le Président de la République :

Left:
The front page of *Excelsior* 3 November 1919 was devoted to the commemorations at Verdun

INSIGNIAS

Six different insignias were produced for this event and all of them came in four different versions - each one bearing one of four quotes in either blue or brown lettering by:

A. Paul Deschanel:
Qui n'écoute pas nos Morts n'est pas digne de vivre. La Mort éclaire la Vie.

B. Maréchal F Foch:
Gloire à cet héroïque soldat. La reconnaissance d'un peuple, plus encore celle du Monde, lui est à jamais acquise.

C. Ernest Lavisse:
Voici les trois commendements des Morts: Aimez-vous les uns les autres. Aimez notre Patrie plus que vous-mêmes. Travaillez de toutes vos forces et de tout votre coeur au relèvement de la France. Travaillez! Travaillez! Travaillez!

D. Raymond Poincaré:
Honneur aux Morts, immortels conseillers des Vivants.

The legend in blue lettering is on the reverse: *Jour de Deuil National - 2 Novembre 1919.* Set just below this is the Poincaré quotation (D). Both the legend and quotation are encircled with: *Offert par l'Union des Grandes Associations Françaises.*

Dimensions: 50(H) x 40 (W) mm

2. A vertical oval badge on which the image is in a gold rectangular frame. On a purple background, Marianne (symbolising France) wears a Phrygian cap and is clearly protecting two young children. The reverse is quotation B - Foch.

Dimensions: 40 mm

3. A square shaped insignia with a multi-coloured image set in a gold frame. The background depicts a deserted battlefield and graveyard. Two young children, one of whom is holding a bouquet of flowers stand in front of a grave decorated with a tricoloured cockade.
The reverse is quotation A - Deschanel

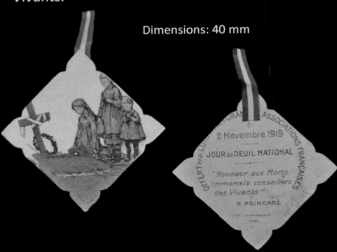

Dimensions: 40 mm

1. A square shaped insignia with printing in purple and gold/brown. The image depicts three children standing in front of a grave. A tricolour ribbon is draped over the cross and a wreath lies at the base.

4. A crest shaped insignia with a golden frame encloses a tricolour flag background. Underneath its wings, a Gallic cockerel is protecting two young children who are holding hands.

The reverse in brown lettering is legend C - Lavisse.

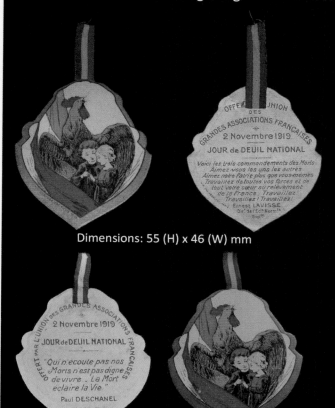

Dimensions: 55 (H) x 46 (W) mm

Above:
A Deschanel version in blue lettering.

Dimensions: 43mm

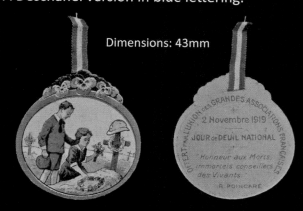

5. Circular in shape, with pansies on the top of a golden frame. Within an internal oval frame, a boy and a girl lay flowers on a grave - the cross has a wreath and a poilu helmet on top of it.

Reverse: In brown lettering legend D - Poincaré.

Dimensions: 53(H) x 38 (W) mm

6. A vertical rectangular insignia is bordered with a golden frame which encloses a triumphal arch composed of ochre and brown colours. A lion rests on top of the arch while a poilu stands alert with his rifle on the right. On the left, a robed female figure is writing the words: *Reconnaissance / Nationale / Aux Morts / de la / Grande Guerre.*

In the centre of the image, a second female figure is seated and appearing to cry. Just behind her are a flag, palm leaves and a laurel wreath. On the reverse the Poincaré legend is set in blue lettering against a plain white background - no other legend appears to have been used for this insignia.

Below:
The 'Diplôme aux Morts pour la Patrie' which was distributed to 1,500,000 families of soldiers who gave their lives fighting for France. The diploma is the central image of the insignia featured above.

SECTION TWO

Journée de la Ville de Paris
14 July 1915

Journée de la Ville de Paris 14 July 1915

On August 19, 1914, the Office Departemental des Œuvres de Guerre de l'Hôtel de Ville was founded in order to centralize and coordinate fundraising efforts and assume responsibity for distributing clothes and food through seven different Sections:

1. Section du Tricot du Soldat
2. Section d'Assistance Publique et d'Aide aux Blessés Militaires
3. Section des Trains de Blessés
4. Section des Prisonniers
5. Section des Réfugiés
6. Section d'Aide aux Mutilés
7. Vestiaire Parisien

The 'Office Departemental' had particular financial responsibility for the donations, subsidies and the fundraising efforts of the three *Journées de Paris* which took place on 14 July 1915-1917.

The three societies collectively known as the 'Croix-Rouge française' (CRF) - La Société française de Secours aux blessés militaires (SSBM), Union des Femmes de France (UFF) and the Association des Dames françaises (ADF) - gave permission for their personnel to be at the disposal of the City of Paris and this one factor undoubtedly contributed to the success of the three fundraising days.

The choice of the 14 July was an obvious one for the three Journées as every year in France the day is held as a National Day, commemorating the Storming of the Bastille in 1789 as well as the Fête de la Fédération in 1790. In 1915, however, the day was marked by a significant event steeped in patriotism which was designed to raise the morale of the French people. The Government decided to transfer the remains of Rouget de L'Isle, the composer of *La Marseillaise* (the French National anthem), from the cemetery of Choisy-le-Roi to Les Invalides.[19] To further acknowledge the great significance of this event, one of the medals that was designed for the Journée de la Ville de Paris commemorated de L'Isle's legacy (see page 146).

Above:
A poster set out the details of the programme for the day and listed the names of the personalities and officials who would attend the ceremony.

At 10.00 a.m. the procession started from l'Arc de Triomphe de l'Etoile down the Champs-Élysées to the Hôtel National des Invalides. A gun carriage drawn by six horses carried the coffin which was covered with a red velvet draperie with a gold thread fringe. In front of the carriage fourteen Tricolours were arranged side by side on a caisson.

The French President, Raymond Poincaré and 15 of 32 members of his government walked behind the carriage. Outside Les Invalides, he delivered an address that generated headlines in all French newspapers the following day. In his address he drew a comparison between the political context of the creation of La Marseillaise in 1792 and the political context of July 14, 1915.

143

Below:

An article from *Le Petit Journal* dated 15 July 1915 page 2 reveals that many of the collectors had sold out of insignias by 10 o'clock in the morning and had to restock . One very successful collector, who was accompanied by his young wife, was a soldier who had lost an arm in the war.

La "Journée de Paris"

Ce fut un nouveau succès. Il y avait surabondance de quêteuses. Rien que le IXe arrondissement avait mobilisé 600 jeunes filles, toutes plus avenantes, plus empressées et plus consciencieuses les unes que les autres. Aussi, à 10 heures du matin, la Permanence centrale de la mairie Drouot, voyait-elle revenir des quêteuses qui avaient à vider leur tirelire et à renouveler leur provision d'insignes, pour s'éparpiller à nouveau à travers rues et boulevards à la conquête de nos porte-monnaie.

Conquête facile ! Ces « journées » qui deviennent classiques, ont habitué quêteuses et public à leur devoir réciproque. Il y a moins de timidité, chez tout le monde, et il s'établit des traditions.

Ainsi, il n'est plus de mise du tout de n'avoir qu'un ou deux insignes à la boutonnière ou au corsage. Il faut au moins la demi-douzaine, et même davantage. Qui n'a pas son insigne ? Mais le commissionnaire du coin, l'agent de service, l'apprenti pâtissier, l'ont des premiers arboré !

Assaut de générosité

Quelques quêteurs aussi à signaler, des boys-scouts, des jeunes gens, et un entre autres qui ne suffisait pas à sa clientèle. C'était un, de nos glorieux blessés, amputé d'un bras, qui quêtait avec sa jeune femme. Le couple sympathique était très entouré. Il fit une brillante recette.

A signaler également de charmantes et gracieuses Alsaciennes, et trois jeunes filles qui, vêtues l'une de bleu, l'autre de blanc, la troisième de rouge, formaient un drapeau vivant.

Aux Halles, la recette a dû être fabuleuse. Non seulement tout le monde versait dans les innombrables troncs présen-

Une petite Alsacienne décore un soldat de l'Insigne de la Ville de Paris

tés, mais marchands et marchandes du carreau prenaient, par paquets, des insignes, parce qu'ils avaient des commissions de leurs voisins restés dans la banlieue et qui voulaient participer quand même à la « Journée de Paris ».

Above:

Interestingly, not all the press coverage of the *Journée* was as eulogistic as *Le Petit Journal*. An illustrated French political magazine - *Le Cri de Paris* (18 July 1915 pages 10-11) - was scathing in its assessment and questioned the organizational abilities of the City of Paris authorities as well as the insignias and medals which were described as being: "d'une regrettable insignifiance".

It went on to state that it might have been helpful, given the huge success of previous *Journées*, to have commissioned the likes of Hippolyte Lefèbvre and René Lalique who in the past had designed: "de petits chefs-d'oeuvre que les collectionneurs ont soigneusement gardés".

Such a stance was in total contrast to the article written by Paul Appell in *Le Matin* 28 October 1916 (see page 86) which was so critical of having to involve famous artists and medallists and resort to selling 'luxury' items which, in his words, amounted almost to "jewellery sales".

Two cardboard insignias were manufactured by Devambez for the first of the three *Journées*.

1. An oval insignia with a purple background and golden border. The eight Allied flags are central to the design. On the reverse, on a gold background in black legend on five lines:

Journée / de la / Ville de Paris / 14 Juillet / 1915

2. The obverse of the oval shaped insignia has a purple background with a golden border. The eight Allied flags of France, Great Britain, Belgium, Italy, Japan, Serbia, Russia and Montenegro surround the Paris coat-of-arms.

The legend on the gold reverse background is identical with that of Insignia 1.

Dimensions: 42 (H) x 33 (W) mm

Silver versions also exist of the two insignias. They are identical with the exception of the reverse background colour - gold is replaced with silver.

Dimensions: 36 (H) x 32 (W) mm

Apart from the 'silver' versions of the two main insignias a further version of insignia 2 was also produced but is extremely rare. On the obverse, the purple background is replaced with a cream colour.

The other two insignias produced for the Journée were made 'en étoffe'. These are rare to find as the fabric they are made of was not known for its longevity. Both feature flowers in red, white and blue and are very unusual shapes, almost giving the impression of being handmade. Reference is made to them by de Bayle des Hermens but no images are presented and he only gives a brief description.

Dimensions: 35 (H) x 22 (W) mm

Dimensions: 35 mm

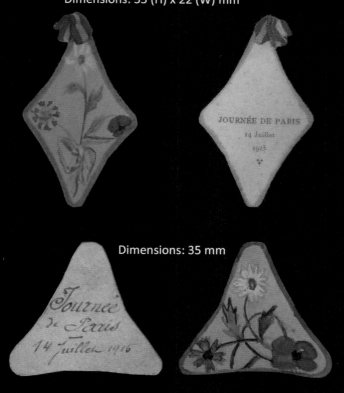

Two medals were produced for this event, one of which featured Rouget de L'Isle. The medal, made of pressed brass in two finishes, featured the side profile of de L'Isle with a legend around the rim:

Rouget de L'Isle/Journée de Paris/1792 1915

The version made of 'cuivre jaune' has the name of the designer ('David') on the neck; the 'cuivre doré' version has no name.

Dimensions: 22 mm

Solid silver and white metal versions of the medal were also produced but whether these were sold to the general public in 1915 remains uncertain.

An oval shaped enamelled medal and brooch were also sold on the day to the general public. Similar in design to the cardboard insignia 2 (see page 145) it had as the central feature the coat of arms of the City of Paris surrounded with the eight flags of the Allies set on a pale blue background with the legend - *Journée de Paris 14 Juillet / 1915.*

Below:
Every street collector was issued with distinctive armbands (brassards) and identity cards, both of which were in the traditional Paris colours of blue and red.

Dimensions: 34 (H) mm

Along with the etiquette (see below), both items bore the same legend in gold lettering:

Journée de Paris / 14 Juillet 1915.

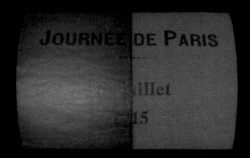

This particular 'Carte d'Identité' was stamped by the 'Mairie du VIIe Arrondissement - Paris'.

Dimensions: 80 (H) x 65 (W) mm

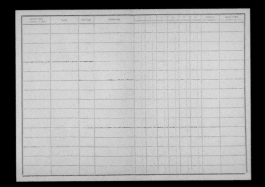

Below:
A letter dated 29 June 1915 inviting individuals to a meeting at the Town Hall set for the 2 July to discuss the arrangements for the fundraising day.

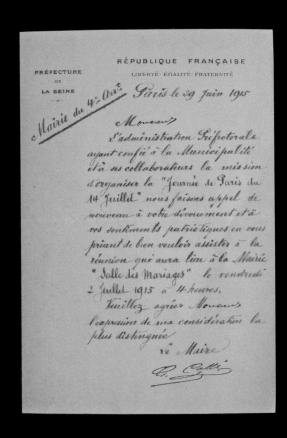

Below and below left:
Documents relating to the recording/receipts of the amounts raised by individual street collectors.

147

POSTERS:

For the first *Journée de Paris* three posters were circulated to advertise the event and promote interest.

One of the posters related to the Government's decision to transfer Rouget de L'Isle's remains from Choisy-le-Roi to Les Invalides. The poster was used mainly for information purposes setting out the details for the day (see page 143).

Below:
A second poster manufactured by Marcel Picard - 'Appel à la Population' - urged all Parisians to show their gratitude to the soldiers for having heroically defended the City of Paris.

It was signed by:
Adrien Mithouard, Président du Conseil Municipal; Marcel Delanney, Préfet de la Seine; Emile Laurent, Préfet de Police; Paris, Président du Conseil Général.

Dimensions: 1400 (H) x 1015 (W) mm

Dimensions: 1200 (H) x 800 (W) mm

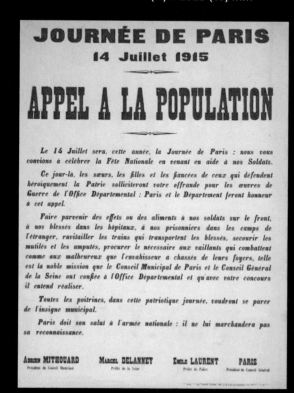

Above:
The poster was designed by Georges Picard (1857-1943) and printed by Devambez.

The text is integrated and positioned across the top edge, in black. Set against a background of the roof of l'Hotel de Ville, a woman cradles a baby and holds out a collection box while two children hide beneath her clutching a shield of Paris. At the foot of the poster, a French soldier stands in front of a small house.

The text:
Journée de Paris 14 Juillet 1915 au Profit des Œuvres de Guerre de l'Hôtel de Ville pour les combattants - les blessés - les convalescents - les mutilés - les réfugiés - les prisonniers.

Journée de Paris
14 July 1916

Journée de Paris 14 July 1916

Dimensions: 115 (H) x 138 (W) mm

Top:
A collection box label - in the City colours with two double yellow borders with three white knots. The Paris coat of arms is in the centre with the legend in white: *Journée de Paris - 14 Juillet 1916*.
Bottom right - Chambrelent Paris.

Below:
A silk/linen armband in the colours of the City of Paris. Legend in gold lettering:

Journée - 1916 - de Paris

Dimensions: 40 (H) mm

Below:
A street collector's identity card in the shape of an escutcheon. The City colours are set within a gold frame; the coat of arms is set below the legend in white: *Journée de Paris / 14 Juillet / 1916*.

Dimensions: 102 (H) x 67 (W) mm

The two articles above reveal the success of the second fundraising event.

The *Excelsior* article dated 15 July 1916 page 3 has as the main focus the magnificent effort of the hundreds of street collectors.

The extract from *Le Figaro* 15 July 1916 page 2 again praises the efforts of the collectors and details the various insignias ('vignettes') and also the Gallieni[20] medal designed by Auguste Maillard.

It is interesting to note that the authorities gave permission for the street collections to continue for a further two days.

INSIGNIAS

Five cardboard insignias were produced for sale in the 1916 *Journée de Paris*.

1. The image on the obverse is enclosed within a circular golden frame. A helmeted female figure, representing the City of Paris, is dressed in red with the Paris coat of arms and is holding an oar with both her hands and standing out against the Hôtel de Ville of Paris. The City's motto - "Flvctvat nec mergitvr" (She [Paris] may be tossed by the waves, but she will never sink) - is set in gold lettering against a blue sky.
The intertwined initials of the artist 'GP' can be seen on the right (4 o'clock).

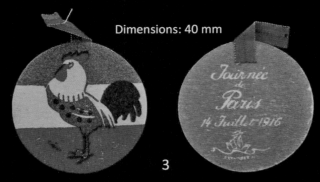

Dimensions: 40 mm

3

3. A simple design of the defiant Gallic cockerel is set against the French colours. The wording on the bronze reverse is identical to the other insignias but is italicised. The Devambez name is set below the small image of the sailing ship.

Dimensions: 35 mm

1

The reverse has a three line legend set in white lettering on a gold background: *Journée/de Paris/ 14 Juillet 1916*. The manufacturer's name is set along the bottom edge: J Barreau Imp. Paris.

2.The obverse features the Paris coat of arms set in a gold tricolour cockade. The reverse is identical to insignia 1.

Dimensions: 35 mm

4

4. The obverse features the ship which is central in the Paris coat of arms. It is coloured silver in relief, on a blue and red background and above it is the legend - *Journée de Paris*. The reverse is a gold background with the legend in white letters on two lines: 14 Juillet/1916 with Lapina Imp. Paris.

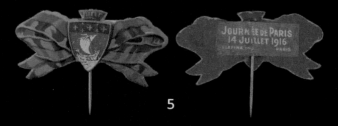

5

Dimensions: 45 (W) x 20 (H) mm

5. An insignia in the shape of a blue and red ribbon bow. The Paris coat of arms feature in the centre. The reverse is brown and a small étiquette holds the pin in place. The two line legend is printed in white on the étiquette: Journée de Paris/14 Juillet 1916. Lapina Imp. Paris is set below.

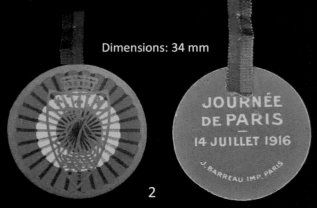

Dimensions: 34 mm

2

MEDALS

1. A circular shaped medal made of aluminium. The scene depicts a winged female figure who represents victory wielding a sword in her right hand urging a group of six armed soldiers from various different regiments into the attack. A biplane can be seen in the far distance. The legend *'Journée de Paris'* is along the top edge and the designer's signature - A Bargas - is in the bottom right (4 o'clock).

Dimensions: 26 mm

2. A silvered bronze medal which has the same design on the obverse as the above medal. The surround of the medal is made up of an oak branch on the left and a laurel branch on the right, all held in place by a knotted ribbon at the bottom. Above the figures is a mural crown which has a suspension ring through it.

The reverse features the City of Paris coat of arms decorated with the Legion of Honour which had been added to the coat of arms through a decree of 9 October 1900. The shield is supported by a branch of laurel on the left and oak on the right.

Dimensions: 35 (W) x 35 (H) mm

3. The brooch is identical to the medal form. Rather than using a suspension ring a horizontal pin and 'C' clasp is fixed to the reverse side.

Dimensions: 35 (W) x 35 (H) mm

After a successful military career, Joseph Gallieni was recalled from retirement when war broke out. Despite ill health he became Minister of War and Military Governor of Paris, charged with organizing the defence of the City. Having died just seven weeks before the fundraising day, the Parisian authorities felt that the critical role he played in the defence of Paris should be acknowledged.

4. Two finishes were produced for this design - silvered metal and bronze. The obverse features Gallieni's bare headed profile. The name of the engraver is set on the right: Aug^{te} Maillard / 1916. Just underneath is the foliage branch stamp of Paris-Art and a square punch is set on the lower left rim (7 o'clock). An embossed three line legend is on a plain reverse background: *Paris / 1914-1916 / "Jusqu'au bout"*. The Gallieni signature is just below with 'Paris Art' along the rim (7 o'clock).

Dimensions: 28 mm

5. This medal, made in two finishes (silvered and bronze), features a bare headed profile of General Gallieni on the obverse surrounded by a circular legend on two lines:
Au. Défenseur. de. Paris. MDCCCCXVI - G^{AL} Gallieni 1849-1916. The interwoven initials of the engraver 'GI' are engraved on the bottom left (7 o'clock).
The reverse has an embossed horizontal legend set on seven lines on a plain background:
J'ai reçu / le mandat de / défendre Paris / contre l'envahisseur / ce mandate / je le remplirai / jusqu'au bout.

Dimensions: 31 mm

6. A gilt bronze medal of Gallieni. The obverse bears his profile with the circular legend: *General Gallieni. 1849-1916.* The embossed signature of Aug^{te} Maillard is also set along the rim (7 o'clock).
The reverse is plain with a legend on eight lines:
Armée de Paris / Habitants de Paris - J'ai reçu le mandat de / défendre Paris contre / l'envahisseur/ ce mandate je le remplirai/jusqu'au bout.
Hollow signature: Gallieni . Paris-Art.

Dimensions: 27 mm

7. A solid silver medal of this design was also produced at this time but was not offered for sale to the general public. It is more than likely that this particular medal was presented to individuals who made significant contributions to the event.

Dimensions: 27 mm

The silver medal is identical to the bronze gilt version.

On the reverse, below the signature of Gallieni, the silver maker's lozenge poinçon can be clearly seen.
The medal is also clearly marked on the edge with the small silver boar's head poinçon.

POSTERS

Two posters were used to publicise the fundraising event.

1. The text of the 'Appel À La Population' (Appeal to the Population) poster urged all Parisians to celebrate July 14 by helping the soldiers who were defending all of them from the German armies.

The names of Adrien Mithouard (President of the Municipal Council), Marcel Delanney (Prefect of the Seine), Emile Laurent (Prefect of the Police) and Henri Rousselle (President of the General Council) were set out below the main text.

The Publisher's name - Marcel Picard - is set out along the bottom right edge.

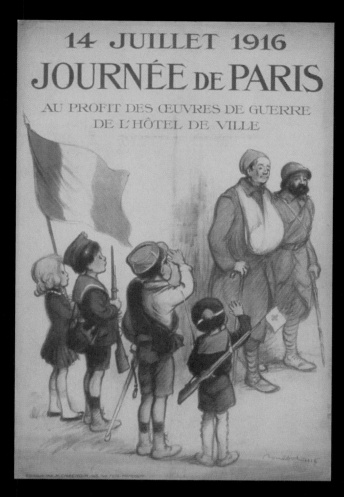

Dimensions: 1210 (H) x 800 (W) mm

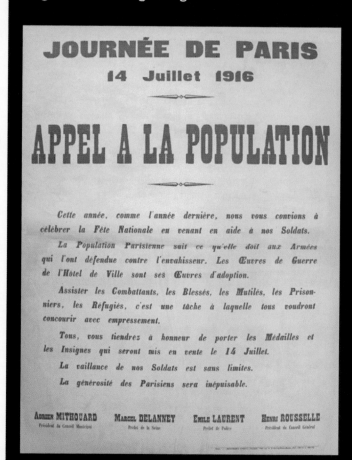

Dimensions: 1400 (H) x 1000 (W) mm

The poster was designed by Francisque Poulbot. The image occupies the whole, with the title and accompanying text placed across the top in black. It features a group of four young children including three boys wearing various French servicemen's uniforms and a girl holding a Tricolour flag. They are standing and watching as two wounded French soldiers pass by.

The poster is headed with a four line caption in black lettering:

14 Juillet 1916/Journée de Paris/Au Profit des Œuvres de Guerre/de l'Hôtel de Ville.

The publisher's name and address is set out on the lower left edge: Editeur Imp. H. Chachoin, 108 rue Folie-Méricourt.

Journée de Paris
14 July 1917

Journée de Paris
14 July 1917

Three insignias and two medal designs were produced for the 1917 *Journée de Paris*.

1 The upper part of the insignia is dominated by the Hôtel de Ville of Paris which is situated in the IVe arrondissement. Immediately below are eight Allied flags and the Paris coat of arms.

The reverse background is gold coloured and has a simple legend in white lettering: *14 Juillet / 1917*. The printer's name - Lapina Imp. Paris - is located just below the legend.

3 An oval shaped insignia features the Statue of Liberty on a background of the American flag. The coat of arms of the City of Paris lying on leaves of oak and laurel is in the foreground.

The reverse has a plain pink-red background with a blue oval centre frame with a five line legend in white: *Journée/de/Paris/14 Juillet/1917*

The name of the printer - 'J Barreau Paris' is set along the bottom edge.

Dimensions: 43 (H) x 32 (W) mm

Dimensions: 50 (H) x 38 (W) mm

2 The two profiles of the Marquis de La Fayette and George Washington are set on two oval shapes on a crimson red background. The flags of France and the United States of America surmount their heads with the Paris coat of arms set below. The reverse is identical to Insignia 1.

A second, much rarer version to this one was also produced. The insignia is identical but also has a ribbon in American colours, pinned with a tricolour linen flower.

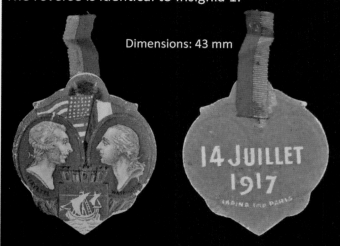

Dimensions: 43 mm

MEDALS

1 A circular medal made of pressed aluminium. The image in low relief features an allegorical female figure representing the City of Paris with a wounded poilu who has his left arm in a sling. She has her left hand resting on his shoulder and is holding his right hand.

The embossed legend around the edge of the medal: *Journée de Paris - 14 Juillet 1917.*

The 'Paris-Art' name is engraved (8 o'clock) and the motif is just below Juillet (4 o'clock).

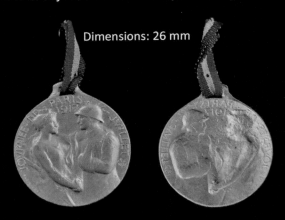

Dimensions: 26 mm

2. A uniface medal of the same dimensions with the exact image composition made of silvered metal with a plain reverse.

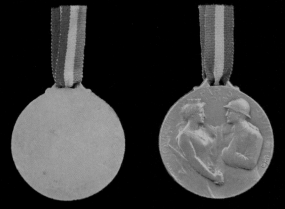

3. An identical uniface medal was also produced made of gilt bronze with a plain reverse.

4. Identical uniface bronze medal with a plain reverse.

5. Circular medal designed by Gaston Lavrillier in silvered metal. The obverse features the joint busts of George Washington and La Fayette. The embossed legend: *Washington/Lafayette/Paris-Art* with the name of the medallist set on La Fayette's shoulder.

The reverse has a six line embossed legend:
> *4 Juillet 1776 / 14 Juillet 1789 / Journée / de /Paris / 1917.*

Just underneath the sixth line, one of four capital letters (A, B, C and D). No authority appears to understand what the letters signified - whether this was a ploy to attract multiple purchases remains speculative.

Dimensions: 28 mm

6. An identical medal in bronze.

Dimensions: 82 (H) x 57 (W) mm

Below:

A rectangular shaped collection box label printed by Lapina used very similar imagery to that of the identity cards. The legend, set within a tricolour and silver frame, in black/blue lettering on a white background: *Journée de Paris / 14 Juillet 1917*.

Dimensions: 118 (H) x 84 (W) mm

Above:

An oval shaped identity card of a street collector. The background colour is silver with the City coat of arms set in a small circular frame with ribbons in the traditional red and blue colours of Paris on each side. The legend in white lettering on a blue ribbon background reads - *Journée de Paris* with the date *14 Juillet 1917* in blue lettering on a white background just below the coat of arms.

The reverse is a plain white background with the legend: Carte d'Identité and a name space. 'Lapina Paris' is set along the bottom edge.

The stamp is that of the Mairie de Pantheon 5ᵐᵉ Arrondᵀ de Paris.

Above:

All those involved in the collection were expected to wear a distinctive armband (brassard) made of silk/linen in the red and blue colours associated with Paris. The lettering was in gold:

Journée / 1917/ de Paris

Une « *Journée de Paris* »

L'Office départemental des œuvres de guerre de l'Hôtel de Ville a été autorisé, comme en 1915 et 1916, à organiser une « Journée de Paris » le jour de la fête nationale.

L'Office départemental fera mettre en vente le 14 juillet prochain :

Deux médailles, l'une qui évoque les traits de Washington et de La Fayette, l'autre qui représente la Ville de Paris accueillant un soldat blessé.

Trois insignes en couleurs reproduisant : 1° la double effigie de Washington et de La Fayette ; 2° la statue de la Liberté éclairant le monde ; 3° l'Hôtel de Ville, le vaisseau de la Ville de Paris et les drapeaux des nations alliées.

Above:

Le Matin 8 July 1917 page 2 sets out the various insignias/medals to be sold on the day.

Below:

This front page article in *Le Petit Parisien* dated 14 July states that the collections continued over several days and were very successful.

La journée de Paris

Si l'on s'en tient aux premiers résultats, la « Journée de Paris » s'annonce comme devant être très fructueuse.

Dès hier, de nombreuses quêteuses — beaucoup de fillettes — parcoururent les voies parisiennes, offrant aux promeneurs les médailles et insignes artistiques, vendus au bénéfice des œuvres de guerre.

POSTERS

Two posters were issued for the third Journée de Paris.

1. The text of the 'Appel À La Population' poster reminded all Parisians that, when approached by street collectors selling the insignias and medals, they should remember that they owe their safety and security to the soldiers defending them.

The names of Adrien Mithouard (President of the Municipal Council) and Marcel Delanney (Prefect of the Seine) were set out at the bottom of the poster along with two new appointments - Emile Deslandres (President of the General Council) and Louis Hudelo (Prefect of the Police).

The Publisher's name is set out along the bottom right edge: Imprimerie Marcel Picard, Paris 140 Rue du Faubourg Saint-Martin.

Dimensions: 1187 (H) x 784 (W) mm

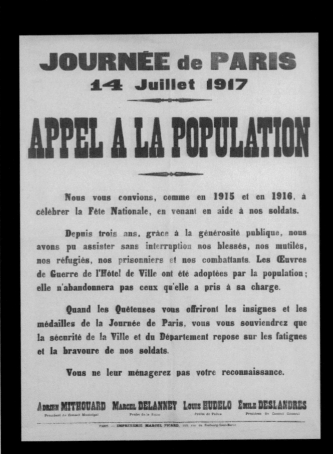

Dimensions: 1245 (H) x 875 (W) mm

2. The illustrated poster by Francisque Poulbot (VISÉ No. 5.936) has as the central image a young girl with a tricolour cockade in her hair playing with a bandaged toy soldier. At her side, a poodle holds a begging bowl in its mouth.

The image occupies the whole, with the title and accompanying text placed across the top in black.
Text: *Journée de Paris au Profit des Œuvres de Guerre de l'Hôtel de Ville 14 juillet 1917.*

The circular stamp states that the poster cannot be sold but special proofs can be purchased from the offices of Maison H. CHACHOIN, 108, Rue Folie -Méricourt PARIS.

Journée du Chrysanthème
5 December 1915

Journée du Chrysanthème
5 December 1915

Even before the declaration by President Raymond Poincaré and Prime Minister Georges Clemenceau that the First World War dead should be honoured on 11 November 1919 by placing flowers on their graves, chrysanthemums were already being used early on in the war as a symbol of immortality.

In *Les Insignes de Journées de la Guerre 1914-1918* de Bayle des Hermens includes this *Journée* but doubted whether it was a national fundraising day. He ventured the view that it might have some connection with the graves of those fallen on the 'Champ d'Honneur'.

On his website, Christian Doué also states that it was likely that the Journée du Chrysanthème was not a national fundraising day but rather a regional one. Doué refers to documentation that clearly shows that the event was organized by the City of Rouen. This view is confirmed in an article from the *Journal de Rouen* (4 December 1915 page 2 - see right).

Below:

An example of a 'chrysanthème en carton' and a 'Sceau de Rouen'.

Below:

The main document that Doué refers to is a letter titled 'Journée du Chrysanthème' which sets out clear details of where the street collections should take place and on which particular days. A price list is also included for seven different items including the only one referenced by de Bayle des Hermens (in red).

Above:

An identity card worn by the 'vendeuses'.

Right:

A detailed map plan of a specific area in Rouen (Saint Gervais) was also included with the letter setting out clearly the area that the 'vendeuses' were expected to cover.

Bottom right:

A card sent from Madame Joseph Lafond, who was charged with the supervision of Saint-Gervais, with a plea for help on the actual fundraising day.

JOURNÉE DU CHRYSANTHÈME

PRIX DE VENTE

Chrysanthèmes en carton...... A partir de	0 F.10
Chrysanthèmes artificiels	0 F.25
Moutons	0 F.25
Sceau de Rouen	0 F.50
Chrysanthèmes en métal	I F.--
Médaillons de Jeanne Darc	I F.--
Médaillons des Alliés	I F.--

Il est expressément recommandé de ne pas vendre au-dessous de ces prix.

En outre, Mesdemoiselles les vendeuses sont instamment priées de bien vouloir se conformer aux instructions suivantes:

I.- La vente commencera le samedi à midi, mais seulement dans les administrations et maisons de chaque secteur et non sur la voie publique où l'autorisation n'est donnée que pour le dimanche.

II.- Le dimanche matin, prière de suivre très exactement les indications qui seront données par Mesdames les Directrices des secteurs relativement à l'itinéraire de chaque vendeuse et de ne vendre, sous aucun prétexte, en dehors des limites du secteur.

III.- A partir de midi la vente est permise dans toute la ville mais Mlles les vendeuses sont priées de ne pas abandonner complètement leur secteur et d'y faire des tournées, afin que les quartiers excentriques ne soient pas complètement délaissés tandis que ceux du centre seraient envahis par un trop grand nombre de vendeuses.

IV.- Il sera indispensable que les vendeuses se munissent de petite monnaie.

V.- Elles devront se réapprovisionner exclusivement auprès des directrices de leur secteur. Il est interdit d'employer une partie des recettes pour acheter des objets et les revendre ensuite, le nombre des objets à vendre étant suffisant pour assurer le résultat désirable.

La commission d'organisation remercie très vivement Mesdemoiselles les vendeuses pour le concours si précieux qu'elles lui apportent. Elle confie à leur dévouement le sort de la Journée dont le produit est destiné à soulager de grandes misères qui menacent des milliers de vieillards, de femmes et d'enfants victimes indirectes de la Guerre.

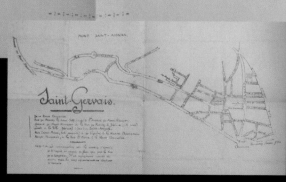

Journée Des Meubles des Foyers Dévastés
24 September 1916

Journée Des Meubles des Foyers Dévastés
24 September 1916

A cardboard insignia in the shape of a cross with a printed tricolour ribbon.

The surround of the obverse is a golden patterned frame in the form of rays surrounding a circle 29 mm in diameter. In the foreground, an evacuated family push a handcart loaded with furniture.

The background image is of a ruined village with a French flag flying.

A legend in blue print on five lines is set on the reverse within a blue circle:

Journée/des Meubles/des Foyers/Dévastés/1916

The printer's name of 'Chambrelent Paris' is set below.

Dimensions: 82 (H) x 57 (W) mm

Above:

A brief reference to the 'Journée' in *Le Figaro* 22 September 1916 page 3. Clearly the event was centred at Versailles and was held on Sunday 24 September.

The writer of the article hopes that:

"cette vente sera très fructueuse et permettra de subvenir largement aux besoins de cette oeuvre si éminemment utile".

("This sale will be very successful and will enable the needs of this eminent [fundraising] event to be met.")

Left:

The event was officially recorded in the *Journal officiel de la République française. Lois et décrets* 26 January 1917 page 759

Journée des Artistes
25 December 1916

Journée des Artistes
25 December 1916

A circular insignia. The obverse features two poilus in the foreground in their horizon blue uniforms watching a show with two actors performing in front of an audience. The legend of *'Noël 1916'* in white lettering is set below the two poilus.

The reverse features two 'masks' on an orange background. The legend set at the top in black lettering: *'Journée des Artistes'*. Under the 'masks' is a second legend in black: *'Tragoedia-Comoedia'* with *'1916'* in white.

The signature of the famous French illustrator Gus Bofa (Gustave Henri Emile Blanchot 1883-1968) is on the right (3 o'clock).

La Journée des artistes

Le ministre de l'Intérieur vient d'autoriser la « Journée des artistes ».

Elle est organisée par l'Association des artistes dramatiques, la Société de secours mutuels des artistes lyriques, la Maison de retraite de Pont-aux-Dames, les Prévoyants des théâtres, la Maison de retraite de Bis-Orangis et l'Amicale des régisseurs de théâtres, au profit de leurs caisses respectives et de leurs orphelins.

Au cours des représentations de dimanche prochain et du jour de Noël, les artistes de nos théâtres, concerts, music-halls, cirques et cinémas, vendront au public de ces établissements les insignes de cette Journée.

La recette, centralisée par les délégués des associations sera transmise à la caisse centrale de la « Journée des artistes ».

Above:
Le Petit Parisien 22 December page 3 - one of the few references to the sale of insignias which was held on Sunday 24 December and Christmas Day.

Below:
Gus Bofa aged 24: When German troops invaded France, despite already having completed his military service in 1904, Bofa joined an infantry division. While on patrol in December 1914 he came under German machine gun fire and suffered severe leg injuries. Awarded medals for bravery, he refused to allow doctors to amputate his leg. His left foot was irreparably damaged and it would be several years before he could walk again. Often bedridden, Bofa developed his artistic talents and by the end of 1915 *Le Petit Parisien, Excelsior, Le Journal* and the newly launched satirical weekly *La Baïonnette*, were regularly publishing his drawings (see bottom left).

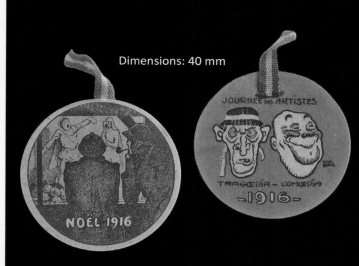

Dimensions: 40 mm

15 June 1916

23 March 1916

8 November 1917

Journée du Bébé du Soldat
1916

Journée du Bébé du Soldat
1916

A circular insignia with a tricolour ribbon bow. The obverse features a baby wearing a soldier's cap. A semi-circle legend is located near the top edge in dark brown print: *Journée du Bébé du Soldat.*

The reverse is plain - however, with this example there is a handwritten date of 21 Avril 1918.

The insignia is dated by de Bayles des Hermens as being 1916. No evidence, however, could be found to confirm whether this particular dating or the handwritten date was accurate.

Dimensions: 38 mm

Ligue fraternelle des enfants de France

An association is made by de Bayle des Hermens with this organization and the *Journée du Bébé du Soldat* insignia. Again this connection is difficult to confirm.

The League was founded in 1895 by Henri Rollet, Apolline de Gourlet and Lucie Faure who was the daughter of Félix Faure (French President 1895-1899). The aim of the League was to "create the bonds of true friendship between the children, young people and young girls of wealthy families and the poor children, orphans or those that have been abandoned - such is our goal".

In order to promote their cause and to raise funds for the various projects undertaken, the League released a set of postcards during the war period which were produced by Breger & Javal - Paris.

Above:
Two versions of postcards by Charles Léandre and Olive - dated 1916.

Above:

Further postcards produced to raise funds for the Ligue fraternelle des enfants de France included:

'La petite alsacienne fait de la pâtisserie' by Hansi

'Chez nous aussi vous pourrez venir' by Lison

'Je n'ai pas d'argent. Accepte mon Coeur' designed by Henri Gerbault.

The other two postcards are by unidentified artists.

Right:

Article from *Le Figaro* dated 10 May 1916 page 2 which refers to the sale of the postcards which was taking place from 8 - 14 May and giving details relating to the 'Ligue'.

Far right:

The founding members of the 'Ligue': Lucie Faure and Henri Rollet.

COMMUNIQUÉS

Une collecte. — La « Ligue fraternelle des Enfants de France », fondée par Mme Lucie Félix Faure-Goyau, et dont Mme Raymond Poincaré est la présidente d'honneur, a été autorisée à faire dans tous les établissements d'enseignement une collecte qui, commencée avant-hier, sera continuée jusqu'au 14 mai.

L'œuvre s'adresse au cœur des enfants heureux : elle leur demande de venir en aide à leurs frères — aux malheureux que sont les enfants des départements envahis.

En accordant l'autorisation d'une *journée* dans les établissements d'enseignement, M. le ministre de l'instruction publique a indiqué qu'il approuvait la pensée patriotique et humanitaire dont la « Ligue des enfants de France » s'était inspirée.

MM. les professeurs voudront certainement s'associer, à leur tour, à l'initiative de la ligue, en recueillant dans leurs classes le plus de « gros sous » possible, grâce à quoi les petits Français éprouvés par la guerre pourront être ramenés des départements envahis et placés en lieu sûr.

La collecte s'effectue principalement sous la forme de ventes de cartes postales, éditées spécialement, et dont le prix minimum est seul fixé...

La ligue, dont le siège social est 50, rue Saint-André-des-Arts, se tient, pour tous renseignements, à la disposition de MM. les professeurs.

Journée Foyer du Soldat
25 March 1917

Journée Foyer du Soldat
25 March 1917

Dimensions: 43 (H) x 32 (W) mm.

A second insignia with a slightly different title - *Le Foyer du Soldat* - was also produced by the City of Rouen as part of a local event.

Dimensions: 65 (H) x 55 (W) mm.

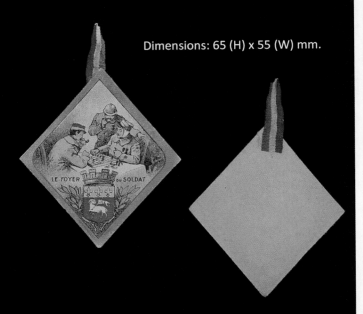

Les Foyers du Soldat was one of the three official welfare organizations along with La Croix Rouge and the Y.M.C.A. They set up canteens for soldiers to go to while on leave, providing a place to sleep, relax and eat. They also provided entertainment such as music or films.

Although de Bayle des Hermens categorizes the *Journée Foyer du Soldat* as a national event, it is more than likely that this rectangular insignia was part of a regional fundraising day.

The image is of a Chasseur Alpin with his left arm in a sling sitting in front of a table and writing a letter. A 'Croix Rouge' sign is on the white wall and just below the table is the signature: 'B Pavec'. At the top is the legend: *Journée Foyer du Soldat* with the date set below - *25 Mars 1917* - all in black print against a white background.

The reverse has the official stamp in red ink of the 'Union des Femmes de France' with 'Comité de Cannes' set below on a cream white background.

A vertical diamond shaped insignia. Set in a golden frame, three soldiers are depicted playing chess. The Rouen coat of arms is set below them with the legend: *Le Foyer du Soldat.* The reverse is plain and the insignia is undated.

The printer's name - 'Chambrelent' - can be seen along the edge of the frame (7 o'clock).

Below:
A 'Foyer du Soldat' set up by La Croix Rouge - unknown location and undated.

Aide aux Aveugles de Guerre
10 February 1918

Aide aux Aveugles de Guerre
Février 1918

Sadly the fundraising events held for the benefit of the war blind are not well known or documented because they did not always have the benefit of the huge publicity that accompanied some of the great national days. They were only mentioned in very brief press articles.

In 1916, a poster designed by the French Symbolist - Art Nouveau artist Lucien Lévy-Dhurmer (1865-1953), helped to alert the general public to this deserving cause. Two of his designs were also used on postcards and sold to the general public to raise funds for the blind (see above right).

Dimensions: 48 (H) x 33 (W) mm

Two insignias are listed by de Bayle des Hermens.

The first one is in the form of a circular golden shape supported at the bottom by a foliage design and surmounted by a tricolour ribbon bow. A young boy is sitting on the knees of a blind soldier reading a newspaper to him.
The reverse has a four line legend in blue lettering on a white background:
Aide aux / aveugles / de la / Guerre.
The date is set below - *Février 1918*

The second insignia is almost certainly dated post 1918 and is in the form of a crest/shield. The obverse features a helmeted soldier supporting one of his comrades who is wearing a blindfold. The image is set within a frame of golden foliage with a legend in gold lettering:
Pour les yeux qui s'eteignent

The reverse is set in brown lettering on a plain background:
Féderation Nationale/des/Mutilés des Yeux/ 12 rue Pergolese/Paris (16e)
The printers name - Imp. Chambrelent Paris - is set below.

Dimensions: 46 (H) x 38 (W) mm

Manifestation Nationale en l'Honneur de l'Alsace-Lorraine 17 November 1918

Manifestation Nationale en l'Honneur de l'Alsace-Lorraine 17 November 1918

Undoubtedly November 1918 was a momentous transition period for the region of Alsace-Lorraine as it passed from German to French sovereignty at the end of the war. When Georges Clemenceau addressed the Chamber of Deputies on Armistice Day (11 November 1918), his opening words very pointedly referred to the Alsace-Lorraine region:

"Au nom du peuple français, au nom du Gouvernement de la République française, j'envoie le salut de la France une et indivisible à l'Alsace et la Lorraine retrouvées".

The focal point of the *Manifestation Nationale* was in Paris on Sunday 17 November but celebrations were held throughout France and on the same day the 2nd Army, commanded by General Hirschauer, triumphantly entered the City of Mulhouse in Southern Alsace.

Above:
Huge crowds greeted the French troops as they entered Mulhouse on 17 November 1918.

Below:
The *Excelsior* copy from 18 November reveals the high profile given to the 'Manifestation'.

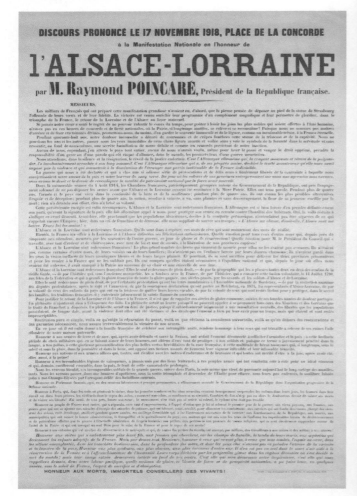

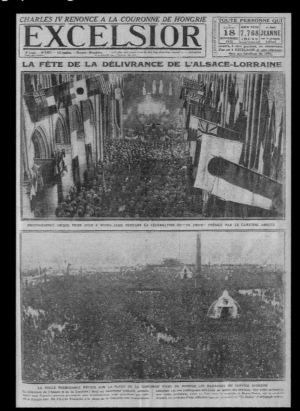

Left:
Posters of Raymond Poincaré's address made from La Place de la Concorde in Paris were displayed throughout the country.

There appears to be very little doubt that the *Manifestation Nationale en l'Honneur de l'Alsace Lorraine* was a celebratory event rather than a *Journée* devoted to fundraising for a worthy cause.

One insignia was produced to commemorate the event but whether these were sold on the day or freely distributed to children remains a matter of conjecture.

Dimensions: 55 (H) x 39 (W) mm

The insignia was an irregular hexagonal shape surmounted by a printed tricolour ribbon bow. A hole just below this allowed a fabric ribbon to be threaded through so the insignia could then be fixed with a pin to clothing.

The images on both sides are set within a golden frame. One side portrays an Alsatian woman in her full traditional dress in the foreground with the French tricolour flag in the background. Laurel branches support the coat of arms of Alsace.
The four line legend in brown print is set below on a plain 'plaque':
Manifestation/Nationale/du 17 Novembre/1918

The other side is exactly the same composition as for side one but the laurel branches support the Lorraine coat of arms and the woman is wearing the traditional costume of the Lorraine region.

As well as the insignia, de Bayle des Hermens also refers to a medal which he relates to this particular event. There is, however, no clear evidence to support the view that the medal was produced for the *Manifestation Nationale*.

Dimensions: 28 mm

Circular in shape and with a suspension loop (bélière) to accommodate a tricolour ribbon, the medal is made of silvered repoussé metal. It features an Alsatian woman placing her right hand on the shoulder of a Lorrainer. Both woman are depicted with traditional headdresses. The dates '1870-1918' are just below the suspension loop and a bouquet of flowers is set just below them with the legend: *'Toujours Françaises'*.

The stencilled signature of the designer is set on the right (3 o'clock) - 'Baudouin'.

Exactly the same image was used for a small lapel pin made of silvered repoussé metal.

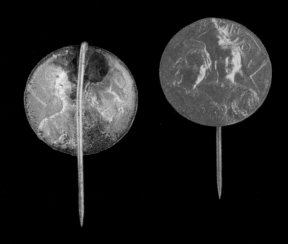

Journée du Président Wilson
14 December 1918

Journée du Président Wilson
14 December 1918

President Woodrow Wilson arrived in France on 13 December to take part in preliminary World War I peace negotiations and also to promote his plan for establishing a 'League of Nations' which he hoped would be able to arbitrate international conflicts in the future and prevent another war like the one that had just ended. The following day, Wilson travelled in an open carriage through the streets of Paris accompanied by President Poincaré and numerous other dignitaries.

Undoubtedly this *Journée du Président Wilson* was "le moment Wilson". It was a celebratory day, not one devoted to fundraising. This observation was partially acknowledged by de Bayle des Hermens - he stated that the insignia and medals which are sometimes associated with this particular day were more likely to have been produced and sold from the time when the United States declared war on Germany on April 6, 1917.

Above:
The coverage of Wilson's visit dominated all the French newspapers.

Below:
Over a million French people thronged the Parisian streets greeting Wilson as "le grand homme de la paix".

Dimensions: 37 (H) x 33 (W) mm

The oval shaped insignia features President Wilson with a background of the American flag. The image is set within a golden frame. The reverse is a plain gold colour with the printer's name set near the bottom edge: 'Devambez Gr. Paris'.

It is more than likely that it was first produced for sale in 1917 rather than for Wilson's Paris visit in 1918.

Fête des Familles Nombreuses
Ligue française 1918

Fête des Familles Nombreuses
Ligue française 1918

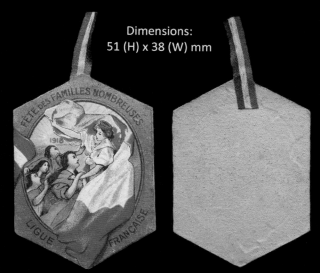

Dimensions:
51 (H) x 38 (W) mm

The *'Ligue française pour la défense des intérêts vitaux de la France et de ses colonies'* was founded by Ernest Lavisse and General Paul Pau on 30 March 1914. Louis-Émile Bertin was appointed President of the movement and Lavisse and Pau became honorary Presidents (see below right).

The aim of La Ligue française was to defend the vital interests of France and its colonies. The group fully supported Georges Clemenceau who had served as Prime Minister (1906-09) and who was a vehement critic of the government, asserting that it was not doing enough to win the war. He was reappointed Prime Minister in 1917 and set about earning his nicknames - 'Le Tigre' (the Tiger) or 'Père la Victoire' (Father of Victory).

Not only did La Ligue française throw its support behind Clemenceau, it also worked tirelessly to fight what it regarded as the 'ills of society' which undermined the vitality of France. Alcoholism, crime and disruption of family life were seen as causing great problems for the future of France.

In researching this particular insignia, no reference could be found to *La Fête des Familles Nombreuses* apart from mentions in two bulletins issued by *La Ligue française:* Janvier 1918 Numéro 28 (see below) and Mars-Avril 1918 Numéro 30. It is likely that the insignia was sold to raise funds to enable *La Ligue* to financially support *La Fête des Familles Nombreuses* but this view remains speculative.

Above:
An irregular hexagonal shape with a gold frame enclosing the image of a female figure personifying France and draped in a tricolour flag, welcoming a family of four. A rising sun with the date *'1918'* in red is in the background. The legend *Fête des Familles Nombreuses* is set along the top of the insignia with *Ligue française* at the bottom.

Below:
An application form and membership card for La Ligue française.

Below (left to right):
Ernest Lavisse
Louis-Émile Bertin
Paul Pau

Journée des Pupilles de la Nation
25 December 1918

Journée des Pupilles de la Nation
Noël 1918

'Pupilles de la Nation' translates as 'Wards of the Nation' - defined as "a French civil status with certain attendant rights allocated by the State to those who have a parent who was injured or killed in war". In other words orphaned children became the adopted children of the Nation.

The institution of the 'Office National des Pupilles de la Nation' was created towards the end of the First World War by the law of July 27, 1917. Its main purpose was to provide moral and material protection, until they came of age, to the many war orphans and children of the badly injured. With a conservative estimate of 750,000 for this group by the end of 1918, it is clear that the State programme was faced with an enormous task.

Above:
A poster setting out the law of July 27, 1917.
The title is positioned across the top, in black. The image, designed by Adolphe Willette, occupies the upper centre, with further text, in black, against a plain white background. The image is of a woman holding a baby, flanked by a girl and a boy wearing soldiers' caps. Text: Office National des Pupilles de la Nation République Française 14 Juillet 1918 Loi du 27 Juillet 1917. Printer: Devambez.

According to the definition of the law, the 'Pupilles de la Nation' are:

1. Orphans under the age of 21 whose father, mother or breadwinner:
- has been killed by the enemy (or in an external theatre of operations);
-died of injuries received or illnesses contracted or aggravated as a result of the war;
- is unable to meet his/her obligations and family responsibilities as a result of injuries and illnesses received, contracted or aggravated as a result of the war.

2. Children born before the end of operations in a theatre of war operations defined by decree, or within 300 days of their cessation, when the father /breadwinner is, due to the injuries received or the illnesses contracted during these operations, unable to fulfil their family responsibilities and obligations.

3. Children and young people under the age of 21 who are themselves victims of war.

Above:
Two 'Carte d'Identités' issued by 'Office National des Pupilles de la Nation'.

Dimensions: 90 (H) 58 (W) mm

Dimensions: 53 (H) x 31 (W) mm

Above:
A silvered bronze plaquette designed by Émile Séraphin Vernier, recognised as one of France's most famous engravers and medallists.

Above:
A vertical oval shaped insignia printed in brown. Despite the insignia being described by de Bayle des Hermens as dating from 1915 and having been part of a national fundraising event, it almost certainly dates from December 1918 and was more than likely a Department of Rhône regional event. The obverse replicates the imagery of the poster.

Left:
The law of July 24, 1917 profoundly changed the status of children whose parents were war victims.

Dimensions - 1190 (H) x 800 (W) mm

The imagery on the poster depicts an allegorical female figure still wearing her breastplate who represents the French nation. Standing near a sword set on a branch of laurels, she is holding a baby in her arms and extending her hand to a little boy. The scene takes place against a backdrop of the landscape with a house on the left and a rising sun bearing the word *'Pax'*; the legend *'Pupilles de la Nation'* is set along the top edge.

World War One - The Legacy

The outbreak of war in 1914 plunged France and much of Europe into a catastrophe of monumental proportions. Neither the leaders nor the civilians from the warring nations were prepared for the length and brutality of the war which would take the lives of millions. During the war period France mobilized over eight million soldiers and suffered the most grievous proportionate losses of all the great powers. In addition, many of the regions in northern France were desolated as they paid dearly for becoming the foremost theatre of war.

The French High Command overestimated the strength of their armies and had been very slow in coming to terms with the fact that reliance on the much vaunted 'cran' (guts/courage) and the 'élan vital' of the poilus would not be enough to secure victory. Whatever illusions they had were swiftly shattered as in 1914 alone, in the space of just five months, France suffered over a million casualties (soldiers killed, missing, wounded or captured) and this included 329,000 dead.

Even today, the exact figures of casualties and death are still disputed and will never be conclusively resolved. This is mainly because of the loss or destruction of a huge number of official documents, questions relating to the different definitions used for each category and the somewhat debatable accuracy of the recording system. There was, however, very little doubt that by the end of the war, the total French casualties numbered over six million which represented 73.3% of the forces. The sheer magnitude of the statistics of soldiers missing in action, prisoners of war and dead are set out in *Le Républicain Landais* (dated 29 December 1918 - see right).

Les Pertes Françaises pendant la guerre

A la séance de jeudi, à la Chambre, le Gouvernement a fait la déclaration suivante :
Au 1er novembre 1918, le chiffre total des disparus tués ou prisonniers était de 1 million 831,000, dont 42,600 officiers, 1 million 789,000 hommes de troupe, se décomposant comme suit :
Décédés : 31,300 officiers, 1 million 40,000 hommes de troupe.
Disparus : 3,000 officiers, 311,000 hommes de troupe.

Prisonniers : 8,300 officiers, 438,000 hommes de troupe.
A la même date, le chiffre des pensions était le suivant :
Pensionnés, 76,000 ; réformés, n° 1, 113,000 ; réformès n° 2, 374,000 ; réformés temporaires, 131,000.

Much of the responsibility for this catastrophe lay with many of the French commanders. They failed to exercise greater economy with the lives of their troops and often exhibited a conspicuous callousness about the death toll. It was not without reason that in the early part of the war, Joseph Joffre, the Commander-in-Chief of the French forces on the Western Front, earned the disdainful sobriquet of 'abattoir superintendent'.

This sombre assessment of Joffre's leadership qualities and military acumen could have been equally applied to a plethora of other military commanders. Sadly the nation's government failed to nullify the shortcomings of the High Command, displaying a lack of 'cran', as it decamped to Bordeaux on 30 August taking with it the gold reserves of the Bank of France. Equally, many wealthy Parisians wasted little time in following their government's example, finding it far more congenial to linger in comfortable urban and suburban homes located in South or South-West France out of earshot of gunfire. Admittedly, the French government returned from its unheroic Bordeaux exile in December 1915 but the prestige of President Poincaré suffered lasting injury.

Little surprise then, that the poilus regarded most of them with disdain and felt betrayed. The war of attrition that the French frontline troops found themselves embroiled in gradually eroded their optimism and engendered a feeling that they were une génération sacrifiée. A contrast was drawn between l'avant and l'arrière, the gulf between savagery and civilization, between those on the frontline and the civilians

apparently pursuing their normal lives undisturbed by suffering. Many emerged from the war embittered by the immense loss of life and the destruction they had witnessed and this perspective undoubtedly reinforced their visceral sense of grievance.

From the start of the war, as reservists were called up, the loss of the main wage-earner often created severe hardship for many families. Government officials soon appreciated that men would be reluctant to volunteer to fight if they felt that their homes and loved ones would not be looked after. It was left largely to the work of civilian volunteers and charities to help assuage these concerns and to create a social cohesion that undoubtedly bolstered the faltering morale among French troops and their families. The fundraising, in the form of nationwide and regional *Journées*, was to play a critical role in buoying the nation's spirit and establishing a bridge in understanding and empathy between soldiers and civilians.

Contributing to the war effort was promoted as a national duty. While it is fair to state that initially the French fundraising efforts lagged behind those across the Channel, by the second quarter of 1915 appeals for the relief of distress steadily gained momentum. It made individual giving part of the French culture - not only was the donation an act of generosity, it was also a test of nationalism.

The sheer scale of help required was totally unprecedented and fundraising became almost part of daily life. Local schools were encouraged to promote enthusiasm for the *Journées* and children played a very significant role in many of the fundraising efforts. National and regional newspapers promoted events and carried details of the revenues collected. Extensive use was made of the promotional posters sent through to all the prefectures which also regularly received leaflets from authorized bodies giving detailed instructions regarding the sale of items, setting up systems for the matching of supply with demand and organizing the collections.

In truth, the fundraising could not really fail: at the very core of any appeal for the funds that would help provide for the servicemen and their beneficiaries was the indisputable fact that, no matter what type of sacrifices volunteers were making by giving up their time and money, by definition there were always others making a far larger sacrifice. By the end of the war, over 1.3 million poilus had made the ultimate 'donation' with their lives and a further 3 million were wounded.

The end of the war, however, did not bring about any cessation of the urgent need for fundraising. The actual 'human cost' of the war, which quite often neglects the additional 450,000 Spanish influenza victims, resulted in a mourning society. The ghostly shadow of the war was to pervade the French nation throughout the entire interwar period. Large areas of Northern France had been totally devastated which resulted in over 1.4 million refugees and incalculable damage not just to private properties but also to treasured historical sites. Even today, over 100 years later, certain areas in North-East France are still designated as 'Zone Rouge'. An area over 1200 square kilometres was isolated by the French government after the war as it was deemed too damaged by the conflict and too dangerous for human habitation. The control areas have now been greatly reduced but any land still designated 'Red Zone' remains abandoned - agricultural use and public entry is prohibited by law because of the risk of unexploded munitions and contamination.

Reintegrating the demobilized soldiers back into civil society constituted a major challenge, particularly as so many of them bore the mental and physical scars inflicted by the war. On returning home, veterans often faced hardship as war production gave way to a peacetime economy of inflated food prices and insufficient wages made worse by high figures of unemployment.

Above left:
A refugee family from an invaded region receiving emergency aid at the Seminary of St. Sulpice, Paris. The father is wearing the Médaille Militaire awarded for bravery in action. Having lost his leg fighting on the front line in 1914, he was demobilized because of his injuries and returned to his farm work until driven from his home by approaching German forces.

Above middle:
Teaching the blind how to play draughts (checkers) on a board adapted for the blind.

Above right:
A disabled French soldier learning to write a letter with the help of a Red Cross nurse.

The Prime Minister George Clemenceau had stated when he addressed the Chamber of Deputies on 20 November 1917:

"Ces Français que nous fûmes contraints de jeter dans la bataille, ils ont des droits sur nous ...
Nous leur devons tout, sans aucune réserve".

Such a declaration resonated throughout the nation and the immense urge to express gratitude to these veterans found an outlet between 1918 and the early 1920s through the organization of thousands of festivals and celebrations at national as well as local levels. The successful leadership, ingenuity, broad participation and popular support that had been instrumental in the success of the *Journées* during the war period were once again employed to ensure the success of these events.

An under-reported component of France's war effort is undoubtedly the fundraising activities undertaken by numerous organizations but it undoubtedly had an enormous impact. The war years prompted a new wave of voluntary activity and witnessed the foundation of numerous charities, many of which are still active today. The fundraising involved huge numbers of people, especially women and children, who regularly gave their time and effort to the innumerable nationwide and regional causes. Admittedly, many of the individuals who formed part of the organizing bodies of the *Journées* were from privileged, upper class backgrounds but the scope and very nature of the fundraising work resulted in the *Journées* acting as an integrating mechanism between social classes - fundraising was no longer regarded as the sole preserve of the upper and middle classes 'doing their bit'.

Before the war, fundraising and charity work were often 'top-down' processes either involving small numbers of exclusive charities run by middle and upper-middle class individuals or a small number of extremely wealthy and well-connected people raising significant sums often through personal donations. The war period still accommodated these two systems but they were both totally overshadowed by the *Journées* which relied on an essentially 'bottom-up' approach of voluntary activity involving every section of society as well as incorporating an astonishing range of fund-raising techniques. However small their individual contribution, those individuals volunteering their time and energy for the *Journées* could be comforted in knowing that they had done 'their bit' in what is often described as the 'people's war'.

REFERENCES

1. Page iv - One of the most comprehensive and accurate assessments of World War One casualty figures can be found in Samuel Dumas and K. O. Vedel-Petersen (Edited by Harald Westergaard) - *Losses of life caused by war*. The Clarendon Press 1923. This work has been digitized by the Internet Archive and can be found on: https://archive.org/stream/lossesoflifecaus00samu#page/n0/mode/2up
Part II of the book, entitled 'Total losses occasioned by war' focuses in part on 'French Military losses' (pages 137-141) and 'French Civil losses' (pages 155-161) during World War One.

2. Page iv - A superb insight into the grim reality of the trench warfare can be found in Louis Barthas and Edward Strauss, *Poilu: The World War I Notebooks of Corporal Louis Barthas, Barrelmaker, 1914-1918*. Publisher: Yale University Press 2015.
Louis Barthas was a 'Poilu' and his notebooks, written shortly after he returned home in 1919, fully captured the futility of the war, the grotesque and numerous hardships that were experienced by frontline troops on a daily basis, and the total ineptness as well as the callousness exhibited by the majority of officers.

3. Page iv - The French soldiers preferred to describe themselves as 'les hommes' or 'les bonhommes'.
The evolution of the word 'poilu' derives from the Old French (pelu) and the Modern French word for animal hair/fur (poil). Well before the outbreak of war, the military slang phrase "il a du poil" was often used to denote that an individual was "a courageous chap". A story by Honoré de Balzac, *Le Médecin de Campagne* (1833) is often cited as the source for the term 'poilu'.
Balzac describes a situation where a French General can only find 42 French soldiers suitable ("assez poilus") for a mission requiring great courage:
"Le général Eblé… n'en a pu trouver que quarante-deux assez poilus… pour entreprendre cet ouvrage".

4. Page iv - The poilus undoubtedly felt a sense of isolation from the generals directing the war, the officers disseminating the orders and those in the military not directly involved on the front line. The *Bourreurs de crane* (press propagandists), feeding their readers heavily censored reports and the *embusqués*, who avoided military service, were particular targets of derision.

5. Page iv - Paul Dubrulle, a Roman Catholic priest who fought at Verdun and the Somme, described "… les pauvres sauvages que l'on transportait, comme des colis, dans des wagons à bestiaux" (the poor savages being moved around like parcels in cattle trucks).
Mon regiment dans la Fournaise de Verdun et dans la Bataille de la Somme: impressions de guerre d'un prêtre soldat. Paris - Librairie Plon 1917, page 78. Digitized by the Internet Archive in 2013: https://archive.org/stream/monrgimentdansla00dubr/monrgimentdansla00dubr_djvu.txt

6. Page iv - Nous les étudiâmes quelque temps dans un froid silence. N'était-ce pas la fine fleur de cet «arrière» tant exécré? Cette cargaison, de quoi était-elle composée? De jouisseurs peut-être qui profitaient, pour se donner du bon temps, de nos peines et de notre sang. Ces gros bourgeois? N'étaient-ils pas de ces fournisseurs sans conscience qui s'engraissaient à nos dépens? … N'étaient-ils pas de ces financiers éhontés qui spéculent sur notre vie? Et surtout, ces figures à l'insignifiance importante, n'étaient-elles pas celles de ces politiciens, les grands ennemis du soldat, de ces stratèges de cabi-net… qui enrayent les mouvements opportuns et décident les offensives désastreuses?

(For a while we studied them in stony silence. So this was the very best of those at the «rear» that we hated so much? The complacent perhaps who were benefiting from our pain and blood, to give themselves a good time. Those fat bourgeois? Weren't they the industrialists feeding well at our expense? Weren't they the shameless financiers who were speculating on our lives? And, above all, those immensely insignificant figures, weren't they politicians, the soldier's greatest enemy, the cabinet strategists… who vetoed sensible tactics and elected instead for disastrous attacks). Ibid, page 79.

7. Page v - The most exhaustive (albeit extremely rare) reference book on the subject of the various insignias produced for these fundraising days is by Roger de Bayle des Hermens (Chargé de Recherche au C.R.N.S.), *Les Insignes de Journées de la Guerre 1914-1918 No 12*. Réservé aux Membres de L'Arc-en-ciel 1985.

8. Page v - Christian Doué: journees-pgm14-18.jimdofree.com/
Bernard Andre: 87dit.canalblog.com/archives/2021/03/21/38875502.html
Other very useful and informative websites include: https://www.medailles1914-1918.fr
www.centenaire.org/fr/fonds-privees/archives/collection-privee-les-enfants-dans-les-affiches-de-la-grande-guerre

9. Page 5 - The Belgian refugee crisis was the focus of the first fundraising Journée held in France during the war period. The 'Small Belgian Flag Day' was organized for 20 December 1914 by a Franco-Belgian Central Committee. All Department Prefects were contacted in November asking them to ascertain the quantity of flags needed in their respective regions. Schools, in particular, were encouraged to promote this nationwide event.

10. Page 12 - Roger de Bayle des Hermens, page 15.

11. Page 29 - According to several leading historians, during the war years, the French press was subject to some of the strictest censorship in Europe. Mindful of a humiliating episode in August 1870 when the newspaper *Le Temps* had inadvertently allowed the enemy to anticipate the movement of the French Army which led to it being encircled by German forces at Sedan, a law was adopted without debate in the Chamber of Deputies on 5 August 1914. The law provided for the suppression of information that could potentially inform the enemy. Newspapers were banned from reporting any details regarding the makeup and position of armies, troop movement, losses etc as well as any articles deemed 'defeatist'. In addition, Le Bureau de la Presse was created on 3 August 1914 within the War Ministry. It had a dual role which entailed presenting detailed censorship guidelines on the basis of instructions sent by General Headquarters and the Ministries of War and Foreign Affairs and, at the same time supervising the guidelines application by the press and the news agencies.

12. Page 29 - Professor Alfred Croiset (1845 - 1923) was Dean of the Faculty of Letters at the University of Paris (known as La Sorbonne). In 1913 he was appointed a Grand Officer of the Legion of Honour. Along with his younger brother Maurice (1846 - 1935), who in turn was also appointed a Grand Officer of the Legion of Honour, he helped in the organization of several of the fundraising *Journées*.

13. Page 51 - Léon Gambetta (1838 - 1882) was a lawyer of Italian-French extraction who became a Republican statesman who assisted the foundation of the Third Republic and the defence of France during the Franco-German War of 1870-1. After the disastrous defeat of the French at Sedan, in which Napoleon III was captured, Gambetta played a principal role in proclaiming the Republic and forming a provisional government of national defence. He became Minister of the Interior in this government. When the Republican Party failed to gain a majority in the 1871 general election, he went into voluntary exile in Spain but was persuaded to return to France later that year and was again elected to the Chamber in July 1871 and chose to represent Paris. An astute parliamentary tactician as well as one of the greatest orators of modern France, he was briefly Prime Minister in 1881. He retired when his government fell in January 1882 and died on the 31 December 1882.

14. Page 54 - Paul Déroulède (1846 - 1914) was a Nationalist politician and author who served during the Franco-Prussian War before an injury forced him out of the army. He subsequently became an author, publishing patriotic poems ('Le Chant du Soldat', 1872). He founded the Ligue des Patriotes in 1882 and attempted to use it to support the rise of Georges Boulanger, a French general and politician who was an enormously popular public figure during the Third Republic. The Ligue was dissolved following Boulanger's tragic downfall in 1889. In the same year, Déroulède was elected to the Deputy of Chambers representing Angoulême. After the funeral of President Félix Faure, on 23 February 1899, he tried to persuade General Gaudérique Roget to lead his troops to the presidential palace. At his own instigation he then demanded to be arrested for treason but was acquitted only to be arrested again a few weeks later. This time he was sentenced to banishment from France for 10 years and he retired to Spain but in 1905 an amnesty allowed him to return to France. Déroulède remained a popular figure and when he died in January 1914 his funeral in Paris was attended by the largest crowds since that of the writer Victor Hugo.

15. **Page 68** - Pascal Ceccaldi (1876 - 1918) was born in Corsica. He studied law in Aix-en-Provence and on his return to Corsica he enrolled at the bar of Ajaccio at the age of 20. It was in this city that he met Henry Maret, a French journalist and politician who was a prominent member of the Radical Party and member of the Chamber of Deputies. Having had to leave Corsica following a duel, Ceccaldi followed Maret to Paris and supported him in his electoral campaign. On 7 June, 1902, he joined the cabinet of Emile Combes, President of the Council and shortly after, he was appointed Secretary General of the Basses-Alpes Prefecture, then sub-prefect at Vervins in the Aisne in 1903. On resigning from this post, he founded Le Démocrate de l'Aisne and in the spring of 1906 he campaigned in the legislative elections and, at the age of 29 he was elected to the Chamber of Deputies and was re-elected in 1910 and 1914. Courageously, in 1914 he joined the army becoming a Sergeant then Sub-Lieutenant at Verdun before commanding a company on the front line.

At the end of 1916 he resumed his seat in the Chamber of Deputies and worked for the inhabitants of the Aisne organizing supplies, creating canteens, inexpensive restaurants and lodgings for refugees from the Aisne. Sadly, just before the war ended he contracted Spanish influenza and died on November 6 in Paris. Describing Ceccaldi's achievements, President Paul Deschanel stated:

> "This Corsican carried in all his person, in all his nature, the quintessential traits of his race: the taste for the fight, bravery, faithfulness ... Pascal Ceccaldi was able, during his short and stormy existence, to make enemies, to provoke, even to deserve anger but no one will contradict me if I affirm that, by his generosity and his courage, he was worthy of our unanimous respect and sorrow."

16. **Page 83** - The posters by Fouqueray and Mourgue feature the Mostar bridge over the River Drina into Albania which became a focal point for the 'Great Retreat' which is the name given to the strategic withdrawal of the Royal Serbian Army, considered by the Serbs as one of the greatest tragedies in their nation's history. Using biblical symbolism it would be remembered as the Albanian Golgotha, a sacred sacrifice followed by the national 'resurrection' when the remnants of Serbia's army, along with French, British and Greek forces liberated Serbia in September 1918.

In late October 1915, the combined forces of Germany, Austria-Hungary and Bulgaria launched a massive offensive against Serbia. Apart from surrender, the only option open to the Serbian government and Supreme Command was to escape by a full retreat in the middle of a harsh winter across some of the roughest terrains in Europe including the mountains of Montenegro and Albania. The hope was to reach the Adriatic coast and then embark on Allied ships transporting them to various Greek islands (many to Corfu) before being sent to Salonika. As they retreated, the army had to help hundreds of thousands of refugees who retreated alongside them with almost no supplies or food left and facing appalling weather. During the journey across the mountains 77,500 soldiers and 160,000 civilians died from the freezing temperatures, hunger, disease and attacks by enemy forces which included 'the first aerial bombardment of civilians' by Austrian pilots. Tragically, even after their rescue, survivors were so weakened that in the following weeks 11,000 more Serbs died from sheer exhaustion, malnutrition or exposure.

17. **Page 99** - The Rockefeller Foundation (RF) was established by the Rockefeller family in 1913. John Davison Rockefeller Sr. (1839 - 1937) was an American business magnate and philanthropist, considered by many scholars as the wealthiest American of all time and the richest person in modern history. At the start of the war the RF organized and funded the provision of food, clothing and medical aid to Belgian refugees. It established military hospitals and funded research on the sterilization and treatment of wounds, the diagnosis of nervous disorders including shell shock and the treatment of meningitis, dysentery and tuberculosis. After the USA entered the war in 1917, the RF continued to coordinate its work through organizations such as the American Red Cross and the Young Men's Christian Association (YMCA).

18. **Page 120** - Henry de Waroquier (1881 - 1970) was a Parisian born painter, sculptor and printmaker. In his teens he lived in the rue Laffitte (in the IXe arrondissement of Paris) almost opposite the famous art gallery of Ambroise Vollard and not far from the Durand-Ruel Gallery and the sales exhibitions of the art dealer Siegfried Bing. He was an admirer of the works of the Impressionists and the Far East. He had an exceptionally long career and his works figured prominently in major annual exhibitions including the Salon d'Automne, which he served as President and also the influential Société des peintres-graveurs français.

19. Page 143 - Claude-Joseph Rouget de L'Isle (1760-1836), a French army officer, wrote 'La Marseillaise' in 1792 to inspire French troops fighting against Prussia and Austria. Supporters of the French Revolution adopted the song, most famously a volunteer army from Marseilles who sang it while marching on Paris - giving the song its name. In the aftermath of the Revolution, Napoleon banned the Marseillaise but it was permitted again by King Louis Philippe after 1830, and was declared the official national anthem for France in 1879 during the Third Republic. On Bastille Day in 1915 Rouget's ashes were brought to Paris from his birthplace and placed in the Hôtel des Invalides, as a grand patriotic gesture.

20. Page 150 - Joseph Simon Gallieni (24 April 1849 – 27 May 1916) was born at Saint-Beat on 24 April 1849. After training at the Saint-Cyr military academy he served in the Franco-Prussian War of 1870-71 and was then posted to Africa in the mid-1870s where he spent most of the rest of his career. After serving in Martinique Gallieni was made Governor of French Sudan, during which time he successfully quelled rebellion by Sudanese rebels. From 1892-96 he served in French Indochina before being dispatched to Madagascar, where he again suppressed revolt, this time of monarchist forces. He served as Governor-General of Madagascar from 1897 until 1905. Gallieni was the favourite to become supreme commander of the French Army in 1911, however, pleading advancing age and ill-health he declined the position in favour of Joseph Joffre.

Retiring from the army in April 1914, Gallieni was recalled in August and given the task of organizing the defence of Paris. Wary of Gallieni's influence and reputation, Joffre attempted to marginalise his role but failed as the older General's energy, organization and foresight undoubtedly saved the City. When Gallieni realised that the German First Army was turning east in early September, he sent the Sixth Army from Paris to strike its flank, even rushing reserves to the front in taxis in response to German counter-attacks. The military acumen that he displayed was to prove instrumental in the subsequent victory of the French at the First Battle of the Marne.

Although at the time Joffre was credited with these successes there was increasing public debate, much of it politically motivated, about which of them had 'won' the First Battle of the Marne - a contentious issue which still divides military historians today. Interestingly, Winston Churchill in his writings, credited Gallieni rather than Joffre:

> "He [Gallieni] is not thinking only of the local situation around Paris. He thinks for France and he behaves with the spontaneous confidence of genius in action."

Gallieni subsequently served as Minister of War in October 1915 before retiring, again citing ill-health in March 1916. In truth, he had repeatedly clashed with Joffre and was critical of his handling of Verdun which became known by the poilus as the 'meat-grinder'. The strain of high office had exacerbated his already fragile health and he died on 27 May 1916. In 1921 he received the highest accolade from his nation when he was posthumously appointed Marshal of France.

TRANSLATIONS

Page 2
THE LITTLE BELGIAN FLAG
Remember that today, all over France, the day belongs to the Belgians. The number of flags required by the province comes to more than ten million! In Paris, the societies of the Red Cross have volunteered their wonderful staff to the Committee for the sales; four million flags have been reserved for Paris and 700,000 for the suburbs.

Page 3
BELGIAN FLAG DAY
Today our flag will flutter in every French hand as a symbol of love and gratitude. This day should be a day of hope and glory for all Belgium.

Let us forget for a moment our terrible distress; let us forget our fields and meadows, the fairest and most fertile in Europe, now ravaged to such a degree that the best description is hopeless in giving any idea of the desolation which seems irremediable. Let us forget - if to forget them is possible - the women, the children, the old men, peaceful and innocent, who have been massacred in their thousands, the stories which will amaze the world once the war is over, behind which so many secret horrors are being committed. Let us not forget those who are dying of hunger in our country, a land without harvests and without homes, a land methodically taxed, pillaged and crushed until it is drained of the last drop of its lifeblood. Let us not forget those remnants of our people who are scattered everywhere, who have trodden the path of exile, who are living on public charity, which though it shows itself full of kinship and affection, is yet so oppressive to those supremely industrious hands, which have never had to rely on charity. Let us not even forget the last of our cities to be menaced, the fairest, the proudest, the most beloved of our cities, which are part of the very face of our country and which only a miracle can now save. Let us not forget in a word, the greatest calamity and the most crying injustice of history and think today only of our approaching deliverance. It is not too early to hail it. It is already in all our thoughts, as it is in all our hearts. It is already in the air which we breathe, in all the eyes that smile at us, in all the voices that welcome us, in all the hands outstretched to us, waving the laurel branches which they hold; for what is bringing us deliverance is the wonder, the admiration of the whole world!

Tomorrow we shall go back to our homes. We shall not mourn though we find them in ruins. They will rise again more beautiful than of old from the ashes and the shards. We shall know days of heroic poverty but we have learnt that poverty is powerless to sadden souls upheld by a great love and nourished by a noble ideal. We shall return with heads erect in a regenerated Europe, rejuvenated by our magnificent misfortune, purified by victory and cleansed of the pettiness that obscured the virtues which lay asleep within us and of which we were not aware. We shall have lost all the goods that perish but as readily come to live again. And in their place we shall have acquired those riches which shall not again perish within our hearts. Our eyes were closed to many things; now they have opened upon wider horizons. In the past we dared not avert our gaze from our wealth, our petty comforts, our little rooted habits. But now our eyes have been wrested from the soil; now they have achieved the sight of heights that were hitherto unnoticed. We did not know ourselves; we used not to love one another sufficiently; but we have learnt to know ourselves in the amazement of glory and to love one another in the grievous ardour of the most stupendous sacrifice that any people has ever accomplished. We were on the point of forgetting the heroic virtues, the unfettered thoughts, the eternal ideas that lead humanity. Today, not only do we know that they exist: we have taught the world that they are always triumphant, that nothing is lost while faith is left, while honour is intact, while love continues, while the soul does not surrender and that the most monstrous of powers will never prevail against those ideal forces which are the happiness and the glory of people and the sole reason for their existence.   MAETERLINCK

Page 4
In Belgium the Belgians are hungry
Artistic tombola to raise funds for feeding the people of Belgium. Every five-franc ticket entitles the holder to:
A - A souvenir: either an engraving by the painter Firmin Baes or a medal by the sculptor Devreese.
B - The tombola draw of gifts of applied art (lacework, embroidery, vase paintings, silks, etc., made by Belgian women).
Tickets can be obtained from the Head Office Franco-Belgian Alliance, 58, rue de la Victoire, Paris. Honorary Presidents of the Franco-Belgian Alliance: Baron Guillaume, Minister of H.M. the King of the Belgians in Paris, M. Louis Barthou, Member of Parliament, former President of the Council of Ministers of State of Belgium. The Honorary Vice President: M. Dalimier, Under-Secretary of State to the Ministry of Fine Arts. President: M. Steeg, Senator, former Minister.

Page 5

Aux Enfants des Écoles

FRENCH REPUBLIC / Liberty - Equality - Fraternity / PREFECTURE OF THE DEPARTMENT OF THE SEINE / TO / CHILDREN OF SCHOOLS / THE LITTLE BELGE FLAG /

On 20 December the sale of the 'Little Belgian Flag' will take place throughout France. Unanimously the French public will show their national friendship for Belgium. By buying your flag in the colours of our friends, think of Belgium which has put honour and freedom above all.

Paris, 12th December 1914. / The Prefect of the Seine, / M. DELANNEY

Paris. - Imp. HEMMERLE et Cie, rue de Damiette, 2, 4, and 4 bis.

Page 9

"From October 1914 the T.C.F., unable to continue its routine tourist work, thought that it was its duty to undertake patriotic work. While our young comrades fulfilled their military duties, the older people wanted to make themselves useful and contribute in their own way to the national defence ... to do something for those who are fighting".

Page 10

FRENCH REPUBLIC - JOURNÉE DU 75 - Sunday February 7, 1915 - THE WORK OF THE SOLDIER ON THE FRONT

Under the high patronage of the President of the Republic and the representatives of the Public Authorities, of the Presidents of the Senate, of the Chamber of Deputies, of the President of the Council, of Ministers of War, of the Navy, of the Interior, of the Presidents of the Council General and of the Municipal Council, of the Prefect of the Seine and of the Prefect of Police, a 'Journée du 75' is in preparation in all of France. The initiative for this day is due to the Touring-Club of France which created 'l'Oeuvre du Soldat au Front' to send to our combatants objects of nature to improve their well-being: Seen and approved, January 16, 1915. The Minister of the Interior, L J MALVY./ The President of the Touring-Club de France, Abel BALLIF."

Letter - B.G. Paris.- Imp. L. Pochy, 52, rue du Château.

A letter from Henri Defert (Vice President of T.C.B.)

Note on the sale of the 75 insignias

To our wonderful sellers

The insignias sold to the general public during the Day of the 75 are of different types. The reason for this diversity is the very diversity of tastes and financial means at which they are targeted.

It is felt that the differences of the insignias has a consequence of being reflected in their manufacturing price and leads us to express to "Mesdames les Questeuses" de la Journée du 75 the following small observation:

The essential principle: the amount of the donation paid by the public must always be left entirely to their generosity, whichever type of insignia it chooses.

But in most cases, our collectors will know how to obtain a certain graduation in the sums which will be paid to them, in harmony with the rather different values of the insignias of the 'Journée du 75'. To achieve this, their diplomacy and customary skills will suffice.

The President of the Committee for the Work of the Soldier at the Front

Henry Defert Vice President of T.C.F.

LA JOURNÉE DU 75

"Give, donate Parisians, it's for our soldiers".

Today is the Journée du 75. In Paris and in the cities of France, you will be invited to accept, in exchange for a donation that you will be able to make generously, the lovely insignias which will, for you and for the future, enforce the immortal glory of our field gun.

There is no doubt that our happy support for the 75, which our troops already have so much reason to be grateful for, will help our soldiers. Because it is for them, it is for the artillerymen in charge of the 75, it is for the infantrymen who complete its work, it is for the cavalry and the aviators who support it. It is for all those who are at front that, during this day, you will be invited to open your wallets.

You will open them wide, and I assure you that what you will receive will be one of the best, one of the most vivid memories that you will keep of this war, which the 75 and our soldiers knew how to make glorious.

Page 10 (continued)

LA JOURNÉE DU 75
To the 75
Let it be shouted very loud, let it vibrate and resound
May an equal fervour illuminate this name
That from our educated hearts, a hymn of justice
Rises to it, our friend, the field gun
May a noble day of honour become its Day
That in a touching, tender and grateful gesture,
The work offering is given everywhere
To this Seventy-Five, alert and quivering
At the edge of the trench, watching over us like a sentry.
Its presence defends our eternal France
It looks after her, its bronze protecting her.
Our sons are its servants and love him like a father,
The 75 tracking down the barbarian in the depths of his lair,
If it stops thundering, the Rhine [enemy] will sing.
MARCEL LAUREM.

Page 17

Le Produit des Journées
It is never in vain that we appeal to the generosity of the people whenever there are collections for worthy or patriotic causes. In exchange for little insignias that everyone wants to keep, millions have been raised and all the goals have been accomplished. We will only give here the results that have been achieved up to the end of August 1917.

Page 20

Comité du Secours National Journee Française
Monsieur le Maire
Along with the Parliamentary Group for Invaded Departments, the Committee of Secours National is organizing a "Journée Française" for the Sunday and Monday of Pentecost 23 and 24 May.

You know, M Le Maire that the Secours National was created at the very beginning of the hostilities to bring aid to Paris and the provinces for women, children and the elderly in need without any interest in personal or religious beliefs.

A group of people from all parties, representatives of all the social pressure groups have been brought together under one mission - to overcome misery and all its repercussions as long as our soldiers are battling against the enemy.

The country has understood the importance and need for the work of the Secours National and, in an admirable gesture of generosity, has responded to its appeal.

From abroad we have received precious donations bearing testimony of the importance and the steadfast attachment they have to France.

A portion of the donations received has been allocated as subsidies: to soup kitchens, canteens, workhouses, locker rooms, orphanages, maternal, infant and apprenticeship works, etc.

Most aid organizations of all kinds, large and small, have requested and obtained, in various forms, the help and support of the Secours National.

But the course of events has naturally widened its task. It has had to be concerned above all with the fate of the people in the regions of our country which were momentarily or are still invaded, of the families who remained in their ruined villages and of those who were forced to abandon their homes.

Throughout the invaded part of France, like the Central Committee, it has set up regional Secours National Commissions which are already operating in Haute-Alsace, in the Vosges, in Nancy, in Belfort, etc., etc. These Commissions study the needs on the spot and provide the means to meet them by distributing food, clothing, bedding, etc.

To civilian prisoners sent back to France, the Secours National has already shipped thousands of clothes and provided large sums of money distributed to our unfortunate compatriots upon their arrival in Switzerland.

Page 20 (continued)

Comité du Secours National Journee Française

Useful and beneficial action of the Secours National Committee asserts itself more and more every day. From all parts of France, works which support the unfortunate war victims are addressed by it. It knows, on the other hand, what efforts it will have to make for immediate relief when the enemy is driven out of France, leaving behind so many desolated homes and wasteland.

The Group of Representatives of invaded regions join it [Secours National Committee] in making an appeal to the whole of France to obtain from its inexhaustible generosity new resources which will allow the war victims to wait, without too much suffering, until the hour of victory.

M le Maire, help us to give our brave soldiers the certainty that those who are deprived of their support are surrounded by our care and that they can do their duty without having to look behind.

Please accept M. le Maire, my best wishes

The Secretary General - A Guillet
The President - P Appell

Le Petit Journal 28 April 1915 Front page
La Médaille de la 'Journée Française'.
The attraction of the 'Journée Française' organized by the Committee of the Secours National and the interparliamentary group of the invaded departments will be, as the *Petit Journal* has already announced: a very artistic medal engraved especially for this occasion by the 'eminent artist' M. Hippolyte Lefèbvre.

We are pleased to reproduce the design of this medal. The kind hearted collectors will offer it on the streets during the two days of the upcoming feast of Pentecost (23-24 May). They will also have available the original postcards that all families will want to send to those on the front lines.

Page 22
RÉPUBLIQUE FRANÇAISE
Journée Française du Secours National organized by the Committee of 'National Secours' and by the Parliamentary Group of the invaded Departments for Sunday and Monday - 23 and 24 May.

The Committee of the 'National Relief' was formed at the beginning of the War, in order to provide for the miseries which it anticipated but which were to exceed all expectations. This Committee represents all beliefs and opinions. The very existence of France is endangered. We are intimately united in the common love of the Nation to accomplish the common duty towards it. This duty imposes the appeal that we address to you, together with the Representatives of the invaded Departments.

After showing your generous solidarity to our Belgian friends and our soldiers at the front, you will not show less generosity to alleviate the miseries of our French populations:
Miseries of women, children and the elderly.
Miseries of widows and orphans.
Miseries of the French who were driven from their homes by the invasion.
Miseries of those who remained in their devastated countries.
Miseries of these hostages that our barbaric enemies have transported by the thousands to Germany and that it makes us exhausted and dying.

Everyone is suffering in this war but not always equally. Those who suffer the least owe a national solidarity debt to those who suffer the most: fatherless children, homeless families, all victims of this war that our enemies have imposed on us and that they atrociously created. Each of us must pay this sacred debt so that we have an equal right to the great emotion and the sublime joy that the Victory of France and of Civilization will bring us.

The National Rescue Committee set up under the high patronage of the President of the Republic and with the support of the Government [a list of 'Honorary Presidents' follows.] Parliamentary Group of Invaded Departments [a members' list follows, including Léon Bourgeois.] The Members of the National Rescue Committee [a list of members follows] Seen and approved, April 23, 1915. The Minister of the Interior, L J MALVY. 17817. Paris. - Imprimerie MARCEL PICARD, 140, rue de Faubourg-Saint-Martin (Telephones 132-74 and 139-5).

Page 25
Excelsior 24 May 1915 page 6
We again witnessed the amiable and irresistible smiles of the young collectors who were distributing, in the squares and avenues, the medal of the French Day and the small flags with which everyone was honoured to decorate themselves with. Like the other great days which have already proved the people's generosity which is never solicited in vain for a noble cause and for a work of solidarity, the French Day will have contributed to the establishment of a magnificent 'war chest' which will bring relief to many misfortunes of the wounded, refugees, convalescents, orphans and widows of war.

Page 29
Extract from an article in La Presse (18 June 1915) Page 1
For its part, the Central Committee of the French Red Cross composed of representatives from the three relief societies recognised [as being] in the public interest, namely: La Société de secours aux blessés militaires (French Relief Society for Wounded Soldiers), L'Union des femmes de France (Union of French Women) and L'Association des dames françaises (Association of French Women), at the meeting held on 15 June, took the following decision:

"The French Red Cross was happy to pledge its assistance for the fundraising campaign organised by the 'Army Orphanages', believing that an agreement had been made by all the connected organisations promoting the same cause. Regrettably we have learnt that disagreements have arisen between them. Everyone will understand that under these conditions, for as long as an agreement has not been reached, the Red Cross will not be involved".

Page 30
Top right: An article from La Presse (23 June 1915) Page 1
One of our counterparts, *The Free Speech* [a French political anti-Semitic newspaper founded in 1892 by the journalist and writer Édouard Drumont] states that "the emblem to be distributed for the 'Day' proposed by Mrs Diek May had been formally rejected by a certain number of associations, which feel that such an emblem is not of a kind that can be distributed on public streets by respectable young girls".

We wanted to obtain this insignia or to be more exact the small medal which is going to be sold by the young female collectors for the benefit of orphans. This work by the engraver Lalique is a beautiful artistic inspiration, but it has too much of a Greek style and is unduly stripped of all veils [modesty]; our poilus cannot be viewed as conquerors of Salamis [a famous battle between Greeks and Persians fought in 480 BCE]. What we can say is that it is not suitable for the public which it is aimed at, be it via the sellers or the families who are offered it. Again from this perspective, it seems to us that the Army Orphanage Day campaign leaders have been misguided.

Bottom right: Le Temps 28 June 1915 Page 4
The War Orphans Day
From early this morning, the collections began for the "Orphans Day". The agreement by the different organisations which organise the 'Day' was largely endorsed by the public and significantly everyone eagerly gave their contribution. One saw, in the same buttonhole however, not just one of the authorised insignias but rather a real selection, made up of Lalique's plaquette, small Army Orphanage flag pins and some charming flowers, roses, daisies, forget-me-nots, which filled the baskets - quickly emptied - of the collectors. The sun helped, ready made to predict that in Paris and in the provinces, the "Orphans Day" would succeed as brilliantly as previous 'Days', the memory of which is not forgotten.

One touching detail: the wounded soldiers, the war invalids are shown the renewed commitment, if that is possible, that the 'civilians' are coming to the aid of war orphans. In the endeavour, the sacred union continues with sacrifice as well as solidarity. Paris is packed with emotional scenes where it is already apparent that everyone's desire is to guarantee the salvation of the country.

Page 31
Top left - La Presse (18 June 1915) Front page
The Army Orphanage Day
As feared, the day or, more precisely, the "Army Orphanage" question, seems likely to create some regrettable incidents that the most basic precautions and the least sophisticated patriotism would have needed to avoid at this time.

The intransigence of the political committee of Mr Croiset and Mrs Paquin has provoked some less than flattering comments and opinions for the promoters of a charity which is both an unacceptable monopoly and distasteful split.

Page 31 continued

It is not only amongst Catholic circles that the discontent comes from: regardless of opinions and beliefs, independent minds and enlightened souls are unanimous in protesting against this power grab of a "Journée" that belongs to all the organizations looking after war orphans.

Top right - Letter from Madame Jeanne Paquin
The Army Orphanage Day 20 June 1915

Paris, 14 June 1915
Mr. Deputy Prefect,
We have the honour to inform you that today we are promptly sending:
Two boxes that contain the following items:

    7,000 metal medals/pendants
    23,000 cardboard medals/pendants
    70,000 [paper] flags
    500 collector [identity] cards
    50 commissioner [identity] cards
    500 labels for collection boxes
    1 packet of posters

We would be very much obliged if you would collect them at the station and then take measures over the distribution. The number of metal medals is relatively small because of the difficulty we have had in procuring copper, this is the method we chose (in rounding off)

    Metal medals 7%
    Cardboard medals and flowers 23%
    Flags (3 types) 70%

Thanking you in advance, please accept M. Deputy Prefect, the assurance of our highest consideration.
Mrs Paquin - Appointed to organize the "Day of the 20 June".

Bottom left - Letter from Madame Jeanne Paquin
The Army Orphanage Day Sunday, June 20, 1915

Enclosed you will find you a notice explaining the purpose of the 'The Army Orphanage Day'.

To enable us to support, educate and raise as many children as possible, the Minister of the Interior has agreed to grant us a 'Day', to be held Sunday, 20 June. We have undoubtedly asked the public for a big effort since the beginning of the war but it has been evident that for worthy causes, the [public] charity is inexhaustible. And our charity is one of the most worthy!

Secondly, the Minister of Public Instruction, has done us the honour of giving us his benevolent support in assuring us that you would grant us your most dedicated support for our work.

We would therefore be most obliged if you would, along with the Mayor, help him in his task and at the same time give more sparkle [publicity] to the charity event for the benefit of the children of those who have died on the Field of Honour.

With our thanks in advance, please accept the assurance of our highest consideration [Yours sincerely].
On behalf of the Committee

Mrs Paquin Appointed to organize the "Day of the 20 June".

Stamped: Any communication relating to the "The Army Orphanage Day" should be sent to Mrs PAQUIN, 3, Rue de la Paix.

Bottom right - Handwritten note from Jeanne Paquin
The organizing Committee have requested to send on 12 June or later:
1. To the Aurillac Prefecture
100,000 insignias
500 collector [identity] cards
30 commissioner [identity] cards

Page 31 continued

2. To the Mauriac Prefecture
50,000 insignias
200 collector [identity] cards
10 commissioner [identity] cards

Page 32
Le Matin 28 June 1915 page 1
The Day of the War Orphans

Once more, the Parisians showed yesterday that one never questions their patriotism and their good hearts. As they have done during the previous fundraising days to help other relief works, perhaps with even greater eagerness because this time it was a question of repaying to the orphaned children, the sacred gratitude to their fathers, all of them, people around the world and common people, competing against each other in order to strip the baskets wrapped in ribbons of the kind hearted collectors. Further, these (the collectors) did not spare their pace or their pains. At dawn, standing at their posts on the boulevards, in the streets, at the Metro gates, at the cafes, in the restaurants, they valiantly did their duty until eight o'clock in the evening. They had not forgotten the Bois de Boulogne, where the walkers were numerous, on this last Sunday of June, despite the withdrawal of the Grand Prix.

Slipping amongst the groups, they imposed themselves between the stacked rows of chairs, in the alleyways, through to the clearings without any fuss where courageous suburban households celebrated with picnics in the presence of the soldiers convalescing or on leave, they had soon covered jackets, blousons, cretonne or silk blouses with their multi-coloured emblems, Lalique's gold gilt plaquette, small flag pins of the Army orphanages, blue or pinky-red flowers, all representing the various organizing bodies of the 'Day', truly achieving, pins side by side on the same person, the sacred union of the charity.

And the French or allied soldiers, whether fit or wounded, were no less committed to make it a success.

Page 33
Le Gaulois 4 June 1915 - Interview with M. Lalique Page 2

We have previously reported that the day of the 20th June will be dedicated to the cause, sadly so necessary, of the Army Orphanages. The issue at stake, both now and in the future, is the existence of legions of little children left without parents due to the war. On their behalf, young women and girls will sell on public roads throughout France, an insignia which will go down as testimony of the national solidarity.

The people, always ready to donate when it a question of our gallant soldiers, will have the honour more than ever before of making this act of generosity towards the innocent victims, who have become the wards of the nation. Yet again, it will be a rousing reception to the new souvenir being offered, not only to the noble cause that inspired it but also because of its artistic character.

This insignia is the work of the famous jeweller Lalique, the renovator of modern taste, who felt obliged to sign it.

M. Lalique, who we had the pleasure to meet in his hotel on the Champs-Elysées, told us:

"I am very happy to have contributed to the Army Orphanages. It is one of the most interesting that I know about and it demands, from its organisers, a great deal of devotion, because it is called to continue [its work] for a long time after the war; I therefore thought it appropriate in the design and execution of the work which had been entrusted to me, all my artist's awareness and my French spirit (heart)".

The insignia, which will be sold on 20th June consists of a small golden plaquette, measuring 32 mm in the approximate shape of a Maltese cross. The central motif is the figure of a woman symbolising the charity with her arms around two small children. These plaquettes are struck 'au mouton', that is to say using machines that drop a huge weight on the selected moulds in a manner that the tiniest details are imprinted on the material. And you know, added M. Lalique with a smile, "these machines are totally French. They have nothing to do with German machines so imposing with their size and complexity but which function badly and do a bad job. I want to make it perfectly clear that no plaquette is put into circulation that is not perfect. So I supervise the manufacturing process myself and I relentlessly eliminate any examples with an imperfection, no matter how many. Check these examples".

And Mr Lalique pointed out to us three boxes filled with rejects, which we pulled out with both hands; admittedly it needed the eye of an expert to determine that they were not perfect.

Page 33 continued

"Besides, this is a small matter compared to the enormous quantity of insignias that we have struck: twenty two million in fact. Altogether this represents the contents of five large removal cars; and the tricolour ribbon used for attaching them, at three centimetres per insignia, makes up a respectable length of 290 kilometres. Despite these figures, I fear that we are going to run out of them. From everywhere we are being deluged with requests and we are demanding considerable quantities of them. So the day of the 20th June looks like being an auspicious occasion".

We were able to examine a final flawless plaquette of M. Lalique's. It really is a work of art. The hollows and the reliefs are particularly well modelled, the draperies have an exquisite finesse and the whole piece has a beautiful harmony, leaving you with a touching impression of gentleness and charm. It will really be a success.

Page 35 Top right - Poster by Riom
THE ARMY ORPHANAGE DAY
Regional Group of the Lower Loire
[Fundraising] Day of 1 November 1917
The fathers died so that France is free.
Give so that their children do not go without.

Page 39
Le Petit Parisien 7 August 1915 page 2
The 'Journée' of the 26 September - A great tombola for the Éprouvés de la Guerre

The Parisian Press Union has never failed, in the painful circumstances we are going through, to lend its most active support to all the charitable works which have requested their help. Not content, however, with this role, the Press Union wanted to do even better and mark, once again, its desire to actively get involved.

Thus, faced with the impossibility of making a choice among so many equally deserving works, it asked the government for authorization to organize a global 'Day' - a 'Day' of the victims of war, military or civilians - which will make it possible to alleviate the burdens of these glorious and worthy victims.

The Minister of the Interior, entering into the views of the Union and realizing the results that could be expected from such an initiative, did not hesitate to authorize the requested "Journée" for September 26: it goes without saying that after prior agreement, the benefits are to be distributed in the most eclectic and generous spirit.

But works of this nature are numerous and, in order to be able to benefit as much as possible from this day, it is very important that the sale receipts exceed the most optimistic forecasts. In order to achieve this goal, the Press Union, while knowing what can be expected from the public's generosity, considered it necessary to create a novel attraction, so it requested and obtained the very great favour of a raffle, the ingenious mechanism of which will make it possible both to distribute large sums to numerous works and to circulate in trade, both in Paris and in the provinces, a million at least and perhaps two.

We will soon have the opportunity to come back to this subject and clarify some additional details.

Page 40
Letter – Note on the Éprouvés de la Guerre which will take place on 26 September.
1. The allocated day will take place on 26 September
2. It will have the title Éprouvés de la Guerre; it will include, therefore, the most interesting works among those which deal with coming to the aid of the military or civilian victims of the war.
3. For the choice of these [deserving] works, as with the distribution of potential fundraising, it will be preceded by agreement between the Ministry of the Interior and the Parisian Press Syndicate.
4. To help the number of works requiring considerable funds, the Parisian Press Syndicate has adopted and made us agree for the Journée des Éprouvés de la Guerre a completely new distribution process that does not include flags, medals or emblems.
5. The Parisian Press Syndicate has made, for this purpose, small envelopes - familiarly called pochettes - adorned with an original composition by the eminent master Luc-Olivier Merson.
6. Each one of these envelopes will contain a coloured reproduction/image making up part of a series of 30 military designs by very famous artists, a series the list of which will be sent through to you.
7. 100,000 of these envelopes, however, will contain numbers ranging from 1 to 100,000 which will be inserted at the rate of one per envelope: these numbers, to avoid any fraud, will be of the same size and weight as the images; the

Page 40 continued

envelopes containing them will be mixed with the others without any external sign allowing them to be in any way recognized and will be put into circulation and sold under the same conditions as all the others. Following the example of what was done during the previous days, the prices of the envelopes will be entirely optional; but it will be up to the sellers to promote the indisputable advantages of the combination.

8. The lucky winners of the 100,000 numbers will benefit from a draw which will be carried out at Crédit Foncier, in the fortnight following the Journée des Éprouvés de la Guerre.

Page 40
Advertising Posters for La Journée des Éprouvés de la Guerre le 26 Septembre 1915 Grande Tombola organisée par le Syndicat de la Presse Française

Grand tombola organized by the French Press Association. Do you want to come to the aid of the civilian and military war-stricken? Yes!

Do you want to pay your debt of gratitude to all those who have suffered and are still suffering for you? Yes!

Buy the little envelopes.

What will you find in them?

Superb drawings signed by our greatest Masters. Is that all? No!

In 100,000 envelopes you will find vouchers from 25,000 down to 5 francs. One million from 25,000 down to 5 francs. And with these vouchers? With each of these vouchers, depending on your luck, you can buy what you want in the shop you want as if with a banknote.

Buy the little envelopes for the price you want.

'AFFICHES-CAMIS, PARIS'

Page 42
Le Figaro 25 September 1915 page 2

GRANDE TOMBOLA of the Journée des Éprouvés de la Guerre (Prize of the Grand Tombola)

NOTICE TO ALL BUYERS

Each pochette has a design, and there are 30 different designs.

The purchaser who is the first to present the 30 drawings will be entitled to a "Unie "automobile, worth 12,000 francs.

The second will be entitled to a silverware service, worth 4,000 francs.

Finally, the buyer who is the first to present 29 drawings out of 30 will be entitled to furniture, worth 3,000 francs.

The second will be entitled to a Pleyel piano, worth 1,800 fr.

So buy the pochettes and pay at least 25 centimes for them.

Page 45
'La Journée de la Pochette' Le Figaro 27 September page 2

After the incessant days of rain that we have just endured, we were not without apprehension for this Sunday of the Pochette. The weather fortunately, was much more favourable yesterday and, from seven in the morning, the street collectors - young women, young girls, very young girls accompanied by young boys, boy scouts and wounded soldiers - spread through the streets, boulevards, gardens, woods of Boulogne and Vincennes. And everywhere, the walkers and passers-by eagerly responded to their call. Everyone, rich and poor alike, bought [them]. There are people who only bought one or two but many wanted ten, twenty, fifty and sometimes even more.

It was like that all day until the night time. It is impossible to say what the receipts will be, or even to put forward a prediction. It is shaping up to be superb and all we know is that it will meet and exceed the most optimistic forecasts. We owe our thanks to the directors of the theatres, cinemas, concerts in Paris, who authorized the sale of the pochettes during yesterday's matinée: large sums of money were collected during intermissions. Because, everywhere and in all places, Paris wanted to show that it was always appreciative of a beautiful work of charity.

The 'Journée des Éprouvés' was very successful

Le Journal 27 September page 2

The 'Journée des Éprouvés' was very successful. Once again, the lovely collectors, boys and girls, travelled through Paris asking passers-by for donations to the 'Journée des Éprouvés'.

This time it was the 'Journée des Éprouvés'; each small envelope contained a drawing and sometimes a voucher for a large prize. In addition, the Syndicat de la Presse française who organized this day, had decided that the subscribers who

Page 45 continued

were the first to present the collection of the thirty drawings contained in the pockets would benefit from a bonus. You could win a car, a silverware set, 3,000 francs for furniture, a piano, etc. It was a question of collecting the thirty drawings. Some subscribers bought a hundred or two hundred envelopes to try to achieve it and not all of them were successful but the subscription benefited greatly.

At 3 o'clock in the afternoon, certain little collectors had sold more than five hundred envelopes; by 5 o'clock their baskets were empty.

It was at the Gaulois, 2 rue Drouot, that we had to drop off the collections and from 11 am participants were presenting themselves; soon the offices of colleagues were invaded and in the rue Drouot we had to organize a security service because here is what happened: Among the happy owners of drawings, many, in spite of the considerable number of envelopes they had bought, had in their possession only twenty-nine drawings instead of thirty, or twenty-eight instead of twenty-nine.

But sellers kept watch; those who had one or the other of the missing drawings offered, for a fee - twenty sous, even forty sous - to give it up.

By 3 o'clock, when the Gaulois counters were forced to refuse to accept deposits, more than three hundred envelopes, containing the thirty or twenty-nine drawings required to win one or the other of the lots which we have described were entrusted to the treasurer of the Syndicat de la Presse Parisienne.

The provinces had also been in touch; the telegrams were pouring in and, in the morning, Arthur Meyer (the treasurer), had been notified by the Prefect of Puy-de-Dôme that a lady from Clermont-Ferrand had arrived at quarter past eight at the Prefecture to show that she had collected the thirty vignettes.

Everything seems to indicate that the receipts of the day will greatly exceed the previous collections.

Le Temps 28 September page 4
La Grande Journée des Eprouvés de la Guerre
Yesterday, the 'Journée des Éprouvés' achieved great success in Paris and the provinces.

Around four o'clock, when the first numbers of the evening papers appeared on news stands, bringing news of victories, Paris presented an especially poignant dimension. A restrained joy shone in everyone's eyes; we would stop in the middle of the boulevard, in the middle of the road, to read and reread the press release, and the crowds, always calm and collected, without vain displays, kept that admirable calm and that dignity which they have not shied away from for more than a year. So the sale of pochettes resumed with greater enthusiasm than ever and soon most of the poor street collectors were forced to declare that they had no more supplies.

In the provinces, the 'Journée des Éprouvés' obtained a success, the impact of which will be measured by this fact alone: the Press Union was notified yesterday, telegraphically by twenty Prefects, that collections of 29 and 30 pochettes were already being submitted, in several numbers in their respective Departments. At half past eight in the morning, Mme Daille, from Clermont-Ferrand, informed the Prefect of Puy-de-Dôme that she had collected the thirty different drawings distributed in the pochettes. Mme Daille is an 'individual' buyer, that is to say, she bought the pochettes herself. This detail is important, given that a real "Stock Exchange" of drawings had been formed yesterday, entered by many people who bought the missing drawings in order to complete their "collection of thirty".

During yesterday morning, more than a thousand people came to rue Drouot, 2, at the office of the work of the 'Éprouvés de la Guerre' in order to show that they were indeed in possession of the thirty drawings required. But how to decide between all the owners of the collection of the thirty drawings who made their declarations at the same time? We understand that we will add prizes to those that exist and thus form a new raffle in which all the beneficiaries will participate.

Page 47
Journal Des Débats Politiques et Litéraires 19 November 1915
We are informed of the following note: We believed that the so-called 'Poilu Day' was organized by Parliament. In reality the initiative belongs to Senators, Deputies and Councillors of Paris without any distinction between political differences.

Le Matin 30 July page 2
The Journée du Poilu
We are given the following note:
Parliamentarians, who have taken the lead in agreeing a benefit day for the combatants, met yesterday in the House. The government have supported this project and all the measures will be taken jointly between the parliamentarians of the two Chambers for the organization of this day known as the 'Poilu'.

Page 56
Le Petit Parisien, Thursday 18 November 1915 Front page
The 'Poilu Day'
It will take place in all French municipalities on 25 and 26 December. The initiative comes from Members of Parliament who have acted cross party, having provided assistance to national and departmental works of solidarity, thought that the Poilus, too, should have their day. Why? To give those of them who have no family or whose family is in need, the means to take advantage in turn of their periods of leave. Because it was right, this simple idea has caught on.

The monies raised on the Day will be distributed in full to those given permission for leave by the commanding officers. Medals, postcards, insignias, jewellery, souvenirs will be displayed in stores and outlets and sold publicly by regions and municipalities, professional and corporate organizations. The purchase of the postcards, all of which are numbered, will give [the purchaser] the right to be placed in the draw for the Tombola du Poilu which will include works of master sculptors and designers chosen for the competition.

After the medal of Hippolyte Lefèbvre, which wonderfully symbolizes the Poilus' tenacity and invincibility of France, the posters of the Day are no less suggestive. Here is Jonas' admirable infantryman in the position of the marksman standing near a tree, looking for a minute at his colleague happily looking at his box of medals and keepsakes. Behind them on a wall blown open by shelling, an old parliamentary poster carries Gambetta's proud appeal "With you and by you, we swear to save France!"

Another print by Maurice Neumont, depicts a huge soldier, scaling the hills of Champagne among the barbed wire to throw a vengeful grenade into the enemy trenches. Shells are raining and exploding around him. Nothing stops him. Proud, with a solid hand, sure in his actions, he will fight the black eagle to the end! It is tragic, impressive and superb, like a colossal challenge!

Here is Léandre's good old mother. Sitting at the corner of the fireplace, by the light of the blazing hearth, having just read the letter from her son. She's thinking! And in the smoke of the dream looms the glorious scene. The cavalry and infantry rush forward, under the folds of the flag, behind the bugles, to the song of the Marseillaise, shouting at the top of their lungs "Good old woman, what are you doing there?" "I'm waiting for my lad who fought". Déroulède would have applauded this stirring memory of a good shelter!

After the mother, here is the woman or the bride Jenny the worker or Mimi-Pinson. How many nights has she spent sewing on her machine the shirts for the soldier's package, of her soldier! She expects him today. He enters. She knocks over her straw chair and threw herself around his neck "Alone at last" says the legend. Alone? No, not quite! Because the little hairy dog with its wide eyes contemplates this family scene where Willette has put all the playfulness of his mind and all the tenderness of his heart.

It's Christmas, in the street! Poulbot was not afraid to depict there the slim figures of his two children, the big sister [dressed] as a nurse, targeting the generosity of the passers with her sealed collecting box and the nursery school boy proudly wearing a soldier's képi, abandoning the small war for the big one, offering to the buyers his basket all covered with flags and insignias "so daddy can come home on leave, please!"

And behold break over, the two Poilus, strong and tough - the old timer with his scrutinizing gaze, his bushy moustache, his pipe and his stick with the other [new recruit] enthusiastic and dreamy, a rose in the corner of his mouth - both returning to their positions to relieve comrades whose turn it is to leave their post and go over there, towards the warmth of the friendly hearth. This poster, signed by Master Steinlen, is a masterpiece of energy and sincerity.

You will admire all these posters on the walls. You must remember that these original or lithographed prints, in black or in colour, before or after the communication will, along with the medals, constitute the tombola prizes. But as there will be only a limited number of winners, because of the great need for the advertising and sale, the 'Poilu Day' Committee thought everyone would be more comfortable to have a reduced image. So they had these prints copied as postcards.

Page 56 continued

For two sous [10 centimes], you will be able to send one to a Poilu on the front line. Generous godmothers will add to the collection of eight cards by sending a designed pin. And it will be perfect!

In this way the poorest people will keep an artistic memory of this day of friendship. And the wealthiest, the enthusiasts, the collectors will not hesitate to pay one hundred francs for the magnificent gold brooch by Lalique or the large table medal by Lefèbvre which the parliamentarians, whose day it is also, will undoubtedly subscribe to. Everyone will make their contribution to the sacred bond which joins those who have gone, those who remain and those who do not forget. The President of the Republic, the Presidents of the Senate and of the Chamber and members of the government have accepted the high patronage of the 'Journée du Poilu'.

Our allies will join in the same way - the English for whom Christmas is a quasi-national holiday, the Belgians, the Italians, the Russians, the Montenegrins and the Serbs - our soldiers will wear our medals and our good wishes. The neutrals, with the Americans leading the way, are already vying for the Poilu jewels. This bodes well for success.

With us, every week, the Prefects receive the boxes of posters, cards, insignias that the railway companies transport free of charge from the Committee which is installed at the town hall of the fourth arrondissement in Paris. Vendors will have them soon enough in every town and village in France, Algeria and the colonies. Bishops, priests, rabbis, teachers, artists zealously promote it. The directors of theatres, concerts and cinemas have committed to a day of collections. The entire press will give its support to Parliament so that our Poilu heroes have a day worthy of them! Christmas! Christmas!

While waiting for the final victory La 'Journée du Poilu' will be France's day! Ch. M. COUYBA

Page 58
Official circular sent out to all Prefectures - December 1915
POILU DAY
Under the Honorary Presidency of
THE PRESIDENT OF THE REPUBLIC
The President of the Senate
The President of the Chamber [of Deputies] and Under the Distinguished Patronage of the President of the Council and all Members of Government.

M. Prefect
We felt we should send you some additional explanations about the Poilu Day, which you are graciously assisting with. The Committee has decided, as we have already informed you, that there will be three categories of badges sold to the public.

1 Ordinary cardboard insignias which will be sold on 25 and 26 December - price will be determined by the generosity of the general public;
2 Medals made by Bargas, bronze silver-plated sold for 1 franc, and gilt bronze 1 fr. 50. The payment will be noted in the counterfoil booklet which we will distribute to the traders, dealers and others who in addition will have possession of an exemplar medal. The purchase vouchers will be detached from the counterfoil book as the sale of the medal is made, then as soon as the counterfoil booklet is sold up or the seller's efforts are exhausted, the medals and jewellery will be shipped to each Regional Committee.
3 The jewels, featuring brooches and lapel pins, are in gilt bronze, silver and gold, with respective prices of 2 francs, 10 francs and 100 francs for the brooches; 1 fr. 50, 5 francs and 35 francs for the lapel pins. These jewels, that our great artist Lalique was commissioned to design and manufacture, are offered for sale, from now on, using voucher booklets that you will receive at the same time as the vendors' samples.

Page 59
Le Figaro 25 December 1915
POILU DAY
Today - Poilu Day - will carry on until tomorrow evening. In every French city and village young women and girls, who have responded with admirable eagerness to the Parliamentary Committee's call, will be on the streets offering insignias and Poilu medals designed by our most famous artists. As we know, the buyer's generosity will decide the price.

Because of the demands for the Bargas medal, the young Prix de Rome winner, as well as some jewels of the great artist Lalique, those who want to possess these gems and in doing so, contribute to the success of the work of the 'Poilu Day', should ask for a subscription ticket reserving them in the prefectures, sub-prefectures, town halls and at merchants.

Page 64
Subscription Booklet - Lalique
To recognise the dedication and the enthusiasm of the women charged with the sales for our brave soldiers' benefit, the organizing Committee has decided to offer them, depending on the number of subscriptions they obtain, the items whether in gold, silver or gilt bronze of the Lalique beautiful jewellery with their unique initials engraved for them. These items will be allocated according to the instructions given on the second page of this booklet.

Page 65
Left - Handwritten note dated Paris 20 January 1916
René Lalique 40, COURS LA REINE, PARIS

M. Préfet
On the orders of the Poilu Day Committee, M. Lalique will ship to you via railway the following for the agreed amounts:
    1 gold lapel pin in a presentation box
    25 silver brooches in boxes
    6 silver lapel pins in boxes
    686 gilt bronze brooches in boxes
    689 gilt bronze lapel pins in boxes
Please accept, M. Prefect, my best regards.
P.S. You will shortly receive the silver lapel pins.

Right - dated 28 January 1916
M. Préfet
On the orders of the Poilu Day Committee, M. Lalique will ship to you via railway the following for the agreed amounts:
    3 silver brooches in boxes
    30 silver lapel pins in boxes
Please accept, M. Prefect, my best regards.

Page 66
Headed letter dated 7 January 1916
Donated to the Secretary General of the Library of Historical Works of the City of Paris - Hôtel Le Pelletier de Saint-Fargeau -23 rue de Sévigné
    1 set of posters
    1 set of insignias
    2 sets of the postcard series
    7 insignias for Lalique sellers
    1 Commissaire armband
    1 bronze gilt Bargas medal at 1f 50
    1 silvered Bargas medal at 1f
    1 subscription booklet for bronze gilt Bargas medal at 1f 50
    1 subscription booklet for silvered Bargas medal at 1f
    1 gold gilt Lalique brooch 2f
    1 gold gilt Lalique lapel pin 1f 50
    1 subscription booklet for Lalique items
    1 sheet of stamps
    1 cardboard poster
    2 identity cards
    1 receipt sheet
    2 bulletins of individual receipts
    2 collecting box labels
    2 lists of instructions

Display Card - Journées du Poilu
25 & 26 December 1915
These postcards and medals are sold exclusively for the 'Journée du Poilu'.
Each postcard is numbered with the right to be entered for the Tombola draw (many artistic lots).

Page 73
Le Figaro 24 June page 2
Serbia Day

In response to the government's views, the National Relief Committee agreed to organize a 'Serbia Day' for Sunday June 25th. The eminent Minister of Serbia, M. Vesnitch, on this subject has just sent Mr Paul Appell, President of the National Relief Committee, a letter from which we extract this passage:

The Serbia Day that the National Relief Committee has agreed to organize, in order to come to the aid of our families in distress, will mark a new debt of our gratitude to your noble country. In the most remote of Serbian homes, it will bring, with the comfort of hope, the certainty of common victory; it will be, in our regard, a clear demonstration of French friendship and generosity that no Serb will ever forget.

It is for all Serbs that the National Relief is addressed today to the hearts of all the men and women of our country.

Page 74
Letter 24 May 1916 from Le Comité du Secours National
M le Préfet
To reply to the Government viewpoint, the Committee for National Relief has agreed to organise a Serbia Day on Sunday 25 June. The Ministry of the Interior wants you to throw your weight of authority behind our efforts.

Today the Committee is asking for your support in our common duties of solidarity towards the heroic Serbian nation, to agree to represent them in your Department and to take in hand the organisation responsibility of the Serbia Day.

You alone, M le Préfet, have the personal responsibility and administrative powers to ensure the efficient coordination of the elements and various appeals needed to support our actions.

Just like the Journée Française, the different branch groups throughout France represented within the Committee, have promised their total commitment; the same goes for the French Red Cross, Railway Trade Union, Union of Postal and Telecommunications Workers etc... etc.

M le Préfet, it will be up to you to take the measure you think that are needed to ensure the success of the Day and, bearing in mind we have no knowledge of the local area, we could not wisely dwell for example on the following:

   - relations with the municipalities and the networks of the different organizations involved
   - centralisation and coordination of the teams of collectors and the allocation of zones for their respective action
   - delivery of materials in the various cities and towns: posters, circular letters to Mayors, insignia boxes, identity cards
     for [street] collectors and commissioners, etc ... etc .
   - police measures to protect [street[collectors, control and prevent illegal sales or counterfeit insignias
   - distribution of measures for the reservation of insignias and deposit of used collection boxes;
   - the picking up of collection boxes and depositing at the Bank of France, for the account of the "Serbia Day".
   - and any other instructions imposed by the conditions;

As far as the items are available at the time, we will be guided in our shipments by your previous requests.

The Committee is confident that you will agree, M. Prefect, to the heavy task we have given you and that you will make every effort to raise money so that the women and children of our noble [Serbian] soldiers, our Allies, survive, and that the Serbian renaissance is fulfilled after the joint victory.

Please accept M. Prefect, my devoted [sincere] thanks.
The Secretary General

Bottom Right
Standard letter sent out by the National Relief Committee to Department Prefects
NATIONAL RELIEF COMMITTEE
SERBIA DAY - INFORMATION

The National Relief Committee will send you:

1. posters intended to advertise the "Serbia Day"
   One [information] text poster
   Three posters illustrated by STEINLEN, FOUQUERAY and MOURGUE;
2. circulars for the Mayors;

Page 74 continued

3. prices for the insignias (see additional instructions);
4. the following insignias:

Prud'homme medals with suspension loops and tricolour ribbons, in stamped copper or aluminium;
four sets of different types of cardboard insignias, with striking imagery;
four sets of flags carrying the Serbian colours: "Retreat in the snow" "Comradeship in arms" "Serbian Forces".

In the event that it is impossible, because of the metal shortage due to war needs, to strike a sufficient number of the Prud'homme medals the shipment would be supplemented with medals from the "French Day" (returns).
5. street collector ID cards, commissioner ID cards, printed strips for the collection boxes, receipt [counterfoil] booklets for the collectors.
6. having been certified by the Community Mayor, sheets are to be returned to the "National Relief", 13 rue Suger.

Page 75
Le Matin 26 June page 2
Serbian Day

The aid that flooded in for Serbia Day was like the climax of French solidarity and remembrance. It is because the French people have a clear vision of the gigantic role played by the Great little Serbia in this atrocious war. We know that this glorious defeated [nation] which only gave way when crushed by numbers and treacherously attacked by the Bulgarians, courageously, proudly, endured the greatest miseries to have remained faithful to their honour and sworn faith. And the age old friendship that unites Serbia and France, bonded by blood, that poured out in common for the noblest cause, has been further increased by all the misfortunes of Serbian families in exile, or weeping in the ruins of their destroyed homes.

From the first hour, young girls, young girls dressed in light dresses, walking through the streets, watching at the railway stations or the Metro stations for the arrival of trains, held out to all, the tricolour baskets beautifully filled with insignias and medals. The collection boxes were quickly filled with small change and high denominations and all the Parisians decorated themselves in Serbian colours. Already, although the results are not yet known, it can be said that the 'Serbia Day' will be a great success.

The National Relief Committee, which had been entrusted with the organization of this beautiful event, had also done things with ingenuity. The posters, which touched the hearts of Parisians, were signed by Fonqueray, Mourgue, Steinlen, and the medals, pure masterpieces by Prud'homme, Bargas, Lordonnois, Lalique.

The Prud'homme medal represents Serbia overwhelmed by numbers and by force and claiming its right 'Meum Jus'. Bargas engraved a mother who flees, distraught, carrying her child - the future of Serbia - under the care of an old man moving away from his beloved home that he will perhaps never see again. Lalique's pin shows the genius of Serbia deploying the motto of the reigning dynasty 'Spes mihi prima Deum'. Glory to the intrepid Serbian heroes stated by Lordonnois on his medal. For its part the French League for the Rights of Women, for the benefit of the organizing Committee, organized a special sale of toys and articles made in its workshops.

The Paris Municipal Council had registered for a sum of 10,000 francs.

Page 78
Left - Standard letter sent out by the National Relief Committee to Department Prefects
NATIONAL RELIEF COMMITTEE Paris June 20, 1916
SERBIA DAY - INFORMATION AND INSTRUCTIONS

POSTERS - "Serbia Day" is announced to the public through information posters and illustrated posters.
INSIGNIAS - Illustrated cardboard badges, flags, various motifs, etc and a medal designed and engraved by Prud'homme which will be pressed either in copper or in aluminium. This medal has a suspension loop and a tricolour ribbon with pin. Cardboard badges can be sold for 0.10 [francs], and the Prud'homme medal (with the Serbian motto 'My Right' under the threat of bayonets) will be sold for a minimum price of 0.25 [francs].

With regard to the badges, no special instructions need to be considered.

The same cannot be said for a second category of higher insignias, including:
1 A Lordonnois medal (recalling the decoration of the Order of the White Eagle in Serbia) bearing on one side the images of King Peter and Prince Alexander, popular because of their heroism, and on the other side all the Allied Nations' coats

Page 78 continued

Of arms: Minimum price: gilt bronze: 5 francs; silvered bronze: 3 francs; bronze: 2 francs.

2 Bargas medal, in the form of an orthodox cross, with one side bearing the coats of arms of France and Serbia; on the other side are engraved a woman fleeing the invaded and desolated homeland, while carrying the future, that is to say her child, under the protection of an old man who is also painfully leaving the homeland he will never see again. This medal will be sold for a minimum price of 1 franc.

3 Some Lalique lapel pins and brooches, [made] with great artistry, representing the brilliance of young Serbia holding in his hands the motto of the reigning dynasty "My first hope is in God". These jewels, few in number, can be released [sold] for:
The lapel pin minimum price of 2 francs
The brooch minimum price of 3 francs.

Right - Extract from the second page of the 'Renseignements' circular

It will not have escaped your notice M. Prefect that the category 2 insignias represent, in a sense, some value and it is impossible for me to place these into the hands of all collectors without taking some precautions to avoid a distribution not quantified with matching proceeds.

Here then is the system that is proposed by the executive committee which is simple, does not involve any formalities or any tedious obligations for the public.

Medals by Lordonnois and Bargas and the Lalique gems will not be entrusted except to some older [more experienced] collectors who will be accountable for carrying out their tasks.

Dockets comprising:
First column - List of insignias
Second column -Number of insignias allocated to each designated collector
Third column - Number of insignias issued at the end of the day
Fourth column - The corresponding amount retrieved from the sealed collecting box

It is crucial that the receipts at least match the number of insignias allocated and the minimum expected prices.
This practical system only requires a division between the large numbers of collectors selling the cardboard insignias and Prud'homme medals and the appointed collectors for the second category of insignias where perhaps the numbers are more restricted who can even install themselves at small fixed tables in places which are often frequented and at times when the crowds are particularly large.

Obviously all the collections will be placed in sacks which should be under your care and taken to the branches of the Bank of France. The Bank Governor has kindly opened a Serbia Day account and will take charge of all the responsibilities involved by this decision.

These precautions are taken so that the trillion coins are immediately put back into circulation.

It will be necessary to send the completed report mentioning the collection proceeds to 13 Rue Suger; which you will receive in due time.

Page 80
Le Petit Journal 22 June 1916 page 2
The 'JOURNÉE SERBE'
The medals that will be on sale.

After the Journée du 75, the Journée de la Ville de Paris, that of the Orphelinats des Armées, the Journée dés Réfugiés, the Journées du Poilu soon there will be the "Journée Serbe", under the auspices of the National Relief.

Several souvenirs will be offered on Sunday relying on the generosity of passers-by: a medal from Bargas, one from Prud'homme, a tie pin and a brooch from Lalique and finally a medal from Marcel Lordonnois, former student of the master engravers Ponscarme, Vernon and Mouchon. This is the one that we are reproducing today.

The composition of the two sides is very exciting. On the obverse of a medal stamped with the royal crown are the twin profiles of King Peter I and his son Alexander bordered with the eagles of Serbia and surmounting a cartouche, where we read their famous titles (in French and in Serbian) "defenders of Serbian freedom".

Page 80 continued

The forceful profile of King Peter is in the foreground. The support of the medal represents the white eagle of Serbia, in the heart of which stands out, in a garter, stamped with the royal crown, the inscription: "Glory to the intrepid Serbian heroes". The Gallic cockerel rears up on the escutcheons of the eight allies.

Very few Parisians will deprive themselves of this medal, which is approved by the King of Serbia.

The designer, who has been awarded by the Society of French Artists, is also a courageous child of Paris. After receiving two wounds at the first hostilities in Hirson and Reims, he was discharged and left behind the rifle for art.

Here are the minimum prices fixed for each of the medals (which will be put on sale from Sunday): Prud'homme medals: 0 fr. 25; Bargas: 1 fr. ; Lordonnois: 2 fr., 3 fr. or 5 fr depending on whether it is a bronzed, silver or gilt copy: Lalique: lapel pin, 2 fr. ; brooch 3 fr

Page 82
Journal Des Débats Politiques et Litéraires 23 June 1916
A medal of perfect taste and highly stylized, which is unsurprising since it is signed Lalique - released as a brooch or lapel pin, which illustrates the brilliance of Serbia deploying the motto of the ruling dynasty: 'Spes Mihi Prima Deus' completes this top category.

Finally, various appealing cardboard insignias in a series enriched by the variety and also by the careful attention given to the printing.

Here are the fixed minimum prices: Prud'homme medal, 0 fr. 25; Bargas, 1 fr.; Lordonnois, 2 fr., 3 fr. or 5fr. (depending on whether it is in bronze, silvered or gilded bronze) Lalique, lapel pin 2 fr .; brooch, 3 fr.

Page 85
Poster Guerre 1914-1915-1916 Journée Nationale des Orphelins
National Orphans Day - 1 and 2 November 1916. Men and women of France, it is for the children whose Fathers have fallen on the Field of Honour, it is for those innocent victims of a war imposed on France that we appeal to your hearts.

In these days devoted to thinking of the Dead, you will remember the sublime sacrifice of those who offered their lives to bar the road to the invaders, to defend your homes and yourselves, to save their Native Land and Civilization. Your emotional thoughts will go to those they have left without support: the women and children who weep. In making your contribution to 'National Orphans' Day' you will be thinking of your own children, the grief-stricken life that would be theirs if you were no longer there to ensure their daily bread and fortify them with your love.

Children of those who have nobly shed their blood in defence of our endangered country must be able to live; they have to be brought up as their fathers would have wished to bring them up themselves; the unity achieved in the struggle against the enemy must likewise be achieved for the protection of these little ones who are entitled to the affection and gratitude of all.

In order to save lives essential for the future of the French nation, to guarantee the little orphans of our soldiers the necessities of life, may the hearts of everyone be moved and understand the great duty of nation solidarity. Little boys and girls of France, for the children whose Daddies no longer exist, give what you can, give a little of your happiness, a little of your well-being and a lot of your soul. The War Orphans are your little brothers and sisters. Don't forget them.

The Day has been organized, in agreement with 'National Relief', by the attribution Committee set up to distribute the funds raised on the First Orphans' Day. The Committee includes representatives of every opinion, every creed, and every social background; among people of every opinion and every creed, it distributed millions raised from the First Orphans' Day to over 60,000 needy Orphans, through Charities that assumed moral responsibility for the task. The Committee: [a list of committee members follows] Gifts and donations must be addressed to the Head Office of the Committee, 33, Rue Bonaparte, Paris (6e).

Seen and approved: The Minister for the Interior, L.-J. Malvy [emblem including the words 'MARQUE SYNDICALE' ['Le Papier' Specialist in Posters].

Page 86
Le Matin 28 October 1916 Pages 1 and 2.
On November 1 and 2, on All Saints' Day and on the Day of the Dead, a national collection will be made for the children whose fathers have fallen, on the field of honour, for these innocent victims of a war that the aggression from the two

empires of central Europe imposed on civilized humanity. In these days dedicated to the worship of the dead, all French men and women will remember the sublime sacrifice of those who offered their lives to block the road to the invaders, to save the country and civilization.

Their hearts will fill with a feeling of loving and tender solidarity with the children of these heroes. Each will give all they can give, so that the children, of those who nobly shed their blood for the defence of our threatened country, may live and that they may be brought up as their fathers wanted to raise them themselves. All will want the union, achieved in the fight against the enemy, to be realized also for the protection of the war orphans. But the duty of the Committee, which will collect the funds, is to explain to the public what it is, what it does, how it proceeds, what guarantees of impartiality, efficiency, economy and method are offered for the distribution of the relief funds entrusted to it.

We remember that the First Orphan Day took place on June 25, 1915 and produced a net profit of 3,100,000 francs. To ensure the distribution of these funds, the Minister of the Interior, in a strong sense of impartiality and justice, asked the National Relief to unite the various works helping the orphans of war, with a view to help these children, regardless of religious beliefs or political opinions.

The National Relief responded to this call by helping to constitute, in its image, a Committee which includes twenty members representing all beliefs, all parties and all social backgrounds. This Committee, situated at 33 rue Bonaparte, took the title of Committee for the allocation of funds for the National Day of Orphans. It used the methods of the National Relief, taking as a basis for the distribution the orphans in need under the age of sixteen having lost their usual support because of the war. It helps the orphan through the works, with the reservation that each work must provide the guarantees of morality, proper behaviour and sound financial management which are essential everywhere, but which must be demanded with particular severity when it comes to the children who will form the France of the future.

When a request for help is made for an isolated child, the Committee Secretariat sends the family a list of supported works, from which they freely choose the one that suits their beliefs, opinions and social background.

In view of the large number of requests, the Committee had to limit the monthly subsidy to a maximum of 10 francs per child. The file of each child must contain a request for assistance signed by the person in charge of the child, proof of the death of the father or of the normal support due to the reality of war, a document giving the date of birth of the child, a declaration from the person in charge of the work establishing that an investigation has been made into the situation of the family, an investigation of which the spokesperson may request communication. Grant applications are submitted by this Committee for review to a responsible spokesperson, who verifies the children's records and the justification of expenses, who ensure the smooth performance of the work and presents a written and signed report to the Committee. As the work required by these reports has become very considerable, the Committee was joined by about twenty spokespersons representing the various groups.

To avoid duplication, personal files by families of orphans, are established by the applicant organization itself and are centralized at the Secretariat. This system worked during the eighteen months which separate us from the very first day with a regularity and an efficiency which helps all parties. The number of subsidized works to date is 111, the number of children exceeds 60,000. Relief was given throughout France.

Some of these works have their head office in the provinces; others have their head office in Paris but they nevertheless assist children in all the Departments: This is how the corporate and mutualist works - 43 in number - have received 1,390,000 francs. Among these works we will cite in particular:

l'Orphelinat' des chemins de fer français; l'Orphélinat des sous-agents des P. T. T; celui de la Fédération des tabacs; celui des employés de la Banque de France; la Fédération des amicales d'instituteurs et institutrices publics; la Saint-Cyriénne; l'Orphelinat de l'enseignement primaire de France et celui de l'enseignement secondaire; la Fédération du personnel des Douanes; la Caisse centrale mutualiste de la Franche-Comté ; la Fédération nationale des cooperatives; de consommation les Pupilles de l'école publique; l'Œuvre de la mairie de Lyon, etc.

Philanthropic works (religious or secular), numbering 688, received 1,975,000 francs. We will cite in particular:

l'Œuvre des orphelins de la mer; l'Aide aux veuves des militaires de la grande guerre; la société la Bretagne; l'Œuvre nationale de protection des femmes et enfants victimes de la guerre; l'Association nationale pour la protection des veuves et orphelins de la guerre; la Délégation générale des diaconats réformés; l'Action sociale de Seine-et-Oise; l'Union des familles françaises et alliées; l'Association nationale pour la protection des familles des morts pour la patrie; le Comité de bienfaisance israélite; Alliance catholique savoisienne; l'Orphelinat des armées

Page 86 continued

(sections de Paris. Nice, Rouen, le Havre, Bordeaux, Dieppe, Fécamp); les Pupilles corses; les Unions provincials (aveyronnaise et lozérienne), de l'Ouest, de Guyenne, de Bourgogne, de Lorraine, des dames limousines et creusoises de la Nièvre; la Compagnie des filles de la charité; l'Œuvre de l'assistance aux orphelins de la guerre; la Société dauphinoise de sauvetage de l'enfance; le Comité d'aide et d'assistance coloniale, etc.

Also the Committee is really a national committee of attribution, since all the works, of whatever department that they are, can obtain relief, as long as they send a request based on regularly established files.

The Committee is assisted, in its work, by the relief committee of the American Clearing House, which has been kind enough to be represented by two of its delegates and which has already paid in large grants. I take this opportunity to publicly express the thanks of the French orphans to the generous American donors, free citizens of a fellow Republic which has the same ideal of freedom and justice as our homeland.

Distribution of funds, which during the month of July 1915 was 35,000 francs, now amount to nearly 500,000 francs per month. The Committee's fund has been empty since 1 October. To avoid an interruption of aid, the Committee appealed to the National Relief which generously granted it an advance of 500,000 francs.

The Days of November 1 and 2 were therefore essential for the continuation of the subsidies.

Some previous Journées have multiplied the luxury items offered on the public streets which amount almost to jewellery sales. Experience has shown that this method has resulted in considerable expenses for the manufacturing of insignias and, for easily understandable reasons, in a marked decrease in the percentage of funds available for relief.

The committee returned to the true concept of a national day. It considered, as the Touring-Club had done for the 'Journée du 75' and the Secours national for the 'Journée Française' that the insignia is a souvenir of the day and not an object for sale; that everyone must give all they can - give without being attached to the market value of the insignia and that the day must be the day of the Orphans of the war and not that of the medal and jewel designers.

All the works which help orphans, unite in the appeal to kindness to generosity, to the recognition of the French, to the affection and to the pity of children who have the happiness and the joy of still having their parents. We are confident that this call will be heard. To save lives that are essential for the future of the French race, to ensure the needs of the little orphans of our soldier are met, it is necessary for everyone's heart to be moved and to understand the great duty of national solidarity.
P. Appell

Page 87
La Croix from 8 November 1917 page 7
The Accounts of 'Poilu Day'
The Soleil du Midi and Le Rappel have published the receipts and expenses of 'Poilu Day'. Really astonishing accounts:
They reveal that staff employed by the Committee consisting of a secretary, typist, and 6 - 12 employees and people performing difficult tasks from November 1915 through to September 1917 cost the cause the modest sum of 31,885 fr. 65, an average of 1386 francs per month.

The 'Day of the 75', for the same sort of thing (staff expenses) recorded an amount of 14,435 fr. 10. While the postage, packaging and transport for the 'Day of the 75' amounted to the total sum of 19,939 fr. 70, the 'Poilu Day' has costs for franking, shipping, charges, advice, dispatch of medal consignments with subscription letters, mail postage etc., etc., etc... 59, 346 fr. 10

Can you send the medals and the insignias for that?

On top of that, if you do not mind, to get an idea on the topic, did you know that postage costs for its objects (jewels) amounted to: 424,811 fr. 60

That M. Bargas (Son) provisioned for medals 196, 459 fr. 90 and that M. Bargas (Father) has received (since the Day ????) 321,452 fr. 20 for a similar supply. Lucky Bargas family who bank 517,912 fr. 1 for one single deal!!!

This, along with Lalique's invoice, reveals to us that the 'Poilu Day' dispensed 942, 723 fr. 90 for medals and jewels.

We would be curious, incidentally, to know the address of this great Bargas house, father and son, that we searched for in the Directory.

Extract from Le Petit Parisien 5 February 1917 Page 2
Tuberculosis Day

Once more Paris has witnessed the charming army of gracious insignia sellers. Despite the inclement and icy weather, as was to be expected, Tuberculosis Day took large collections in all Parisian districts. The hearts of Parisians which never tire in expressing generosity for all the victims and miseries of war, could not remain indifferent to the request for the benefit of those poor unfortunate sons of France: no less glorious in the great struggle, the hidden injuries of those suffering from tuberculosis.

Throughout Paris, in grey fog and the chilly morning, young collectors whose courageous efforts were totally undeterred by the chill wind, approached the passers-by shopping for the insignias of the day, medals made of cardboard or in silver, tied in national colours. In the Underground, on tramways, on streets, around stations, squares and the churches, everywhere, young women and children collected for the whole day for the tuberculosis sufferers and everywhere they were given a warm welcome.

In Seine-et-Oise, due to the freeze, the Prefect M. Autrand, authorised the Department Mayors to delay the collections to a future date.

Extract from Le Petit Parisien 5 March 1917

Tuberculosis Day
Tuberculosis Day, which had not been possible to hold due to the great freeze of last month, had been postponed to yesterday - Sunday. The day was graced with splendid weather. The zeal shown by the young girls and women who devoted themselves to this pious and humane cause was rewarded by the good heartedness of Parisians.

Page 98
Left - Le Gaulois (2 February 1917) page 3
4th February - Next Sunday - Throughout France
We are collecting on behalf of ex-service personnel inflicted with tuberculosis
Give your donation
By saving them you preserve the people from contagion.

Top right - Excelsior (dated Friday 2 February 1917) page 6
Snow and ice impeded movement in Paris.
Although yesterday's temperature relented a little bit, the snow that fell nearly everywhere did not melt and, in Paris, ice really hampered circulation:
1. Cars stopped and swerved off the great Boulevards;
2. A horse just fallen on the roadside;
3. A scene repeated hundreds of times in the morning;
4. A coachman on foot leading his loaded cab/carriage;
5. Many horses had their hooves covered with cloths.

Page 99
Extract from an article from Le Temps 2 February 1917
The Relief Effort - The insignias for the 'Tuberculosis Day'
The central committee for the support of ex-service personnel inflicted with tuberculosis, under the chairmanship of M. Léon Bourgeois, decided that the following insignia will be offered to the public on 'Tuberculosis Day' which will be held on 4 February.
Lalique brooch or pendant, offered for the price of 3 francs;
Lalique lapel pins for the price of 2 francs;
a tricolour bow tied to a lozenge shaped medal for the price of 1 franc;
a small envelope containing a selection of insignias for the price of 2 francs. Note that many of these envelopes contain a free voucher for an additional artistic insignia;
some stamped brass medals for the price of 0 fr. 50;
cardboard insignias which are [miniature] reproductions of the Lucien Levy-Dhurmer and Abel Faivre posters for the price of 0 fr. 20;
some less artistic cardboard insignias for the price of 0 fr. 20;

autographs of famous men or of leading personalities associated with the tuberculosis cause. These autographs will be sold starting from 0 fr. 50.

Page 106
Extract from an article from Le Temps 1 February 1917 page 4
The 'Day of support for ex-service personnel inflicted with tuberculosis'.

We have received the following communication from the National Relief Committee.

Our Collectors, whose dedication, enthusiasm and good grace cannot be praised enough, will in several days time, be presenting insignias to the public for the 'Day of support for ex-service personnel inflicted with tuberculosis'.

These insignias will comprise of brooches, lapel pins, some pendants / charms and stamped medals bearing a very strong artistic element based on the Lalique brand. Unfortunately, these insignias are few in number because of shortages in the supply of metal due to war demands. Other varied insignias of a good appearance but less valuable, some of which are designed by Abel Faivre and Lévy-Dhurmer, will complete this collection.

Please give a large donation in the traditional collecting box, as our generosity must serve to restore the health of the valiant disabled soldiers.

Page 110
Le Devoir Social letter, addressed 'Aux Français'
Dear fellow citizens
Among the works that the spirit of solidarity gave birth to during the war, there is one that deserves the benevolence of all French people: it is Le Devoir Social.

The purpose of Le Devoir Social is to reconstruct destroyed homes. This is a task that needs everyone's help.

Le Devoir Social does not intend to substitute its action with that of the State nor to solicit from private initiatives an effort of integral reparation which must above all be a national act; it proposes to attend to the most urgent needs, to immediately relieve the heart breaking distresses of the unfortunate families driven from their country and wandering through France.

According to its resources, Le Devoir Social makes available to refugee families:
furniture with bedding; clothes for children; layettes for young mothers, etc. It thus allows families to group together and rebuild a home. Help [Le Devoir Social] in this mending mission.

Le Devoir Social obtained the support of all the major groups with the very highest patronage. The various mutualist federations, the large organizations of railway workers and postal workers, have given it their precious support.

Le Devoir Social organizes conferences and creates committees in the main towns. It radiates all over France and spreads its propaganda abroad.

The members of the board of the steering committee travel to the main centres; there they make known the work to the general public, an appeal that we cannot encourage too much.

We associate ourselves with the work of Le Devoir Social by offering generous donations or cash payments.

We were confident that all French people will want, according to their means, to participate in this work which is, at the same time as an act of legitimate reparation, a great event of French fraternity and solidarity.

Page 113
'Carte de Sociétaire' for Le Devoir Social dating from 1915
Le Devoir Social Art 3 - The aim of the Society is to come to the aid, within the limits of its resources, to the inhabitants of France and Allied countries, including the Alsatians-Lorrainers, who had to suffer from the invasion.

To reconstitute the destroyed homes with a view to the resumption of family life.

To repair the damage caused by the war to both individuals and communities and to revive as quickly as possible, the recovery in devastated areas.

Page 113 continued

Decision of the General Assembly of March 25, 1915
Each card bears a number, which will be used to designate by drawing lots, those Members called to participate in the great Congress which will be organized in Paris by Le Devoir Social. Travel and subsistence expenses will be borne by the Association. The date of this great Congress will be fixed later. It will coincide with the victory celebrations, which will probably be given by the Allies after the signing of peace.

Page 113 bottom right
Le Devoir Certificate
To Its Colleagues
Homage of Gratitude to M........
To the French
We are confident that all French people will want, according to their means, to participate in this work which is at the same time an act of legitimate reparation, the highest statement of the French fellowship and solidarity.
Honorary President Paul Deschanel Extract from his letter of January 23, 1917

Page 115
Le Figaro 11 June 1917 page 2
La Journée de l'armée d'Afrique et des Troupes Coloniales

The 'Day' of the African and Colonial troops - which is now almost the same thing, since we have incorporated into our Colonial regiments many soldiers of colour - despite dubious weather, received a most favourable response. Insignias were eight in number, representing the various types of our Colonial army - infantry, African hunters, Spahis, Algerian and Moroccan riflemen, Sudanese and Annamese. Passers-by had a choice, but many took the full set.

At the same time the collectors - young girls and adolescent girls and some boys - offered the raffle tickets (at the price of 50 centimes) authorized for the same purpose by the Minister of the Interior and for which lots representing a value of 300,000 francs are deposited with the Crédit Foncier.

Page 120
Henry de Waroquier Poster Journée de l'Armée d'Afrique et des Troupes Coloniales
DAY ORGANIZED ON THE GOVERNMENT'S INITIATIVE FOR THE BENEFIT OF THE WORKS OF ASSISTANCE OF THE AFRICAN ARMY AND THE COLONIAL TROOPS JUNE 10, 1917
On the everlasting unforgettable day of the mobilization, while the cannon and the sound of bells called to arms all French to the Nation's defence, the troops of North Africa, West and East Africa, Madagascar and Reunion, Indo-China, the West Indies and Guyana, Tahiti and New Caledonia, exalted by the purest and most ardent patriotism, rushed to the holiest of causes. The defence of the greatest thing in the world, as the illustrious Gambetta had proclaimed, immortal France. Zouaves, Algerian, Tunisian and Moroccan riflemen, African hunters, colonial troops, Senegalese, Malagasy and Somali riflemen, soldiers from the Atlantic Ocean, the Indian Ocean, the China and the Pacific Seas, all worthy emulators of their illustrious predecessors and whose incomparable bravery has become legendary, wished to prove before the World that having received the benefits of freedom and civilization from French hands , they wanted to be victorious or die ahead and alongside of their older brothers.

In a hundred battles, they asserted their courage and heroism: on the Marne, Yser, in Picardy, in Artois, in Champagne, in Verdun, in Douaumont, in Vaux, on the Somme, on the Aisne, in the Orient. Nothing could stop their irresistible momentum.

The great dead of yesteryear, the Zouaves and Turcos of Alma and Inkermann, Magenta, Solferino, Reichshoffen, the African Hunters of the sublime rush of Sedan, the Colonials of Bazeilles, the brilliant battalions of Senegalese Tirailleurs and the Foreign Legion, who in thousands of battles have secured the magnificent colonial empire of France, all stand up before the heroes of the Great War and cry to them - 'You too have deserved well of the Nation. Thank you.'

The Government of the Republic considered it a duty to ask France and its Colonies to award these incomparable soldiers the homage of its admiration and recognition. The Committee, formed to organize a Day in Favour of the Works of Colonial Assistance, sends a warm appeal to all French people, to all Colonials, to all foreigners who are friends of France. May the mothers, the widows, the children of the heroes who have fallen and the families of the heroes who continue the great battle know that generous France will guard them forever and her love and gratitude.
[a list of committee members follows] H. de WAROQUIER 1917 CRÉTÉ Imp. 2, Rue des Italiens.

Page 124
Le Devoir Certificate
To Its Subscribers
'Souvenir of Recognition' to M ……
Extract from the letter written by the President of the Chamber of Deputies for Le Devoir Social on January 23, 1917
To the French
We are confident that all French people will want, according to their means, to participate in this work which is at the same time an act of legitimate reparation, a high manifestation of the French Fellowship and Solidarity.

Page 126
Le Devoir Certificate - The Social Duty for the Reconstitution of Homes Destroyed by War
To Its Subscribers
'Souvenir of Recognition' to M...
The dawn of entitlement illuminates our French schools.
The children too felt the infinite misery of the great drama, the pain enhanced their souls.
Their burning love will dry up the tears well
Honorary President Paul Deschanel
The President Mayor of the XIe Arrondissement of Paris

Page 135
THE FIFTEEN HUNDRED THOUSAND FAMILIES OF THE DEAD / Will receive on November 2 / The Diploma of "RECOGNITION" / A National Subscription
The Union of Grandes Associations Françaises, chaired by Paul Deschanel, launches a large public subscription to finance the printing of 15,000 "Diplomas of National Recognition", which will be solemnly awarded on November 2, 1919 in each commune of France, to the families and orphans of soldiers who died for the Nation.

Page 138
Journal Officiel de la République Française (Lois et Décrets) No 291 page 2 26 October 1919

LAW on the commemoration and glorification of the dead for France during the Great War

Art 6 - Every year, on November 1st or 2nd, a ceremony will be dedicated in each commune to the memory and to the glorification of the heroes who died for the homeland. It will be organized by the municipality with the help of the civil and military authorities.

Page 143
National Day 14 July
Transfer to 'Les Invalides' of the ashes of Rouget de L'Isle, the author of 'La Marseillaise'.

The Government has decided solemnly to transfer to 'Les Invalides' the ashes of Rouget de L'Isle.

The ceremony will take place on Wednesday 14 July. The remains of the immortal author of 'La Marseillaise', brought from Choisy-le-Roi, will be placed on a gun carriage from the wars of the First Republic and will depart at 10 a.m. from the 'Arc de Triomphe' at the Étoile, preceded by cavalry troops from the Paris garrison.

The President of the Republic, Members of the Government, the administration and members of the Senate, the Chamber of Deputies, the Prefect for Seine, the Police Commissioner, the General Secretaries, the departments and members of the City Council of Paris and the districts of the Seine department, officers and soldiers in uniform, and delegations from corporate bodies will go to the 'Arc de Triomphe' and will accompany it to 'Les Invalides', where a military parade will take place, following which the President of the Republic will make a speech.

The diplomatic corps will be present at the ceremony.

Parisians will be admitted to file past the remains of Rouget de L'Isle until 5 p.m. Official persons will gain access to 'Les Invalides' from Place Vauban, at 10 a.m., on presentation of their credentials. Military preparation societies, veterans, various associations and children from the schools of the City of Paris, will be positioned at 'Les Invalides' and will be allowed in through the door in the Court of Honour, from 8.30 to 9.45. Marcel Picard, Printers [address].

Page 144
Le Petit Journal dated 15 July 1915 page 2
The 'Journée de Paris'

It was another success, there was not an overabundance of collectors. The 9th arrondissement alone had mobilized 600 young girls each more pleasant, more eager and more conscientious than the last. Also, at 10 o'clock in the morning, the Drouot Town Hall, saw the return of collectors who had to empty their collection boxes and renew their supply of insignias, to scatter again through the streets and boulevards to attract the contents of purses.

Job done! These "days" which are becoming normal, have accustomed collectors and public alike to their reciprocal duties. There is less shyness in everyone and traditions are now established.

Thus, it is no longer appropriate to have only one or two insignias on the buttonhole or on the blouse. It takes at least half a dozen, and even more. Who doesn't have their insignia? But the corner commissioner, the duty officer, the apprentice pastry chef, were the first to have it.

Some collectors also reported - boy scouts, young people and others - did not have enough for their clientele. It was one of our glorious wounded, with an amputated arm, who was collecting with his young wife. The friendly couple was surrounded. He made a fabulous collection. Also to be noted are charming and gracious Alsatians, and three young girls who dressed - one in blue, the other in white, the third in red - formed a living flag.

At Hailes, the receipts must have been fabulous. Not only did everyone pour money into the innumerable trunks but merchants took insignias in packages because they had commissions from their neighbours who had remained in the suburbs and who wanted to participate anyway in the 'Paris Day'.

Le Cri de Paris 18 July 1915 pages 10-11
Journée de Paris

Moreover, the insignias sold by the collectors during this day in Paris, the small enamelled badges in the colours of the City, were regrettably insignificant. Without doubt, there was indeed the reproduction of the medal of Rouget de L'Isle by David d'Angers, struck for the occasion. But David d'Angers is long dead and buried. Why not ask a modern sculptor for a plaque?

For previous charity days, we relied on masters like Hippolyte Lefèbvre and René Lalique to design beautiful medals. They executed small masterpieces that collectors have carefully kept. Was it so difficult to still speak to some of our best artists? We have no shortage of them.

We are even convinced that if on these occasions bronze or silver [items] were sold for five or ten francs, they would sell like hot cakes.

In truth, as it was the City of Paris which this time organized the day, it may have been advised not to employ artists. As usual, she had certainly chosen the worst.

Page 147
A letter dated 29 June 1915
Sir

The Prefectoral Administration having entrusted the Municipality and its colleagues with the mission of organizing the July 14th Paris Day, we appeal again to your dedication and your patriotism, asking you to attend the meeting which will have held at the Town Hall 'Salle de Mariages' on Friday July 2 at 4 am. Please accept Mr.

Expression of my best wishes - The Mayor of IVe arrondissement

Page 148
'Appel à la Population'
Paris Day July 14, 1915

Appeal to the Population

This year July 14 will be Paris Day: we invite you to celebrate the National Day by helping our Soldiers.

On this day, the sisters, daughters and brides of those who heroically defend the Nation will ask for your donation for the 'Œuvres de Guerre de l'Office Departemental': Paris and the Department will honour this appeal.

Send goods or food to our soldiers on the front, to our wounded in hospitals, to our prisoners in camps abroad, to supply the trains that transport the wounded, to help the mutilated and amputees, to get essential goods to our defenders and those unfortunate people who the invader has driven from their homes. This is the noble mission that the Municipal

Page 148 continued

Council of Paris and the General Council of the Seine have entrusted to the Departmental Office and that it intends to achieve with your assistance.

All hearts on this patriotic day, will want to adorn themselves with the municipal badge.
Paris owes its salvation to the national army: it will spare no effort to acknowledge it.

Adrien Mithouard (President of the Municipal Council)
Marcel Delanney (Prefect of the Seine)
Emile Laurent (Prefect of the Police)
Paris (President of the General Council)

Page 150
Le Figaro 15 July 1916 page 2
Paris Day

Paris Day, organized by the City Council of Paris and the General Council of the Seine for the benefit of the war works of the Town Hall, obtained a success comparable to that of the previous 'days' if not greater.

The emblems were very well chosen. One can cite in particular small vignettes with the arms of Paris, the very tasteful medal of Maillard with the profile of General Gallieni, carrying on the reverse this inscription: Paris 1914-1916 - Until the end, followed by the facsimile of the signature of the former governor of Paris. Many of the good natured collectors had run out of items before noon.

Nevertheless, the Minister of the Interior had with reasons authorized the City Council to continue today and Sunday the sale of the insignias for the Day of Paris.

Page 154
'Appel À La Population'
Paris Day July 14, 1916

Appeal to the Population

This year, like last year, we invite you to celebrate the national holiday by coming to the aid of our soldiers.

The Parisian population knows what it owes to the armies which defended it against the invader. The war works of the Town Hall are its adopted works.

Assisting the Fighters, the Wounded, the Mutilated and the Prisoners and the Refugees, is a task to which all will eagerly wish to contribute.

All of you will be honoured to wear the Medals and Badges which will be put on sale on July 14th.

The vigilance of our soldiers is limitless. The generosity of Parisians will be inexhaustible.

Adrien Mithouard (President of the Municipal Council)
Marcel Delanney (Prefect of the Seine)
Emile Laurent (Prefect of the Police)
Henri Rousselle (President of the General Council)

Page 158
Le Matin 8 July 1917 page 2
Paris Day
The Departmental Office for War Works at the Hôtel de Ville was authorized, as in 1915 and 1916, to organize a Paris Day on the national holiday. The Departmental Office will sell on July 14:

Two medals, one which evokes the features of Washington and La Fayette, the other which represents the City of Paris welcoming a wounded soldier.

Three colour insignias reproducing:
1 the double effigy of Washington and LaFayette;
2 the Statue of Liberty enlightening the world;
3 the Town Hall of the City of Paris and the flags of the allied nations.

Le Petit Parisien dated 14 July 1917 Front page
Paris day
If we stick to the first results, the Paris Day promises to be very fruitful.

From yesterday, many collectors and many young girls walked the streets of Paris, offering passers by artistic medals and insignias, sold for the benefit of works of war.

Page 159
1917 'Appel À La Population'
Paris Day July 14, 1917

Appeal to the population

We invite you, as in 1915 and 1916, to celebrate the National Day, by helping our soldiers.

For three years, thanks to public generosity, we have been able to provide uninterrupted assistance to our Wounded, our Mutilated, our Refugees, our Prisoners and our Combatants. The Town Hall War Works have been adopted by the population; it will not abandon those it has cared for.

When the collectors present you with the insignias and medals of Paris Day, you will remember that the security of the City and of the Department rests on the toils and bravery of our soldiers.

Show your gratitude.

Adrien Mithouard, (President of the Municipal Council)
Marcel Delanney (Prefet of the Seine)
Louis Hudelo (Prefect of the Police)
Emile Deslandres (President of the General Council)

Page 161
Journal de Rouen dated 4 December page 2
The Day of the Chrysanthemum
Sunday 5 December 1915

We have been asked to make known that the four commissioners responsible for ensuring the sound administration of the sale and guiding the street collectors will be Messrs Falkenstein, Henri Lebourg, Schlumberger, General Relief and Assistance Commission members and Dufayel, assistant to the Organizing Committee.

The Saint-Godard and Saint-Joseph sector, managed by Ms. L Fichet, will have two offices: one at No 14 rue Dulong and the other at Ms. Leon Louvet, No 4 rue de Pleins-Champs.

Chrysanthemum Day which is being prepared for tomorrow for the benefit of the General Commission for Assistance and Relief of the City of Rouen will include, like the other 'Journées', the sale of several small insignias and trinkets, very artistic and very curious souvenirs of this day dedicated to relieving the miseries of the City of Rouen.

First, the Chrysanthemum will appear there, the flower of painful mourning, the flower of winter - which gave its name to this day - It will appear there in the most diverse, unforeseen and most charming forms.

First in silver metal, as a pin or brooch, adorned with the delicately imitated and chiselled petals of the flower so dear to the Japanese. Then, a second model provided by Maison Nee, will be formed by a whole series of small artificial flowers, great copies of nature's corollas and foliage and passing through the infinite ranges of colours, tints and shades, from the crimson reds, deep purples to the softest pinks and brightest yellows.

We can certainly choose from this varied collection, 100,000 copies of which have been reserved for this popular 'Journée'. Finally a third model, in painted cardboard, will represent, in a more modest way, the chrysanthemum flower, drawn in several shades and suspended from a pretty tricolour ribbon.

The organizers of Chrysanthemum Day have not forgotten on the other hand, that it was especially reserved, after so many others for the City of Rouen. So they were well inspired, by reproducing, in reduced form, the old 'leopard seal' of our ancient City which dates from 1262 and which was struck from the original silver mould preserved in the collection of our fellow citizen M Georges Lormier, and about which we will have to speak again.

Page 161 continued

20,000 copies of this ancient seal have been ordered for the commune of Rouen, including 16,000 in pins and the rest in brooches, either in silver metal or in gilded metal. It will be a very artistic memory, very old and very......... Rouen - that everyone will want to have.

No less 'Rouennaise', will also be the reproductions in silver or gilded lapel pins of the Rouen sheep or lamb, holding the traditional banner of the City between its hooves just as it is portrayed in the municipal coat of arms.

Finally our fellow citizens will still be able to choose these delicate charms which are so fashionable today. Under glass, there will be Joan of Arc fighting in the form of the beautiful statue of Fremiet, or the Talisman of the Allies, a silk embroidery formed by the flags of all the nations fighting with France for the 'Right' and 'Freedom'. This double charm can easily be transformed into a photo holder or a lucky charm.

Drawn in large numbers, all these trinkets are recommended for their originality and their great French taste. Our fellow citizens, whose generosity is tireless, will therefore have only the choice between all these charming models. To avoid embarrassment, they will want to have them all, knowing that they will help fulfil a duty of assistance towards the poor, the humble and the unfortunate, always so numerous in a large city - G.D.

The prices of the items are fixed as follows:
Chrysanthemums made of cardboard 10 c, Artificial chrysanthemums 25 c, the Rouen lamb, gilded or silvered 25 c, City Seals of Rouen in brooches or pins 50c, Chrysanthemums in metal 1 fr, medallion of Joan of Arc 1 fr; medallion of the Allies 1 fr.

These are the minimum prices that can be exceeded through the generosity of buyers. The sale of the items will begin today at noon in the administrations and particular houses.

Page 162
Letter - Prix de Vente
Sale Prices

Chrysanthemums made of cardboard minimum price	10 c
Artificial chrysanthemums minimum price	25 c
Rouen lamb, gilded or silvered minimum price	25 c
City Seals of Rouen in brooches or pins minimum price	50c
Chrysanthemums in metal minimum price	1 fr
Medallion of Joan of Arc minimum price	1 fr
Medallion of the Allies minimum price	1 fr

It is expressly forbidden to sell these below the minimum pricing.

Furthermore the collectors are expected to abide by the following instructions:
I.   The sale will begin at midday but only in the administration and particular Houses of each sector and not on the public streets where authorization has only been granted for the Sunday.
II.   On Sunday morning, please follow exactly the instructions given by those women in charge of the particular sectors and do not sell, under any circumstances, beyond the sector limits (boundaries).
III.   From midday the sales can roll out across the entire City but the collectors are urged not to completely abandon their sectors and to undertake regular rounds, so that quirky neighbourhoods are not abandoned (overlooked) whereas those in the City centre could be swamped with too many collectors.
IV.   It is crucial that the collectors have small change on them.
V.   The collectors should replenish their supplies only from those in charge of their sector. It is forbidden to use any part of the collection money to buy items and then resell them - the number of items ordered for the sales are quite sufficient to ensure to ensure a desirable result.

The Organizing Committee would like to thank all the collectors very much for their precious assistance and excellent support. We have confidence in their dedication that the outcome of the Day will help relieve the awful miseries that are inflicting thousands of the elderly, women and children - indirect victims of the war.

Page 165
Le Figaro 10 May page 2
PRESS RELEASES

A fundraiser by the *Ligue des enfants de France* (Fraternal League of the Children of France), founded by Ms. Lucie Félix Faure-Goyau, and including Ms. Raymond Poincaré who is the Honorary President, has been authorized to undertake a collection in all teaching establishments which, started the day before yesterday and will continue until May 14.

The work is addressed to the benevolence of happy children asking them to come to the help of others - the unfortunate children in the invaded Departments.

By granting permission for the day in educational establishments, the Minister of Public Education indicated that he approved of the patriotic and humanitarian thought which inspired the *Ligue des enfants de France.*

The teachers will certainly want to be involved, in their turn, with the initiative of the league, by collecting the largest amounts of money possible in their classes, thanks to which the little children disrupted by the war can be brought back from the invaded departments and placed in a safe environment.

The collection takes place mainly in the form of sales of postcards, specially edited, and for which the minimum price is fixed.

The League's Head Office is 50, rue Saint-André-des-Arts, and is happy to provide teachers with further information.

Page 167
Le Figaro 22 September 1916 page 3.
We remind our readers that the 'Journée au profit de l'Œuvre des meubles pour les foyers dévastés' will take place in Versailles next Sunday, September 24th.

We hope that this sale will be very successful and will allow us to provide ample support to the needs of this eminently useful fundraising work.

Page 169
Le Petit Parisien 22 December page 3
Artists' Day

The Minister of the Interior has just authorized the 'Artists' Day'. It is organized by the Association of Dramatic Artists, the Mutual Aid Society of Lyrical Artists, the Pont-aux-Dames Retirement Home, the Theatre Providers, the Ris-Orangis Retirement Home and the Association of Theatre Directors, for the benefit of their respective funds and their orphans.

During the performances of next Sunday and Christmas Day, the artists of our theatres, concerts, music halls, circuses and cinemas will sell to the public of these establishments the insignia of this ' Day' .

The revenue, centralized by the representatives of the associations, will be sent to the central cashier of 'Artists' Day'.

Page 175
Speech delivered on November 17, 1918, Place de la Concorde, at the National Demonstration in Honour of Alsace-Lorraine by Mr. Raymond Poincare, President of the French Republic
The thousands of French people who prepared this grandiose event had, at first, only the pious thought of placing at the foot of the statue of Strasbourg the offering of their vows and their fidelity. The victory came to enrich their programme with a magnificent complement and to allow them to glorify in the triumph of France, the return of Lorraine and Alsace to the maternal hearth.

If ever our heart has felt regret at not being able to slow down the course of time, to taste at leisure the noblest joys which are offered to human beings, is it not in these hours of harmony and national pride, where the nation, so long mutilated, is rising and reconstituting itself? Since we are not masters of stopping and fixing these divine minutes, let us at least promise to keep the memory of them immaculate and to bequeath it, like an inestimable treasure, to eternal France.

For forty-eight years our inconsolable sorrow has decorated this statue of sorrow and captivity with funeral wreaths. We could not, both of us, pass under the motionless eyes of this dear silent veiled figure, without seeing there the symbol of firmness in servitude and without feeling, deep within ourselves, a secret humiliation of our defeat and a lingering remorse for our inaction.

Page 175 continued

None of us, however, as the whole country attests, none of us would have wanted even to wash away the past and avenge oppressed law, to take responsibility for a gesture or a word that would have risked igniting in the world, the first fires of a deadly war.

We awaited, in silence and resignation, the awakening of sleeping justice. It was Germany itself who, believing it to be dying and dreaming of betraying it, involuntarily snatched it from its long sleep. It was Germany who, with its own hands, clarified the monstrous treaty which it had imposed on us by violence and which submitted to the domination of abroad an inalienable part of France.

The war declared on us, which ended such an odious series of provocations and challenges, has finally freed us from the constraint to which our love of peace and our horror of shed blood subjected us. From the day when the thieves of our provinces undertook an unapologetic aggression on us, we had the right and duty to claim the totality of the national heritage that the force had fragmented.

In the memorable meeting of 4 August 1914, the French Chambers, patriotically grouped around the Government of the Republic, took the solemn undertaking not to lay down their arms before Alsace and Lorraine had been returned to France. They kept their word. For more than four years, the army and the country have lived in the continuity of the struggle and the suffering; for more than four years, they have known the most painful alternatives of disappointment and hope and for more than four years, the nation, determined to conquer, saw, without complaint and without discouragement, the flower of its youth plucked by death; nothing relaxed its effort, nothing broke its will.

This persevering energy is finally rewarded. Alsace and Lorraine have become French again. Germany is forced before the signing of peace, to call on us to protect its retreating army against the hostility of the inhabitants. Yes, there it is reduced to inflicting this cruel denial. The day before yesterday, it proclaimed that the Alsatian populations, docile to the Germanic conquest, did not intend to be separated from what was still called the Empire; yesterday, in a cry of frankness and distress, Germany begged us to save its troops: "Alsace is hunting me," it said, "it wants to beat me, please hold our hands."

Alsace and Lorraine have become French again. How sweet to repeat these dream words which are now the words of reality.

Soon, France will offer Lorraine and Alsace its enthusiastic congratulations. What an emotion for all of us who, for nearly fifty years, have been waiting bruised by the memories of the other war for this day of glory and resurrection. What an emotion for the President of the Council who has worked with so much ardour and foresight, with so much faith and so much success, to the liberation of our captive provinces!

Alsace and Lorraine have become French again. Most of the heroes who just died for them had not known them. They were not, like some of us, their neighbours or relatives; they had not spent their childhood cradled by their gifted songs; they had not kept in their eyes the unobtrusive vision of their blue mountains and their wide plains. And yet, they set out to deliver the two captive provinces and to return them to France, which had not forgotten them. They understood that they were necessary for the national balance and that, since the day they were taken from us, the homeland had lacked a piece of its flesh and a spark of its soul.

Alsace and Lorraine have become French again. They have become so again in their own right because of the geography which placed them both within the confines of old Gaul - due to the history which, under the old monarchy, fused them with France, through history, which consecrated this voluntary merger on July 14, 1790, to the feasts of the Federation and which increased the French glory from all the glory gained in past centuries, by scholars and the soldiers of Alsace and Lorraine.

They have become so again as of right, by the brilliant protest that their representatives read at the National Assembly of Bordeaux, by the unanimous re-election of the protesting Deputies after the kidnapping and annexation, by the courageous declaration that was brought to the Reichstag in 1874 by the representatives of Alsace-Lorraine, by the will of those of the children of the country who had the sadness to leave their invaded homes, by the will of those who remained there to protect French traditions, in the secrecy of families and jealously maintain the holy flame of memory.

To justify the return of Lorraine and Alsace to France, it is only necessary to recall these centuries of common glory, followed by these heavy years of shared pain. A plebiscite would add nothing to the eloquence of the facts. A plebiscite would be an illusion since it could not call for a decision on all those Alsatians and Lorrainers who were dispersed by the Treaty of Frankfurt. A plebiscite would be a denial of justice, since it would subordinate to a new consultation, the

freedoms that the populations had long enjoyed, before the violence of which they were victims and the rights that the enemy could well have taken from them for a time but which were and have remained inalienable.

Pure and simple restitution, this is what the repair of the past requires, this is what the universal conscience demands, this is what, apart from the necessary restorations and guarantees, irrevocably assures us the victory of our arms.

On this day when it is finally given to the French family to celebrate their unbreakable unity, let us pay tribute to all those who have worked to raise from its ruins the collapsed wing of our parental home.

Honour to our armies of land and sea, which, after having defended and saved France, reduced the disconcerted enemy to soliciting armistice and peace; to that brilliant cluster of military leaders who, by making themselves loved by their men, have obtained from them so many wonders; to our soldiers and, since this term has happily entered the language, to our Poilus to this glorious personification of the most beautiful hereditary virtues of the French race, to this multitude of anonymous heroes who, for so long, under the sun and under the rain, in the dust and in the mud, opposed the furious assaults of the enemy with their inflexible vigour and their tireless tenacity!

Honour to the nations and to the allied armies who all rivalled ours in endurance and bravery and who all deserve to be joyful, after having also been so sorrowful! Honour to these innumerable legions of victors, forever united by friendship; to these armed peoples who fought side by side for a common ideal and who tomorrow will collect together, in peace, the fruit of this prolonged comradeship!

We will soon see them, these incomparable soldiers of the Great War, following in Paris the very path that the long procession of demonstrators has just taken today. We will see them pass, in a light of apotheosis, under the Arc de Triomphe de l'Étoile, and descend in their rhythmic steps from the Étoile to erase the stain once left on our Champs-Elysées by the arrogant parade of enemy battalions.

Honour to the French Parliament, which, in laborious, almost permanent sessions, effectively assisted the government of the Republic in the progressive organization of National Defence.

Honour to Paris, which in the nights when the siren moaned, in the dark days when the assassins' shells suddenly came to surprise the playing children, the women in their work or in their prayers, the old men in the rest of the shelters, has kept its calm, its confidence and its serenity! How many times have I then had the painful duty of saluting the dead and visiting its wounded? I have felt its heart beating very closely; the movement was neither activated nor slowed down, the rhythm was not disturbed.

Honour to the entire people of France, who responded with such eagerness to the call for union that I addressed to them on the first day of the war, to the old peasants, to the women, to the young people, who added to the miracles of energy, miracles of patience, which ploughed, sowed, reaped, to feed the combatants; to workers who melted cannons, loaded shells, armed planes, created, developed, improved over four years, this formidable tool which was the essential instrument of victory; to officials of the Republic, to mayors, to municipalities, who have good administration, the tranquillity and the supply of the country; to the teachers, who put before the eyes of the children the imperishable lessons of selflessness and patriotism offered by war to the eternal admiration of the human spirit; to prelates, priests and to the leaders of all religions, who came together closely around the altar of the nation and who called on one God for the salvation of France and for the rest of her dead.

Honour to our colonies who have competed in devotion to the metropolis and who, from all parts of the world, have sent thousands of workers to our factories and soldiers to our armies.

Honour to the mothers who will no longer embrace their daughters, to the women who seek their husbands' graves on the battlefields, to the orphans who have become the adopted children of France. But above all, honour to those who are no longer, to those who have fallen in the bloody furrows, in the overwhelmed trenches, in the depths of the seas and whose closed eyes will not have seen coming the dawn of victory and the light of peace. Honour to the most modest, the most obscure, the most unknown among them. There is not a single one whose death did not help in the resurrection of France and the liberation of humanity. Their bodies, torn by projectiles, lie in the devastated regions where the fate of the world has been decided; but their sacred image will remain intact in the depths of our hearts. From now on they will be our inspiration; it is they who will remind us tomorrow, in our peaceful labour, what harvest of glory and soon of national strength and prosperity, has been able to raise, in a few years, under the French sun, the spirit of sacrifice and self-sacrifice.

HONOUR TO THE DEAD, IMMORTAL ADVISERS OF THE LIVING.

Excelsior copy from 18 November Front page
The huge crowd assembled at La Place de la Concorde has just broken through the barriers of the Service
Only this desired event, awaited for so many years could cause such a grandiose demonstration as that which took place yesterday. From the Arc de Triomphe to the Place de la Concorde 700 groups comprising of 150,000 participants marched in the midst of ovations. Another ceremony, no less grandiose, had taken place in the morning at Notre-Dame, where Cardinal Amette, in the presence of an enormous crowd, presided over a "Te Deum" of thanksgiving.

Page 180

La Ligue française: Janvier 1918 Numero 28
Steering Committee - Presidency of Mr. Emile Bertin
The Board of Directors appointed new delegates and approved the formation of the Committees of Le Havre, Chambéry and Sétif. The Secretary General presented the question of school boards to the Committee.

After a discussion in which MM. E Bertin, Maurice Croiset, Lemonnier, and the Secretary General, the Committee took the decision that the school boards will be viewed as formations of the local sections. They will operate under the authority of the local committee to which they will address their wishes and will focus mainly on publicity.

The Management Committee allocated a subsidy of 200 francs as a one-off contribution for the organization of a 'Fête des Familles Nombreuses' to the Committee of the 7th arrondissement. The Secretary General gave the Executive Committee guidelines on the important conference movement throughout France undertaken by the League.

Page 182

National Office of the Wards of the Nation. French Republic 14 July 1918. Law of 27 July 1917
Men and women of France, the Law of 27 July 1917 on the Wards of the Nation, approved unanimously by the Chamber of Deputies and the Senate, is a law of liberty, fraternity, mutual respect, and social harmony and solidarity. It will be applied in that spirit.
It is a Law of Liberty. The Nation, by adopting the War Orphans, does not want to take the place of their mothers or that their natural guardians; it does not withdraw any right from their relatives, it merely adds its protection to theirs. In addition the State authorises all existing charities that offer adequate safeguards to exercise their patronage over these orphans.
It is a Law of Fraternity and not of assistance. It is made for both the rich and the poor. The State has contracted a sacred debt towards the Wards of the Nation. The law ensures to these children, who are unequal in fortune, the same honourable title. It brings them close to one another by a badge of nobility that is conferred upon them as a reminder of the sacrifice of their fathers who fell for the common good.
It is a Law of Mutual Respect. The wishes of the deceased father or, in his absence, the wishes of the mother will be strictly observed. Their traditions, their beliefs, their feelings will be scrupulously respected, particularly as regards the type of education to be given to the child. The law will endeavour above all to maintain the traditions of the French family whose rights will be safeguarded and the rebirth of which it will encourage.
It is a Law of Harmony and Solidarity. It has as a crucial aim the achievement of sacred unity by accomplishing the noblest of missions: the protection and upbringing of children. Is not the finest way of honouring those who no longer are with us to continue that unity, an integral part of the moral strength of the Nation, born of a deep love of the Country and sealed in the blood of battle?
Men and women of France, in July 1790, at the great celebration of the Federation, the whole of France, through the representative of all its provinces, swore on the Champs-de-Mars, on the altar of our Country, to remain united and indivisible in defence of regained Liberty. On 14 July of last year, through the moving review of the flags, we wished to glorify those who are fighting with such heroism under the folds of the prestigious symbol of our Country. For the 14 July of this year, can we find a more moving symbol than a solemn demonstration in honour of those who have died for France, and whose children, adopted by the Nation, are going to become brothers and sisters? This is the exact meaning and scope of the Law of 27 July 1917 on the Wards of the Nation. It can and must unite all French people in a close community of minds and hearts. The Supreme Board of the National Office. [a list of members follows] DEVAMBEZ

Page 186

Clemenceau's ministerial declaration before the Chamber of Deputies
These people that we were forced to throw into the battle, they have rights over us... we owe them everything, without any reservations.